In the current volume Professor Horváth, one of the most seasoned observer of regional policy in central and eastern Europe, gives a truly interdisciplinary account of the changed role of space in the European perspective. Combining historical, regional, comparative, political and economic approaches he provides new insights in why the role of regions has not changed over the decades. The evidence-based analysis calls for major changes in the cohesion policies of the European Union. A must reading for anyone with serious academic interest in all those subjects.

László Csaba, Professor of international political economy,
Central European University, Hungary

This is an important contribution to the literature on regional development in Europe. It is an interdisciplinary account combining theoretical depth with a real understanding of cases. Instead of assuming that central and eastern European countries are of a single type, it emphasises the specificities of the cases and their historical development. Its stress on the importance of institutions and policies means that it will appeal to economists, geographers, political scientists and sociologists as well as to policy practitioners.

Michael Keating, Professor of Politics, University of Aberdeen, Scotland UK

This book leads the reader into the broad field of transition processes in different regions, with emphasis on the countries of Central and Eastern Europe.

Professor Horváth has conducted a marvellous survey with detailed analyses that help us understand the present challenges of these regions and the component countries in the light of their earlier, but still recent history.

Ulrich Blum, Professor, Martin Luther University of Halle-Wittenberg, Germany

No one else has studied the European process of regionalization for so long and in such detail as Gyula Horváth. I believe we should all be grateful to him and to the work he has done over the past several years finalizing a book that is useful not only to practitioners, economists and politicians, but to anyone who would better understand the process of birth and development of a unified European community.

Vladimir Kvint, Professor, Lomonosov Moscow State University, Russia

Spaces and Places in Central and Eastern Europe

Across Europe there is a rapidly changing context for undertaking regional development. In the twentieth century, development of the former planned economies (Bulgaria, Czech Republic, Hungary, Poland, Romania and Slovakia) was defined by these countries' differences, rather than their common ideological roots. These disparities altered over time and were marked by changing social structures. However, the ranking of regions has remained the same as core areas have strengthened their positions while the structural obstacles to the modernisation of peripheral areas have remained due to a lack of coherent regional policy.

This book examines the specific regional development paths of Central and Eastern European countries and evaluates the effects of the determining factors of this process. Through analysis of the system of objectives, instruments and institutions used in different eras, and case studies of Hungary, East Germany and Germany, development models are established and compared with Western European patterns.

The book summarises the experiences of Central and Eastern European regional cooperation and examines the basic nature of the cohesion problems of the Carpathian Basin trans-national macro region. It confirms by comparative historical analyses that the transformation was indeed unique. This book will make a welcome addition to the literature for students and academics interested in the broader picture of Central and Eastern European politics, future integration within the European Union and the history of regional development processes.

Gyula Horváth is Professor in Regional Economics and Policy at the University of Pécs, Hungary and Scientific Advisor of the Institute of Regional Studies, Hungarian Academy of Sciences.

Regions and Cities

Series Editor in Chief
Susan M. Christopherson, *Cornell University, USA*

Editors
Maryann Feldman, *University of Georgia, USA*
Gernot Grabher, *HafenCity University Hamburg, Germany*
Ron Martin, *University of Cambridge, UK*
Martin Perry, *Massey University, New Zealand*

In today's globalised, knowledge-driven and networked world, regions and cities have assumed heightened significance as the interconnected nodes of economic, social and cultural production, and as sites of new modes of economic and territorial governance and policy experimentation. This book series brings together incisive and critically engaged international and interdisciplinary research on this resurgence of regions and cities, and should be of interest to geographers, economists, sociologists, political scientists and cultural scholars, as well as to policy-makers involved in regional and urban development.

For more information on the Regional Studies Association visit www.regional-studies.org

There is a **30% discount** available to RSA members on books in the *Regions and Cities* series, and other subject related Taylor and Francis books and e-books including Routledge titles. To order just e-mail alex.robinson@tandf.co.uk, or phone on +44 (0) 20 7017 6924 and declare your RSA membership. You can also visit www.routledge.com and use the discount code: **RSA0901**

Spaces and Places in Central and Eastern Europe

Historical trends and perspectives of regional development

Gyula Horváth

LONDON AND NEW YORK

First published 2015
by Routledge
2 Park Square, Milton Park, Abingdon, Oxon OX14 4RN

and by Routledge
711 Third Avenue, New York, NY 10017

Routledge is an imprint of the Taylor & Francis Group, an informa business

British Library Cataloguing in Publication Data
A catalogue record for this book is available from the British Library

Library of Congress Cataloging in Publication Data
Horváth, Gyula
Space and place in Central and Eastern Europe : historical trends and
perspectives / Gyula Horváth.
pages cm. -- (Regions and cities)
Includes bibliographical references and index.
1. Regional planning--Europe, Central. 2. Regional planning--Europe,
Eastern. 3. Sustainable development--Europe, Central. 4. Sustainable
development--Europe, Eastern. I. Title.
HT395.E36H67 2014
307.1'20943--dc23
2014002228

ISBN: 978-0-415-72774-7 (hbk)
ISBN: 978-1-315-85205-8 (ebk)

Typeset in Times New Roman
by Fish Books

I dedicate this work to the memory of the founders of Hungarian regional science: István Bartke, György Enyedi and László Lackó

Contents

Figures

Tables

Introduction

The system of objectives of spatial development

Man, ever since becoming a social creature, has worked to organise the exploitation and functioning of his geographical environment. Planned human activity is oriented towards the evaluation, utilisation and control of various elements and levels of space (the natural environment, the economy and the cultural-intellectual milieu) and the organisation of the relations between independent spatial organisations with the purpose of satisfying the needs of society (Dunford 1988; Enyedi 1987; Gore 1984).

The harmonisation of spatial elements fulfilling basic social functions (housing, work, distribution-provision, training-culture, regeneration, communication, community life) with social needs has taken various forms throughout history, and the presence of organised and spontaneous processes characterise the space used by society. The conscious utilisation of space is a result of the activity of social organisations at various levels (ethnic groups, settlements, regions, states, international communities). Regulation, in an increasingly widening geographical milieu, was initially created by smaller groups within society (e.g. the slash-and-burn, shifting cultivation in Africa was regulated by individual tribes, irrigation farming in the Nile valley resting on strict spatial organisation required collaboration from several settlements and the building of the continental road system of the Roman Empire required central and regional efforts). The role of the state strengthened during the creation of national economies and capitalist, national markets in the nineteenth century. Active state intervention in the domain of spatial organisation began with the regulation of city building and the establishment of modern public administrative organisations to ensure the spatially uniform control of the relationship between the state and the citizen. Industrial capitalism led to a massive reorganisation of the economic field of energy in every country of Europe.

The rapid development of raw material-intensive sectors took place in areas far removed from earlier growth centres (Antwerp, Venice, Florence, Amsterdam, Bordeaux) and the population of settlements in these regions (Northern and Eastern England, Lorraine, the Ruhr Valley, Northern Italy) multiplied. Other regions within a country were deserted due to this massive migration. The industrial agglomerations of large cities were born at the turn of the nineteenth and twentieth centuries and the mono-centric spatial structure of several countries was formed during this era. For instance, between 1880 and 1936 the population of the Paris region increased three times and rose to 3.3 million, and its share of the total population of France increased from 5 per cent to 19 per cent. The Western regions of the country, which occupy 56 per cent of the national territory and were home to 48 per cent of the total population of France in the middle of the previous century, saw their share decline to only 37 per cent by the middle of the century. Over 2 million people migrated to Paris and the Eastern industrial regions. The chaotic state of affairs in the new industrial centres forced state organs to introduce various development regulations. The most comprehensive legal regulations, however, were introduced in Great Britain in 1909. Based on the Housing and Town Planning Act and supported by adequate public subsidies, local authorities elaborated development plans and applied uniform standards.

Between the two World Wars, a partial regulation of spatial development was incorporated into the programmes of several national governments. Post-WWI, new Central and Eastern European nation-states elaborated concepts to strengthen the cohesion of their territories which had formerly belonged to other states, and the economic depression at the beginning of the 1930s led to public intervention and development in areas of Western Europe and the United States affected by the crisis. Complex regional development, however, only appeared in Great Britain during this period. In 1928, the Industrial Relocation Council was established, and the Special Areas Development and Improvement Act, adopted in 1934, established special funds and a separate organisation (the Special Areas Reconstruction Association) for the development of four major districts of heavy industry (South Wales, Northeast England, West Cumberland (a specific area in Northwest England) and West Central Scotland). Comprehensive investigations were launched to organise the spatial restructuring of both industry and population.

The reconstruction euphoria of the post-WW II era temporarily concealed serious regional inequalities, but, at the end of the 1940s, comprehensive regional development programmes were prepared in the market economies. The Eastern European socialist countries worked out their own spatial development concepts much later. For example, the first document on spatial development following several attempts by the Soviet Union on the spatial location of centres of production was prepared in Hungary in 1959 under the title 'Public Tasks in the Location of Industry'.

The paradigm shift of the market economies in the 1970s fostered a basic revision of earlier regional development concepts. Through a comprehensive evaluation of the theoretical and practical experiences of this period of development, the spatial development tasks and objectives of industrial and post-industrial societies were clarified and regional policy became an organic part of social and economic policy (Yuill *et al.* 1980; Vanhove and Klaassen 1979; Wadley 1986).

The task of spatial development is to create favourable conditions for the practice of basic social functions (in other words, for the improvement of the living standards of the population). This is achieved through the detection and utilisation of the laws of interaction among spatial assets, opportunities and elements. The purpose is to validate the principle of social equity and justice (i.e. the intention to reduce the objective disparities in living conditions).

Under current market conditions, the long-term objectives of spatial development are:

1   Job creation, limiting unemployment rates;
2   Relieving demographic pressure on overpopulated city centres;
3   The effective utilisation of domestic resources;
4   The reduction of unreasonable regional development disparities;
5   The preservation of regional culture and identity, with special focus on areas populated by ethnic minorities;
6   The preservation or restoration of the population-environment balance.

The validation of this system of objectives varies, of course, in space and time, and a different combination of elements can be envisaged in the development of various space types.

In order to realise the objectives of spatial development, various *instruments* are required. The tools of spatial development may comprise multiple types of element, and their application may vary. This can be from country to country in terms of the function of their economic policy orientation and from region to region, according to the nature of spatial development problems.

There are instruments which may be used to realise regional development objectives:

1   Financial incentives (capital grants, budgetary support, preferential loan construction, interest rate reduction, tax relief, accelerated amortisation, labour mobility and retraining support);
2   Central regulation (spatially limited development restriction, downsizing or relocating activities, spatial planning and programming, creation of state-owned companies, preference for state orders, decentralisation of public institutions, growth poles, designation of development zones);
3   Infrastructural investment (the complex creation of a favourable environment for economic development: energy and water supply, transport network, industrial parks, research and development capacity, professional training, development of financial-economic-market services).

A vertically and horizontally differentiated system of institutions is responsible for executing spatial development tasks, elaborating general objectives in harmony with regional assets and selecting and applying development tools. The organisational system of spatial development has changed in line with the growing role of the state, the increasing number of spatial development tasks, the changing size and borders of areas involved in development and the increasing assortment of available instruments. Initially, tasks affecting a restricted number of smaller areas were organised by a central organisation as part of its complementary activities. From the 1950s, central government organs were given regional development functions as basic tasks, de-concentrated spatial institutions of central authorities created, and regional and local authorities handled an increasing number of tasks individually and other stakeholders in spatial development (interest groups, social movements, international organisations) gained influence in the phase of decision preparation (Armstrong and Taylor 1993).

Regional development has evolved into a multi-player activity during the past century. Currently each advanced country pursues an independent regional policy encompassing the objectives of the development of spatial elements, spatial structures and the necessary instruments and institutions.

A major obstacle to strengthening competitiveness across the European continent is the existence of excessive regional disparities among the various territorial units. This phenomenon applies to both old and new member-states. The structural and cohesion policies of the European Union are, of course, targeted at alleviating this factor which seriously handicaps or even paralyses economic development. The success of these initiatives depends heavily on the nature of the national past processes, financing and institutional bases created for the implementation of unified EU regulations. The systems of objectives and instruments of regional policy of the individual nation-states do not lose their importance; rather, their role becomes more significant in the efficient absorption of the additional development subsidies provided by the EU. The Structural and Cohesion Funds of the European Union can produce results provided that the systems of instruments and institutions of national regional development function correctly. The policy instruments designed to shape the regional development of European countries have a long history.

Regional policy in Europe

Regions and towns react differently to the impacts of globalisation processes and depending on their features and applied strategies they will end up as winners or losers. In attempts to avoid negative impacts, local and regional authorities introduce a number of measures to protect their interests. At the same time, the applied strategies strengthen the segregation at the expense of amalgamation. For instance, the vital regional cultural movements serve this aim as well as the ethnic organisations acting throughout most of the world with growing success. Yet, it remains questionable, whether a regional strategy favouring identity is appropriate to protect the national or even international position of a given region, and whether it represents an adequate development force in terms of the improvement of the region's productivity. The answer is obviously dependent on the location of the region, which region within what macro-region of the world we talk about.

The Fordist type of industrial centres, rural regional centres or global metropolitan areas have of course different features in terms of the traditionally interpreted reactivity. Yet, the quality of the classical productive factors is only one of the preconditions of adaptation. The second, new adaptation criterion, deriving from the functioning mechanisms of the networking economy, is the type, character of relationships between the organisations and institutions of the region or the town, the possibility of the institutionalisation of common targets, local incentives, the preparation of local decisions and the social concerns. This group of new competitive factors implies that the success of local and regional development is not any more exclusively dependent on some narrow economic aspects, but rather on the close coalition and institutionalised co-operation of the actors interested in regional growth.

The result of the dissemination of the post-modern space theory is the gradual spreading of the new regional development paradigm. The development idea based on endogenous resources and starting from peripheries is slowly naturalised in the strategies of less developed regions and even the central regional policy in a growing number of states consider the "bottom-up" principle as the starting point.

Globalisation gives continuous impulse to the trends of restructuring of the post-modern economy and in many cases even accelerates them (Amin and Tomaney 1995). The accomplishment of the economic paradigm developed in the 1980s can be expected in Europe in the first decades of the new millennium, yet, post-Fordist space shaping forces will also impact for a longer period. The extension of advanced services enforcing agglomeration benefits can be forecasted and the concentrated decentralisation of these activities will continue yet at different speeds in each country. The speed of spreading is highly dependent on the role of mature tertiary and quaternary sectors granted by the region in its development strategy, and on the proportion of sectors organised in clusters producing added high value within the economy. The new approach of regional development, the professional culture's ability to alloy the motive powers of globalisation with local advantages, will be an important selection factor in the reduction or reinforcement of territorial inequalities.

The prospects of the spatial structure of Europe are shaped today only partially by the national state strategies; the motivating power of global processes and common policies, mostly respecting the former, is significantly stronger. It is therefore not unimportant, which ideas will be born to shape the future of the single European space.

The community policy expresses the aim of the member-states completing certain tasks together. The common policies are mostly not the regional developmental type and instead serve specific targets. Yet, the Maastricht Treaty showed the impacts of territorial sectoral policies in a new light. The powers of the Commission were significantly extended since several important community policies (such as the common agricultural policy, transportation policy, Trans-European networks, structural policy, R&D, competition and environment policy) also serve regional development targets.

The reduction of the state borders' restricting power within European integration, the institutionalised development of the European economic space and the eastern enlargement of the European Union showed the development possibilities of cross-border regions into a new light. Besides community and national and sub-national frameworks, European macro-regions may become important strategic units in the future as regards the improvement of continental competitiveness. The regions with high productivity will be able to meet the requirements of the economy of scale and to increase efficiency.

The permanent character of transformation trends of the European economy's development factors, the quality changes within European integration and their impacts on national political systems markedly influence the future arrangement of the target, method and institutional systems of regional policy. Within the interrelations of regional development and macro-policy and within the internal mechanisms of regional policy we can witness significant changes. The most important lesson of the century is that the long development of regional policy became by today an organic part of the European approach.

The national and sectoral policies in the majority of European states and the cohesion strategy of the European Union consider the principle of solidarity as the starting point of social action. This characteristic distinguishes clearly the European model from the social administration practices of other continents. The cohesion model in economic terms means the moderation of inequalities between regions and between social layers, enabling the most social strata to contribute actively to the establishment of the conditions of economic growth and to share the outcomes of growth. The social dimension of cohesion covers the highest possible level of employment, the improvement of the chances of employment for disadvantaged social strata and the moderation of unemployment. Finally, cohesion in political practice is the expression of mutual support within the state and the European Community, not simply in the form of income transfer but rather through the common application of means and methods serving the optimal utilisation of endogenous resources (First Report on Economic and Social Cohesion).

The changes during the previous years imply that the space of regional policy at the very beginning of the new millennium, besides the self-determining rules of economic development, will be determined by two significant factors: first by the organisational, functional and financial reforms of the European Union and its eastern enlargements and second, due to a high extent of the previous factor, by the new distribution of power within the national state, decentralisation.

The reforms within the European Union shall receive special attention, since, as we have seen, regions were granted significantly higher subsidies from the structural and cohesion integration funds in the course of the process of strengthening European cohesion, than from national resources (Bache 1998). The final outcomes of the *c.* €250 billion of community subsidies granted for regional development are not very promising, since the cohesion analyses report a very slow decrease in regional inequalities. One of the reasons for the weak implementation of efficiency requirements is to be detected in the dispersed character of the subsidies. The determinative direction of the reforms being prepared is not accidentally the improvement of concentrated utilisation of the resources. In the course of the designation of eligible regions the indigence must be defined by a strict criterion and the proportion of the eligible population must be restricted to one-third of the total population within the Community. The investment practice is to be reconsidered, since the multiplication effects of the investments did not reach the desirable level and, due to different reasons,– the absorption ability of the regions did not develop in accordance with original expectations. The consistent enforcement of the principle of additionality, the local, regional and national contribution, seems to be the only feasible way. The second key issue is the enforcement of co-operation between the actors of regional development, the partnership, yet, taking the principle of subsidiarity into account. Within the system of subsistence and incentives of the European Union, the 'ex-ante' evaluation of 'cost-benefit' effects are given significant importance which could, depending on the possessed knowledge on the functioning of regional economy and not exclusively on solid capital, launch a new process of differentiation between European regions.

Yet, regionalism must face several serious challenges before its general evolution. National governments still have a significant regulating role in shaping the relationships between the regions and the European Commission. Europe's least advanced regions can enforce their interests somewhat weakly in the integration decisions, since exactly the least affluent states have fewer representatives in the Union's bodies. Also, the competition policy of the Union strengthens the centralisation effects. The common regional policy is not able to balance the inequalities deriving from the competitive abilities. Federal Germany is an expressive example of the fact that regionalism and the moderation of territorial differences can be reconciled in the governmental tier too.

The permanent trends in the transformation of development factors in the European economy, the qualitative changes seen in European integration and their overall effect on national political systems will have a visible impact on the future evolution of the system of regional policy and on national political systems of instruments and institutions. We can already see a fundamental change in the interactions between regional development and macro-economic policy and the internal mechanisms of regional policy.

Changing regional structures in Central and Eastern Europe

In the twentieth-century development of the new Central and Eastern European (CEE) member-states of the EU,– Bulgaria, the Czech Republic, Hungary, Poland, Slovakia, Slovenia and Romania, despite being members of the same alliance and rooted in the same ideology for four decades, apart from a few outward similarities arising from the political system, it was basically the differences that played a dominant role. In the course of history, these countries and areas which united in the beginning of the twentieth century to form the Central European nation-states, were previously bound to different geopolitical spheres. Belonging to the same empire, Hungary and Czechoslovakia, once integrated in the Central European macro-region, were able to connect to the mainstream of European industrial transformation a much longer time ago. This take-off period has left its marks on the spatial structure of other countries as well, and the core regions of most countries exert a non-negligible influence on the spatial structuring forces even in the present.

There are large disparities in the demographic, labour market, economic and environmental processes influencing the spatial structure of the new member-states in Central and Eastern Europe, and the consequences of accession foreshadowed a heterogeneous picture. Even though EU experts tended to regard this area as a homogenous entity, the heritage of state socialism, and more particularly the economic policy instruments and institutional practices applied in the management of regional effects of transition and newly emerged phenomena have produced diverse outcomes. The degree of these disparities differed during the various periods marked by changing social structures, however, no changes can be detected in the ranking of regions. Core areas have strengthened their positions during the different eras, meanwhile, the structural obstacles to the modernisation of peripheral areas have not been eliminated due to the lack of a coherent regional policy.

The crisis preceding and following systematic change has produced similar, yet diverse processes in terms of scale and consequences in Central and Eastern European countries. The specific features of political relations during the first years of parliamentary democracy have resulted in significant disparities in the speed of legislation on market economy and economic performance. A marked differentiation could be observed in the generally homogenous performance of the previous decades in the final years of the 1990s.

Regional policy faces several problems in these countries. The operation of institutions established by the laws on spatial development is characterised by instability. The main organ of regional policy changes with each new government cycle. In Hungary and Romania, there is severe competition between potential regional centres and other important county seats for the location of development organs. Financial management authorities are still underdeveloped. Regionalism, the territorial decentralisation of power and the distribution of tasks among different local governments are objects of debate in several unitary states of CEE. The political transformation, the integration into the globalised European economy and the construction of self-governments built upon the principles of civil democracy have shed a new light on the interrelations of central and territorial-local power and the harmonisation of settlement autonomy with intermediary-level public administrative functions. The economic, political and functional transformation of basic institutions of self-governance has become a major issue in almost all of the former socialist countries.

Despite the similar features of spatial restructuring in the accession countries, the changing ways in which regional development problems are handled and the varying results of the developments undertaken indicate that the 'Eastern European Bloc' is just as heterogeneous as the countries of the former EU-15. Structural policy reforms of the EU must take account of this fact.

EU accession opened up a Pandora's box in the countries of Eastern and Central Europe. The fundamental issue of how unitarily structured states can be set on a decentralised path became the centre of debate. If regionalism progresses, it can bring about the modernisation of regional structures and the need for multi-polar regional development may change the hierarchies of power in those countries still in transition quite profoundly. The sub-national level of the power structure, the region, is a territorial entity which supports the sustainable development of the economy and the modernisation of the spatial structure, with its own financial resources and having at its disposal an autonomous development policy based upon local governmental rights. The regions are becoming the stage for innovative development, and the degree of embeddedness of the fundamental institutions of innovation output is becoming stronger at regional level.

It is now self-evident in the majority of EU member-states that the institutions of power sharing and multi-level governance enhance economic performance and welfare in individual regions. Lobbyist politicians are replaced by development-minded peers, who encourage long-term legal guarantees for auto-nomous local growth, co-operation on the European scale and partnerships among regional stakeholders. The successful development of numerous Western European regions shows the efficacy of this attitude, as well as its eminent role in fostering a regional identity. This new paradigm has emerged in some Eastern European regions.

Regional development in CEE has been a neglected object of scientific research for a long time. The primary focus of Western European social scientific works analysing this region were the various factors of communist political authority and macro-level processes in planned economies. The analysis of the spatial structure of the Central European economy and society was almost entirely monopolised by urban and social geography; it was only around transition that collective works were published in collaboration with Central and Eastern European authors. The era after the signature of the treaties of accession, and the years of the elaboration of pre-accession programmes in particular, saw the proliferation of research programmes on East Central European structural and cohesion policy and publi-cations in their framework. For the most part, thematic volumes contained studies on the regional transformation in individual countries with a focus on one specific theme. Collective works were published for example on the declining industrial regions of East Central Europe, characteristics of the spatial location of FDI, regional components of national development plans, questions of rural develop-ment and transformation, and new directions in urban development (Bachtler 1992; Bachtler, *et al.* 2000; Baun and Marek 2008; Enyedi 1992; Hamilton *et al.* 2005; Müllert *et al.* 2005; Palermo andParolari 2013; Turnock 2004, 2005). Individual monographs by one or more authors still rarely emerge in domestic and interna-tional scientific book markets (Artobolevsky 1997; Gorzelak 1996; Hughes *et al.* 2004; Turnock 1989, 1998; Yoder 2013).

Although two decades have passed, transition from state socialism to capitalism and the switchover to market economy and democracy are far from being a closed issue for anyone striving to understand economic, social, political and spatial processes in the early years of the twenty-first century and place them in the current global processes of transformation.

Target and method

How long will it take for a society that is, with respect to its operation, ridden with all the problems of transition to produce spatial forms that are not simply different from their former socialist counterparts, but expressly capitalistic, namely for spatial processes to pass through the stage of transition, in a new system of parlia-mentary democracy and under the conditions of market economy? If there exists 'post-socialist' production of space, what are its characteristics and what are the characteristics of its end-products?

The objective of the book is to:

- detect the specific regional development paths of Eastern, Central and South-Eastern European countries and the processes impacting spatial reorganisation;
- evaluate the effects of the determining factors of spatial development and the role of modern driving forces of spatial restructuring in the real processes of regional development and the application of the instruments of spatial policy;
- analyse the impact of the system of objectives, instruments and institutions of spatial policy created in various eras on the evolution of the country's spatial structure and regional performance. Three case studies (Hungary, East Germany and Russia) show historical development of spatial structures and changing driving forces of regional cohesion.
- introduce general and unique features of the development paths, categorise the various types of development on the basis of their distinctive characteristics, describe the development models and compare them with Western European development patterns;
- review the positive impacts of the institutionalisation of regions on the strengthening of spatial cohesion and outline the impact of the driving forces of regionalism which has embarked on the road towards decentralisation;
- summarise the experiences of Central and Eastern European regional co-operation and examine the basic nature of the cohesion problems of the Carpathian basin macro-region; and
- list the regional preconditions for the revival of a crisis-stricken Europe, the decentralisation requirements defined by the Lisbon Treaty and provide alternative scenarios for various levels of improvement in regional cohesion.

The book differs from recently published works in three aspects. First, it provides a comparative analysis of the system of objectives, instruments and institutions of spatial development of Eastern and Central European countries in a unified perspective. Second, it evaluates the development experiences of three countries with changing development paths (former East Germany and the incorporation of the eastern *Länder* into the re-unified Germany, Russia and Hungary), detecting the impacts of the various social systems on regional development. Evaluation of various periods of regional development of Eastern Germany and Russia is important issue, because these entities currently show consequences of former socialist territorial development paradigms. Both countries are mainly decentralised today, but state operation and the functions of the regional policy demonstrate huge differences. Third, the book paints a comprehensive picture of two essential factors of European territorial cohesion: the role of research and development and macro-regional integration in the Central and Eastern European transition process. The research area of the European East now includes Balkan countries in that their research capacity should be developed in co-operation with Central and Eastern European research clusters.

The basic concept of the book is to present the huge regional disparities in Central and Eastern European development. In the twentieth century, it was basically the differences that had played a dominant role in the development of the former planned economies, despite being members of the same alliance and rooted in the same ideology for four decades, apart from a few outward similarities arising from the political system.. The degree of these disparities differed during the various periods marked by changing social structures. However, no changes can be detected in the ranking of regions. Core areas have strengthened their positions during different periods, but the structural obstacles to the modernisation of peripheral areas have not been eliminated due to the lack of a coherent regional policy.

The case studies presented in the book (East Germany, Russia, Hungary) further elaborate the theme of historical embeddedness, shedding light on how political and social relations have shaped the evolution of spatial structures. Each of the three countries represents a distinct type. The transition from planned to market economy has resulted in significant disparities in the conditions of regional development.

Comparative analysis provides the other logical framework of this book. During the investigation of the regional transformation processes, attention is focused on comparing the varying extent of the transformations. The characteristic features of the transformation are evaluated in light of Western European trends and the former situation of the regions under examination, and we also attempt to detect the factors behind the transformations and the nature of the specifics of their mechanisms of action. Comparison is a significant source of new knowledge since it compares similarities and differences between territories and localities. It enables evaluation of the roles of various regional development factors by comparing their importance and effects in some areas and lack of them in others.

The third axis of our analysis is to examine whether the present regional structures enable the creation of the conditions for democratic governance and sustainable economic growth. The chapters presenting the differentiated Central and Eastern European area are followed by a section discussing questions related to regional governance and reviewing the regional assets of the knowledge-based economy.

The same logic prevails in the elaboration of the case studies, the evaluation of historical determination, path dependency, differentiated regional structural assets and their causes, the territorial frameworks of power and the capacity to adopt new space shaping forces will be the focus of these chapters. Besides the vertical connections in history, additional important effects arise from the horizontal interrelationships between various regions (Berend 2013).

The main methodological feature of the book is complexity, although it is descriptive in a sense that it contributes a huge body of knowledge to the better understanding of the development processes of this mega-region.

Acknowledgements

I gratefully acknowledge the support and generosity of Hungarian National Research Fund (OTKA), without which the present book could not have been completed. I acknowledge the facilities, and the scientific and technical assistance of my intellectual home, the Institute of Regional Studies of Hungarian Academy of Sciences.

I acknowledge the support and assistance of the University of Pécs, the many students who provided feedback on the European Regional Development and Policy master's course, as well as students of the Regional Policy and Development Doctoral School. I also thank my colleagues in Central and Eastern European research institutions, who have created for me a stimulating intellectual ambience during my research visits.

References

Amin, A. and Tomaney, J. (1995) 'The regional dilemma in a neo-liberal Europe', *European Urban and Regional Studies,* 2: 171–188.

Armstrong, H.W. and Taylor, J. (1993) *Regional Economics and Policy,* London: Harvester-Wheatsheaf.

Artobolevsky, S.S. (1997) *Regional Policy in Europe,* London: Jessica Kingsley.

Bache, I. (1998) *Europeanization and Multi-level Governace in Europe. Cohesion Policy in the European Union and Britain,* Lanham, MD: Rowman and Littlefield .

Bachtler, J. (ed.) (1992) 'Socio-Economic Situation and Development of the Regions in the Neighbouring Countries of the Community in Central and Eastern Europe', Final report to the European Commission, Brussels.

Bachtler, J., Downes, R. and Gorzelak, G. (eds) (2000) *Transition, Cohesion and Regional Policy in the Central and Eastern Europe,* Aldershot: Ashgate.

Baun, M. and Marek, D. (eds) (2008) *EU Cohesion Policy after Enlargement,* Basingstoke: Palgrave Macmillan.

Berend, I.T. (2013) *An Economic History of Nineteenth-Century Europe,* Cambridge: Cambridge University Press.

Dunford, M.F. (1988) *Capital, the State and Regional Development,* London: Pion Ltd.

Enyedi, G. (1987) 'Tér és társadalom' [Space and society], *Janus. II. 1: 3–13.*

Enyedi, G. (ed.) (1992) *Social Transition and Urban Restructuring in Central Europe,* Budapest: European Science Foundation.

'First Report on Economic and Social Cohesion' Brussels: Commission of the European Communities. Commission Communication. COM (2002) 46 final.

Gore, C. (1984) *Regions in Question. Space, Development Theory and Regional Policy,* London: Methuen.

Gorzelak, G. (1996) *The Regional Dimension of Transformation in Central Europe,* London: Jessica Kingsley.

Hamilton, F.I., Dimitrowska-Andrews, K. and Pichler-Milanović, N. (eds) (2005) *Transformation of Cities in Central and Eastern Europe: Towards Globalization,* Tokyo: The United Nations University Press.

Hughes, J., Sasse, G. and Gordon, C. (2004) *Europaization and Regionalization in the EU's Enlargement to Central and Eastern Europe. The Myth of Conditionality,* Basingstoke: Palgrave Macmillan.

Müllert, B., Finka, M. and Lintz, G. (eds) (2005) *Rise and Decline of Industry in Central and Eastern Europe. A Comparative Study of Cities and Regions in Eleven Countries,* Berlin: Springer.

Palermo, F. and Parolari, S. (eds) (2013) *Regional Dynamics in Central and Eastern Europe. New Approaches to Decentralization,* Leiden, Boston: Martinus Nijhoff.

Turnock, D. (1989) *The Human Geography of East Central Europe,* London: Routledge.

Turnock, D. (1998) *The Making of Eastern Europe: From the Earliest Times to 1815,* London, Routledge.

Turnock, D. (2004) *The Eastern European Economy in Context: Communism and Transition,* New York: Taylor & Francis.

Turnock, D. (2005) *The Economy of East Central Europe, 1815–1898. Stages of Transformation in a Peripheral Region,* London: Routledge.

Yoder, J.A. (2013) *Crafting Democracy. Regional Politics in Post-Communist Europe,* Lanham, MD: Rowman & Littlefield.

Yuill, D., Allen, K. and Hull, C. (1980) *Regional Policy in the European Community,* London: Croom Helm.

Vanhove, N. and Klaassen, L.H. (1979) *Regional Policy. A European Approach,* Farnborough: Gower.

Wadley, D. (1986) *Restructuring the Regions,* Paris: OECD.

Part I

Regional development

Processes, frameworks and driving forces

1 Regional transformation in Central and Eastern Europe

Macro-economic position

While the reforms of the European Union's regional and cohesion policies were meant to reduce the spatial inequalities within the Union, and were more or less successful during four decades, expansion to Central and Eastern Europe will result in enhanced regional inequalities. The weak performance of the newer member-states will lead to stronger spatial inequalities and an increasing number of backward areas.

The demographic, economic, employment and environmental processes that affect the spatial structure of the future member-states of Central and Eastern Europe are diverse, and so are the expected impacts of their accession. The experts of the European Union prefer to treat this area as a homogeneous unit. Yet, the heritage of the state socialist system, the regional effects of transformation, and the different economic and political tools and institutional solutions in the management of new phenomena have brought about rather diverse results in the individual countries (Table 1.1).

The *demographic potential* of the newer member-states, with a total of 97 million in population, displays strong differences. Two countries, Poland and Romania, account for 60 per cent of the total population and the rest are small or medium-sized countries. Poland, the Czech Republic, Romania and Bulgaria enjoy a spatially more or less balanced population with a deconcentrated settlement structure. In the settlement structure of countries that were divided for longer periods of time during their historical development, like Poland and Romania, we find several highly concentrated spots: beside the capitals, several regional centres have developed with high populations and significant economic potential.

Changes in the settlement structure in all countries during the state socialism era were primarily quantitative. By the late 1990s, the rate of urban population reached 69 per cent in Bulgaria, 70 per cent in the Czech Republic, and 63 per cent in Hungary. Romania is less urbanised where 55 per cent of the population live in towns and cities.

The weight of capitals, at the top of the urban hierarchy, is remarkable in Bulgaria and in Hungary. Sofia accounts for 14 per cent of the population of the country and Budapest for 18 per cent. Prague, Bratislava and Bucharest have more a moderate share (6–10 per cent) in population of respective counties. The role they play in the economy and in cultural life is more dominant than their share of the population. The important elements of the market economy are concentrated in the capitals (Table 1.2). Several elements of a decentralised development policy could be designed to decrease this unfavourable, decades-long territorial concentration.

Table 1.1 Main macro-statistical data, 2011

	Bulgaria	Czech Republic	Hungary	Poland	Romania	Slovakia
Average population, '000	7,327	10,486	9,983	38,538	20,199	5,392
Total area per, 1,000 km²	111	79	93	313	238	49
Density of population, person per km²	66	134	107	123	94	110
GDP per capita (PPS) in per cent of EU27	46.0	79.8	64.6	64.4	46.8	73.4
Economic activity rate, per cent of population	65.9	70.5	62.7	65.7	63.3	68.7
Unemployment rate, per cent	11.3	8.6	10.9	9.7	7.4	13.7
Urbanisation rate, per cent	73.1	73.4	69.5	60.9	52.8	54.7
Number of human settlements	5,302	6,250	3,154	56,769	13,275	2,792
Number of local governments	264	6,250	3,154	2,479	2,861	2,792
Average population of local governments per, 1,000	27.8	1.7	3.2	15.5	7.1	1.9
Number of meso-level public administration units	28	14	20	16	43	8
Average population of meso-units per, 1,000	261	749	497	2,409	481	674
Railway network, km per 1,000 km²	35	125	80	69	45	74
Length of motorways, km	457	1,192	1,516	1,070	350	419
Density of motorway, km per 1,000 km²	4.1	15.1	16.3	3.4	1.5	8.6
Number of cars per 1,000 inhabitants	368	436	359	470	203	324
Number of subscribers of mobile services per 1,000 inhabitants	1,454	1,355	1,190	1,223	1,128	1,051
Internet penetration, per cent	49	75	72	65	44	79
Persons aged 25–64 with tertiary education attainment, per cent	23.5	18.2	21.1	23.3	14.9	18.6
Gross domestic expenditure on R&D	0.57	1.64	1.22	0.90	0.42	0.82
R&D personnel as per cent of labour force	0.50	1.15	0.82	0.52	0.28	0.67

Source: National statistical yearbooks and Eurostat.

Table 1.2 The weight of capital cities in some activities, in per cent, 2001

Activity	Sofia^{2000}	Prague	Budapest	Warsaw	Bucharest	Bratislava
GDP	24.6	24.5	35.0	n.a.	16.5^{1998}	24.2
Industrial output	15.9	13.0	17.6	11.8	17.0	37.3
Foreign direct investment	49.9	25.7	56.5	33.0	46.7	71.2
Tertiary education students	43.3	31.4	49.2	16.7	32.4	83.0
Employees in R&D	72.7^{1995}	48.0	55.8	30.0	39.0	40.2

Source: Own calculations based on national statistical yearbooks.

Since the early 1990s, processes related to the changes that affected the whole of society have influenced the settlement structure. One of these processes is suburbanisation, that is urban population moving to the countryside, especially into the outskirts of large cities. This trend has emerged gradually, as it is observable in the slight decrease in the population of urban settlements and the increase in the proportion of inhabitants living in smaller and/or rural settlements.

In the shaping of a decentralised development policy, the large and medium cities in the second level of the urban hierarchy play an important role. The endowments of two countries are similar in this respect. Bulgaria has three cities with populations of over 200,000 (Plovdiv, Varna and Bourgas), and three towns (Rousse, Stara Zagora and Pleven) between 130,000 and 170,000. Hungary has one city with a population of over 200,000 (Debrecen), while three regional centres (Miskolc, Szeged and Pécs) have populations of around 160,000. In Bulgaria's two cities (Sliven and Dobrich) the populations are between 100,000 and 130,000, while in Hungary there are three such towns (Győr, Nyíregyháza and Székesfehérvár). The urban network of Poland and Romania shows a relatively balanced hierarchy and regional pattern (Figure 1.1). The second level includes two to eight cities with over 300,000 inhabitants (e.g. Łódź, Cracow, Poznań, Katowice and Gdańsk in Poland; Cluj-Napoca, Timişoara, Craiova, Iaşi, Constanţa in Romania; Brno and Ostrava in the Czech Republic). This figure has to be compared with more than 20–30 similar towns in Western European countries. These towns exert significant influence over a wide area and this is why they are called potential regional centres. They have relatively good amenities to prevent their inhabitants from migrating to capital cities. They have an academic tradition and cultural history. But they are often too weak, from an international point of view, to compete successfully with other large European cities.

The settlement structure of the Czech Republic is characterised by high population density and disintegrated nature of settlements. A large portion of the population lives in urban settlements. Towns with over 50,000 inhabitants were among those most severely affected by the process of urbanisation; between 1993 and 2,000 they showed a migration decrease of over 25,000 inhabitants. On the contrary, in terms of migration, the largest increases took place in settlements with over 10,000 inhabitants.

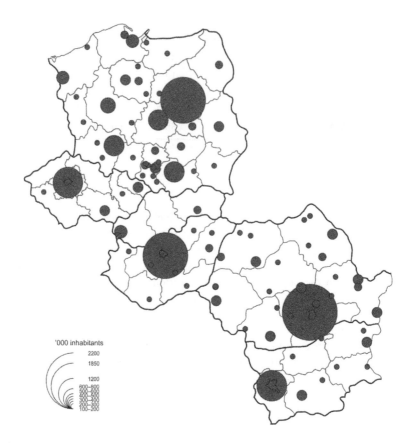

'000 inhabitants

Figure 1.1 Large urban centres in Central and Eastern Europe
Source: Designed by the author.

The settlement structure in Poland is characterised by:

- a moderate, polycentric concentration of population and economic activity in less than 20 medium-sized centres, relatively homogeneously localised over the country's territory;
- 4.5 per cent of the population live in Warsaw – this is a relatively low proportion of Poland's population;
- the low position of Polish metropolises in European rankings (Warsaw is in groups V and VI in the 8-group classifications);
- a low degree of urbanisation (below 61 per cent) that has remained unchanged for the past few years;
- highly dispersed settlements in rural areas, where as much as 40 per cent of Poland's population lives.

One of the reasons for the lack village-town and interregional migration is the housing situation. The insufficient number of dwellings and their low standard is reflected in the generally low level of fulfilment of social needs and the low standard of living of many families. Currently in Poland, approximately 1.5 million households do not have their individual flat. The average age of housing stock in Poland is 40 years and more than 1 million flats have completely deteriorated. More than 10 million people live in Poland in low-standard accommodation (including 44 per cent of rural population). The insufficient number of flats of a reasonable standard and the price of both purchasing and renting (especially with regard to towns) exceed the financial capacities of the majority of interested people. Municipal infrastructure in the majority of cities and communes is obsolete, completely depreciated, and is of low functionality. It is relevant also to big cities and influences their lower competitive position when they try to attract investment, especially of foreign origin.

The large city network in Eastern and Central Europe, except for Romania and Poland, is thin (Figure 1.2). In the whole area, 97 towns or cities are above 100,000 in population terms, and two-thirds of these are found in Poland and Romania. Slovakia has only one major city apart from the capital. In these two countries, the number of regions is much lower than the number of cities but the largest cities are evenly distributed over the whole area and have the potential to become potential regional centres.

For this reason, therefore, designating a regional centre could be much easier. In most of the Eastern and Central European countries the debates over the designation of regional centres have become more intensive as the EU accession

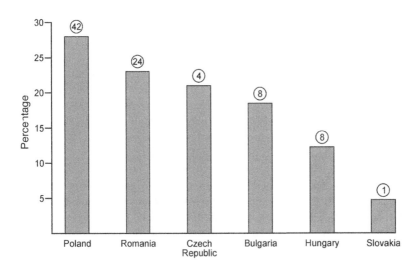

Figure 1.2 Number of towns or cities with over 100,000 inhabitants in Eastern and Central European countries (excluding the capital) and their proportion of national population, 2009

Source: Designed by the author based on national statistical yearbooks.

process progressed. In Poland, after the introduction of the new *voivod*ship public administration, the leading major cities became the centres of the new regions. The only exception is the Kujawsko-pomorske voivodship where the regional centre is not Bydgoszcz, the industrial centre with 361,000 inhabitants, but Toruń, with its historical traditions and a population of 206,000. In the other countries, the competition among towns or cities goes on almost exclusively in establishing the labour organisations of the development agencies and the changing category of the two NUTS regions. The latter is certainly at the centre of debate in Romania. Several cities with traditionally strong regional administrative functions, such as Arad, Oradea, Sibiu, and Târgu-Mureş lost these functions and this demands a change in the national regional system. The dissatisfaction among the counties belonging to the planning-statistical regions is shown by the fact that the head-quarters of the regional development councils were established in smaller county centres throughout Romania. There were also examples of obsolescence of the role by the leading cities in Bulgaria. As a result of the public administration reforms of the 1970s, when six large 'oblasts' were created instead of smaller spatial units, the leading major city was replaced as the regional centre by a smaller town in the geographical centre of the region.

The medium-sized town network, with populations between 50,000 and 100,000, includes 15 towns in Bulgaria and 12 in Hungary. The small town network, with towns of less than 20,000 inhabitants is dense in both countries: it includes 152 towns in Bulgaria and 160 in Hungary. The spatial organising functions of most of the small towns are weak. They can only provide low quality services to the rural settlements in their sphere of gravity, and they do not play an important role in the employment of the inhabitants of these settlements. In most of these towns, the most jobs were lost with the closing down the former industrial sites after the change of regime.

The *rural settlement structure* is also rather different. Bulgaria has a large number of villages (5,100), whereas there are much fewer of them in Hungary (2,900). Although in comparison with other European countries both countries have a high proportion of villages, this type of settlement is far more typical of Bulgaria. In Bulgaria, 83 per cent of all villages have fewer than 1,000 inhabitants, but in Hungary this figure is 59 per cent. While villages of over 5,000 inhabitants are rare in Bulgaria (there were only eight such settlements at the mid-1990s), 38 settlements belonged to this category in Hungary in 2001.

In countries witch several economic centres, like most Western European countries, the difference between the population of the primary city and that of the regional centres is at most five-fold; in the case of countries dominated by the capital, this difference is ten to twelve-fold. In Poland and Romania, for instance, the capitals are followed by six to eight major cities with populations between 300 and 700 thousand, which have an impact on the spatial structure of the entire regions. Contrary to this, in Hungary, there are only four regional centres, whose population exceeds 150 thousand (Table 1.3).

At the same time, a particular Central and Eastern European characteristic is that medium-sized cities play important role in the organisation of the settlement

Table 1.3 Population of the largest urban centres, 2009

Country	Capital city		The seven largest regional centres	
	'000	Percent country = 100	'000	Percent country = 100
Bulgaria	1,190	14.4	1,154	16.7
Czech Republic	1,193	11.7	1,288	12.5
Hungary	1,812	18.0	1,036	10.3
Poland	1,615	4.1	4,064	10.5
Romania	2,027	9.0	2,156	9.6
Slovakia	449	8.3	806	14.9

Source: National statistical yearbooks. Calculations by the author.

structure. Many of these function as territorial administrative centres, and the structure and scope of their institutional system and administrative organisations do not differ significantly from those of major cities. The unitary administrative and political system of the planned economies has worked towards homogeneity: the major cities could not assert their natural and traditional power in organising the spatial structure. It is not surprising therefore that after the first steps towards regionalisation and a decentralised development policy, sharp competition emerged among the territorial centres, different in size but of similar institution structure, to control the new functions of regional organisation.

Historical trends in the twentieth century

There is hardly any period in the millennium-long history of Europe when eastern territories followed an 'outstanding' development path. The long-term trends of marginalisation were only interrupted by short periods of recovery during the prosperous centuries of the Middle Ages, the enlightenment, and, later on. the unfolding of the industrial revolution. General European development had a decisive impact on the metropolitan elements of the Eastern and Central European system of settlements. Core regions did emerge in the spatial structure, but their expansion was limited and they did not exert a decisive influence on regional development outside their immediate catchment areas.

Regional disparities in the 'Eastern Europe of empires' before World War II

Geopolitical factors contributed heavily to the aggravation of spatial disparities in the Central and Eastern European macro-region. During the eighteenth and nineteenth centuries, which saw the spectacular transformation of the spatial structure of the economy and the town network, nations lived under Russian, Turkish, or Prussian control and were later on integrated into the Austrian and Hungarian lands of the Habsburg Empire. Their political dependence restricted the possibility of their autonomous development. Spatial development within the macro-region was primarily a function of what type of economic policy the imperial centres practiced. These disparities were the most spectacular in the economic performance of neighbouring Polish areas which belonged to Tsarist Russia or Prussia.

The institutionalisation of national movements had an indirect effect on the spatial development of future nation-states as well. It was most particularly the countries within the Russian sphere of interest which articulated their objection to the oppressive measures of imperial nationality policy. The Russian state utilised territorial-national strategies in the operation of the public administration of peripheries. The Tsarist General Gubernias were mostly multiethnic entities. The regions' historical, ethnic and geographical factors were also taken into account in the development of various forms of the exertion of the imperial will (Lieven 2000).

At the end of the nineteenth century, 92 per cent of the industrial production of Tsarist Russia was provided by the country's European territories. The concentration of these areas continuously increased. During the last decade of the past century, the most developed industrial areas of the Empire were the Gubernias of Moscow, Warsaw, Vladimir and St Petersburg. The number of industrial employees per thousand persons was between 32 and 82 in these areas, while in the least developed areas this figure was between one and seven. During the first decade of the twentieth century, the industrial production data of macro-regions showed 10- to 12-fold differences. The manufacturing industrial production per capita was 31 RUB in Russia during the first years of the twentieth century; its value was 87 RUB in the North-western regions and the Baltic area, 78 RUB in the Central Russian industrial district, and 8 RUB in Asian Russia (Horváth 2008). The level of the exploitation of the country's natural resources was incredibly low with 90 per cent of the Empire's resources remained unexplored.

The modernisation programmes of Hungary, the construction of railways, water management works, and state financed public works whose main focus was Budapest caused significant transformations in the country's spatial structure at the end of the nineteenth century. These were predominantly aimed at concentration and contributed to strengthening the national and international role of the capital city. The governments of the era did not elaborate their spatial development policy in its current form, yet a response was required for the unfolding modernisation demands of backward areas of the country. The actions of peripheral areas where intensity varied were supported by the National Hungarian Economic Association (OMGE). The moderation of spatial disparities was a key factor in the philosophy of the operation of the Association. The first governmental development programme was launched in the North-eastern Carpathians at the end of the 1890s, and a governmental inclusion strategy was formulated on the basis of the decrees of the Székler (Székely) Congress in 1902 for the modernisation of the Székler Land, one of the most under-developed regions in the country. The congress, which provided an emblematic unified system of the development efforts of the area's stakeholders, can be considered a key element in the tradition of Hungarian spatial development (Székely Congress, 2001). Even though concrete governmental and local actions failed to achieve their ambitious modernisation goals due to the vicissitudes of history, the congress' protocols provide interesting and thought-provoking literature for today's spatial development professionals.

The integration of regions into nation-states in the inter-war period

In the course of history, these countries and areas which formed the Central European nation-states, were previously parts of the Austro-Hungarian, German, and Russian Empires at the beginning of the twentieth century. Being member countries of the same empire, Hungary and Czechoslovakia, once integrated into the Central European macro-region, were able to connect to mainstream European industrial transformation. Romania, formed by the unification of two principalities and with population of 5 million at the end of the nineteenth century, had recently begun to establish a capitalist economy: the economic census of 1886 listed only 150 companies which employed more than 25 workers (Berend and Ránki 1982).

After World War I, significant changes took place in the Central and Eastern European economic and political area. The primary task of national governments was the organisation of the internal administrative-political, and, later on, the infra-structural and economic cohesion of those parts of the country that formerly belonged to different economic spheres.

The most striking territorial disparities were in Romania. In Transylvania, which was ceded to Romania after World War I, the level of urbanisation (density of settlement network) and industrialisation was considerably higher than in Moldavia and Wallachia. The Transylvanian region contained 30 per cent of the enlarged Romania's population, while it had a 40–70 per cent share of industrial capacities in different branches. Significant spatial disparities characterised Czechoslovakia, which manifested themselves not only in the income producing capacity of individual regions, but in the varying development levels of their infrastructural networks. In western parts of the country, the density of the railway network was six times higher than in the east.

The first post-World War I Eastern and Central European governments were not only faced with spatial disparities in economic performance, but spatially hetero-geneous social, political and public administrational institutional systems as well. These problems were considerable in each new state, since the provinces of the new countries formerly belonged to different empires. The creation of a uniform framework for politics and power absorbed a staggering proportion capital. In the realisation of a unified state organisation, the moderation of spatial differences was not a priority. In several countries, however, tasks related to spatial policy did emerge in the integration of the transport network, the expansion of energy production and the construction of social-political institutions of the majority state. The highest number of measures were mobilised in the two largest countries, Poland and the Soviet Union directed at the creation of the economic foundations of regionalisation.

Following the declaration of a unified Poland in 1918, the first tasks included the construction of roads and railways linking the Upper Silesian coal basin and the Baltic Sea. The railway line starting from the Katowice industrial region had to be extended to the coastline, and new port investments and urban development programmes had to be launched in Gdynia as Gdańsk (Danzig) remained under League of Nations control. These objectives were realised in 1926. The expansion of the economic bases required the development of industry in a country where 66 per cent of the population was in agricultural employment in the middle years of the 1930s. Several regions became the focus of political attention. Twelve areas with development difficulties were delimited. One category comprised the German demarcations and politically vulnerable areas (the so-called 'Polish corridor' between Germany and the Free City of Danzig); another comprised overpopulated regions dominated by peasant economies or lacking development intensity due to mountainous terrain (Białysztok, Lwów, the Kielce region, Southern Poland). Historical industrial regions constituted a separate group (Łódź, Poznań, Upper Silesia). And finally, in order to enable Warsaw to perform its capital city functions, total infrastructural modernisation of the agrarian region was necessary (Hamilton 1982).

The development difficulties of these problematic areas did not disappear even after World War II and the resolution of some of them is still unresolved. Still, the programmes had several positive impacts. First and foremost, the important role of spatial aspects was recognised in national economic planning. This led to systematic data collection, population and economic prognoses were made, and the spatial foundations of the post-war planning system were already established during this era (Malisz 1978). The 1932 Conference of the Society of Polish Town Planners (TUP, established in 1923) expressed the need for the application of spatial planning for the first time, and the Regional Planning Association of Warsaw was established in 1936. The Society published the statistical atlas of Poland which divided the country into two entities. 'A' Poland was constituted by developed areas lying west of the Vistula and 'B' Poland consisted of the eastern regions. The Association strived to convince the government that the latter regions should be the main beneficiaries of the public investment plan of 1936–1940. The Polish Ministry of Interior Affairs established planning offices in the former special regions. The backward area in the Krakow-Sandomierz-Lwów triangle was put under the control of the Ministry of Defence as it was designated as the development zone for the Polish armaments industry replacing Upper Silesia close to Germany.

The development of backward peripheral areas was elevated to the level of state ideology in the Soviet Union. The illusionary programme of eradicating the disparities between villages and towns served the needs of a policy oriented to the military, defence, and power interests of nation. The few attempts to develop in the first decades of the Soviet Union caught the attention of international professional public opinion. The concept of the comprehensive electrification of the country, the so-called GOELRO plan could be regarded as the forerunner of complex spatial economic development strategies. This plan articulated the need for the creation of macro-regions. Twenty-one economic districts were created whose tasks were the elaboration and organisation of the implementation of energy and economic development programmes (Tarkhov 2005). The concept of industrialisation focused on the country's territories lying to the west of the Urals. Over a half of industrial investment was located in the proximity of the old industrial areas, the Volga region, the Kuznetzk basin. The new industrial parks in the proximity of raw material sites serving defence purposes and not territorial development contributed to the eastward shift of the industrial potential. This resulted in the rapid settlement of several regions of Siberia. The spectacular regional disparities in the country did not disappear; moreover, in the presence of modern space shaping forces, they continued to rise.

During World War II, a considerable spatial restructuring could be observed in the industrial sector. Two-thirds of the outsourced companies settled in the Ural and Volga region and 16 per cent in Western Siberia (Treivish 2002). In 1941, a large proportion of Moscow firms were evacuated to areas lying east of the city and to Siberia. Consequently, the production of European industrial regions was reduced by half. The weight of Siberia was even less significant according to value data, yet a drastic increase in its position could be observed based on the number of employees. Post-World War II, a rapid development of the western territories took place. In eastern areas, petroleum, gas and other raw material industry developments were launched at the end of the 1940s, deriving from geology research and natural resource extraction of the 1930s. The positions of the eastern regions (Kazahstan, Siberia and the Far East) in raw material production were considerably strengthened during this period.

The scientific groundwork for the elaboration of regional programmes of national economic plans was laid by the Committee for the Research of Natural Forces of Production of the Academy of Sciences (Komissiya po izucheniyu estestvennyh proizvodetel'nyh sil (KEPS)) during the 1920s. The organisation was established by the Imperial Russian Academy in 1915. It was responsible for the regional sub-programmes of the GOELRO plan. The organisation was transformed in 1930 when it became subordinated to the central planning office under the name of the 'Council of the Research of Production Forces' (Soviet po izucheniyu prozvoditle'níh sil (SOPS)) (Adamesku 2012).

The regional consequences of the organisation of various parts of the countries into a unified state could be evaluated in other new states of Eastern and Central Europe. The strategic objective of Hungarian economic policy was to establish the internal cohesion of a country reduced to one-third of its previous size and the adjustment of industrial capacities in the new markets. Spatial disparities were significant in the new Romania. The level of urbanisation in Transylvania (density of city network) and its level of industrialisation was considerably higher than in the regions of the Moldavia and Wallachia. Transylvania contained 30 per cent of the population of the new Romania, while it had a 40–50 per cent share in the industrial capacity of the country. In Czechoslovakia, it was the creation of new Slovakian markets for Czech industry and the harmonisation of the transport infrastructure which determined the integration of Upper Hungary into the new national economic space. The formal power and public administrational structure required for establishing political cohesion had direct and indirect impacts on the development of the settlement network and the evolution of the economic potential of the various urban areas.

As a result of the state organisational and socio-political tasks related to the territorial changes that took place during the short period between both world wars, several scientific disciplines played an increasing part in the analysis of territorial economic processes, the organisational system of territorial public administration and governance models, the settlement system and population redistribution. During this era, the activities of several acknowledged social scientists left their mark on the functioning of the state. To cite a few examples, we can mention works of the Romanian rural sociologist Dimitrie Gusti, the political scientific research of the Hungarian András Rónay and the economic and socio-geographical analyses of the Czech Viktor Dvorský. The research results of significant figures in the generally prominent Russian (later Soviet) field of applied economic geography, Ivan G. Aleksandrov, Nikolay N. Baransky, Nikolay N. Kolosovsky contributed to the creation of economic districts and provided the scientific groundwork for spatial planning.

During World War II, new institutions were established in several parts of Central Europe which regarded the identification of regional assets to be their main task in order to provide a scientific bases for post-war reconstruction. Among these, the Baltic Institute in Toruń, the Silesian Institute in Wroclaw, the Western Institute in Poznań, the Silesian Institute in Opava, Moravia and the Transdanubian Research Institute in Hungary are worth mentioning. Two of these institutes are still functioning now. Currently the main profile of the Institute of Poznań is research into Polish-German relations. The institute founded in Pécs in 1943 became the centre of basic research in Hungarian spatial development, and remained the seat of the Centre for Regional Studies of the HAS (Hungarian Academy of Sciences) from 1984.

The equalizing spatial policy of state socialism

In the years following World War II, agriculture was the main source of employment in every country: 74 per cent in Romania, 51 per cent in Hungary. Its share in the industrialised Czechoslovakia reached 39 per cent. In the other countries, the indices of industrialisation reached only a half or a third of the Western European average. At the beginning of the 1950s, the rate of industrial employment was 14 per cent in Romania, 23 per cent in Hungary and 19 per cent in Yugoslavia. The leading industrial state in the area was Czechoslovakia, where the rate of industrial employment was 39 per cent. The low number of industrial workers (800,000 t, 700, 000 in Hungary) shows strong spatial concentration (Turnock 2006). In most of the countries, apart from capital cities, only large towns could claim a significant number of industrial jobs. The historical Czech and Moravian regions provided the only exceptions, where large-scale industrial centres of the traditionally developed textile industry, coal mining and metallurgy were counter-balanced by a network of smaller hubs.

The forced industrialisation characterising the socialist planned economy produced conflicting results in the 1950s and 1960s. The politics of the era formally supported the growth and spatial diffusion of industrial employment, strongly influenced settlement structure and enhanced the speed of urbanisation. The standard of living in rural areas was raised to a certain extent through its socio-political and cultural. We can observe an apparent change in the indices representing quantitative growth. Between 1950 and 1970, the rate of urban population increased from 23 to 41per cent in Romania, and from 37 to 48 per cent in Hungary. By 1970, the number of industrial workers reached 2 million in Romania and 1.7 million in Hungary. The structural changes of the economy led to decreasing regional disparities, while the relative spatial cohesion meant an even distribution of the basically weak industrial outputs. GNP per capita rates were approximately the same in Hungary, Romania and the Soviet Union in 1975, while spatial discrepancies were largely unequal. GNP values in most spatial administrative units were lagging behind the average GNP of CMEA countries. In Romania, 32 out of 40 counties, and in Hungary, 12 out of 20 counties remained below the Eastern European average. The spatial structure of Czechoslovakia was the most homogenous even at that period, with just one out of 12 districts (East Slovakia) showing weaker performance than the Eastern European average.

The centrally controlled economy appeared in strongly differentiated forms in the region, and the countries showed significant heterogeneity in the organisation of their economies, economic policy instruments and orientations of European relationships. In Hungary, in addition to the instruments of national economic planning, elements of normative regulation also appeared in the control of regional development (Enyedi 1989). The Hungarian government laid down the long-term objectives of spatial and settlement policy in a decree in 1971, and the parliament approved a spatial development act in 1985. Romania, on the other hand, continued to enforce its low technology level, Stalinist industrial policy. The more developed areas and the 17 provincial capitals were affected by the concentrated location of industry until the end of the 1960s, while the industrialisation of rural areas (e.g. Székler Land) increased in the 1970s (Benedek 2006). Forced industrialisation was coupled with a fatal settlement policy in Romania. Strict anti-rural spatial planning norms were introduced at the beginning of the Ceauşescu era, and the excessive urbanisation campaign had peaked in the final years of the 1980s with the launch of the rural rationalisation programme. The objective of the Romanian Communist Party's programme was to reduce by half the number of villages, and in the meantime, to create 558 agro-industrial towns and regional organising centres in order to control the agricultural sector (Turnock 2006).

Socialist planned economies wished to moderate spatial disparities primarily through industrial development programmes. Infrastructural investments linked to industrialisation and the ever-growing speed of urbanisation resulted in the reduction of income disparities of macro-regions.

Spatial planning fulfilled an important role in the system of the planned economy: in Poland, an act on spatial planning was approved in 1961. Long-term spatial plans contained the key elements of regional development strategies. Settlement network development concepts were elaborated in several countries (Bulgaria, Hungary, Romania).

The ideology of the regional and settlement policy of state socialism (classical Marxist theory, urbanist utopias, planning theory) and the objectives derived therof (balanced development, the moderation of disparities in the civilisation of villages and towns, the spatially balanced distribution of free or highly subsidised social transfers) posed serious barriers to scientific disciplines engaged in the study of spatial processes. The notion of an ideally homogeneous society conquered scientific thought in the various countries in a differentiated way. Owing to their intensive links with Western science, Polish and Hungarian social scientists provided significant research results about spatially unequal development, the anomalies of the transformation of the settlement structure at a relatively early period, the middle years of the 1960s. They questioned in expressed words the efficiency of a central planned economy, an economic policy neglecting local-regional assets (Domański 1973; Dziewoński 1967; Enyedi 1981).

The results of the analyses about the spatial transformation of the planned economies pointed to the fact that the economic structure and type of urbanisation characteristics in Eastern and Central Europe did not represent an autonomous model, but a repeat of Western type urbanisation and development cycles with a significant delay. The disparities of spatial development could be attributed to late industrialisation, on one hand, and the functioning of the system of state socialism on the other.

Due to the specific development paths of Eastern and Central Europe, research in the field of social and economic space shows quite a few unique features as well. Socialist science policy, following the guiding principles of the power structure, did not consider spatial research as a priority issue. This was mainly because none of the tiers of the strictly centralised state administration was interested in the analysis of local-regional specifics. Political practice aimed at homogenisation considered spatial aspects only to the extent of central planning requirements.

Even though the era between 1948 and1990 was characterised by challenges related to the research of socio-economic space for different scientific disciplines, the demands of the commissioners were neither complex nor demanding of thematic cooperation between scientific disciplines from the aspect of social management. The traditional scientific disciplines investigating spatial relations (economic geography, settlement and public administration sciences and economics to a certain degree) could all pursue independently of each other their activities in academies or universities. The scientific bases of spatial development research were established primarily in public institutions, national planning offices and urban planning institutes.

The catalytic effect of the investigation of spatial processes can also be detected in the process of the differentiation of Eastern European social sciences. The research results related to the detection of inter-settlement disparities in the structure of society served as an important force behind the greater autonomy of sociology in terms of theory and methodology, while the investigations of spatial-settlement components of public administrative-power relations contributed to the legitimisation of political science (Bihari 1983; Kulcsár 1986; Musil 1977).

The institutional coordination of territorial research was achieved in two countries. The Council for the Investigation of Forces of Production maintained its functioning in the Soviet Union. In Poland, the Polish Academy of Sciences established the Committee of Space Economy and Regional Planning in 1958 (Kukliński 1966). These two institutions had autonomous financial resources at their disposal facilitating the validation of their general coordination competences. In Hungary, the governmental decree on the national spatial development concept delegated the organisation of basic research in spatial development to the Hungarian Academy of Sciences in 1971. However, this did not imply state level coordination.

The major scientific branch involved in the examination of spatial processes was social and economic geography. Almost every scientific academy had their own geographic institutions whose results in applied geographical research had a significant impact on spatial development decisions of the era. Poland was also prominent in the area of institutional innovation. The name of the geographical institute of PAS was changed to Institute of Geography and Spatial Economics at the beginning of the 1970s. In Hungary, the Centre for Regional Studies functioning in the form of a network was established in 1984 whose base was the Transdanubian Research Institute of the HAS performing territorial basic research. The research centre in collaboration with the Faculty of Economics of the University of Pécs launched a post-graduate training programme in spatial development in 1988. The scientific capacities of the geographical departments and institutes of the university were quite significant despite the fact that this discipline was rather more oriented towards teacher training in socialist higher education. Departments of urbanism in polytechnical universities were also recognised research groups in several countries.

A significant factor in the permanent development of Polish and Hungarian spatial research was the reformist spirit in the political systems of the two countries. Consequently, the relations between scientific workshops of the two countries were maintained with Western European research units. Joint research programmes were launched and the national, regional and local political elite expressed interest in their research results. In fact, it is not too bold to state that regional research played an active role in preparing regime change (Maurel 2002). Research results called attention to the fact that the modernisation of the economy required a substantial transformation of the spatial structure and, as a result, the reconceptualisation of objectives, principles and institutions of spatial development policy was inevitable. The cooperation and development coalition between the central state, local-territorial communities, public and private sectors was to become the basis of the new model of social management. Hungarian research analysing the spatial structural transformation of planned economies highlighted the fact that Eastern European economic structure and urbanisation did not constitute an independent model but an imitation of Western type urbanisation and development cycles with a significant delay. The disparities of spatial development were attributed to the lateness of development on the one hand and the functioning of the system of state socialism on the other.

Socio-economic disparities between regions

In the countries of systemic change, depending on their level of urbanisation, the territorial expansion of rural areas and their level of backwardness display significant inequalities. With the exception of Poland, where the urban population is growing, outward migration from rural areas has stopped. Moreover, in some countries, due to reverse migration from the towns and cities, the rural population is growing. These recent demographic trends cannot be considered as unequivocally positive, since the economic bases of these rural areas are weak and most of those who returned there were forced to work in in *agricultural* production. The rate of working-age population is the highest in these rural areas and in the traditional industrial areas. In metropolitan areas, quite the opposite process is happening. In the age structure of the capitals, the weight older age groups is growing. In regions of dynamic development (like Western and Central Transdanubia in Hungary, the North-western regions of Poland, or Southern Moravia in the Czech Republic) as well as in the northern and eastern Romanian and eastern Slovakian regions where birth rates are high, a favourable age structure is emerging, although in the latter regions strong outward migration has negative impact on the working-age population.

The territorial differences between the *labour markets* are the result of the previous economic structure and the structural transformations that have taken place in the emerging market economies. The economic activity rate is high in regions where the structural transformations have not started yet. Several heavy industrial regions in the Czech Republic and Poland have not been set on a new development track, and there are also many rural areas in Eastern Europe where the high rate of agricultural employees (reaching 42 per cent in Moldavia, Romania) is expected to cause sharp tensions. There are regions where the rapid growth of the previously neglected tertiary sector has counter-balanced the shrinking size of other sectors of the economy. A peculiar paradox of the Central and Eastern European transformation is that, with the exception of Hungary and the Czech Republic, the activity rates are the lowest in the more successful regions. Among the new EU member-stages Hungary has the lowest activity rate (51.7 per cent in 2001), while the rates of Central and Western Transdanubia are a few points higher than the national average.

The development of the diverse economic potentials of the CEE countries is hindered by cohesion problems. At low levels of economic development, however, the performance gap among the regions within the same country are not greater than in Western Europe (Table 1.4). Yet, the gap between the worst performing region and the best one (Prague and the Romanian and Bulgarian regions) is greater (750 per cent) than in Western Europe. On the whole, disregarding national inequalities, the Central and Eastern European economic space is relatively homogenous, with the majority of the regions performing below the European average; in Romania and Bulgaria even the capitals are quite under-developed (Figures 1.3 and 1.4).

Obviously, economic differences among the smaller territorial units are stronger than those among the regions; interestingly, at the county (NUTS 2) level the

Table 1.4 Regional differences in GDP per capita in Central and Eastern European countries, 2011

Country	Least developed region		Most developed region		Difference
	Region's GDP per capita in PPS, EU27 = 100				
Bulgaria	South-CTsentral	27	South-west	52	1.93
Czech Republic	Central-Moravia	60	Prague	160	2.67
Poland	Lubelskie	35	Mazowieckie	81	2.31
Hungary	North Great Plain	41	Central Hungary	105	2.56
Romania	North-east	24	Bucharest	75	3.13
Slovakia	Eastern Slovakia	43	Bratislava	148	3.44
EUR15	Anatoliaiki Mackedonia	47	Inner London	303	6.44

Source: The author's calculations on the basis of the Regions: Statistical Yearbook, 2007.

development gap is the widest in Hungary. The GDP per capita figure for Budapest exceeds that of the Szabolcs-Szatmár-Bereg county more than threefold, while the GDP gap between Bucharest and the Vaslui county in Romania is only twofold. The impacts of the market economy are expected to bring about the further strengthening of territorial inequalities. During the territorial restructuring of Hungary, the leading and backward counties have been developing at quite different paces, which indicates that the spatial structuring forces are now more differentiated than they were in the planned economy period. Back then, planned industrialisation was to shape the economic potentials of the various regions; today, their economic development is influenced by the competitive sectors of industry and by adjoining services (Table 1.5).

The disparities between the individual planning regions within Bulgaria are relatively small except for the more pronounced backwardness of the North-west region in its social-economic development. Considerably more significant, however, are the intra-regional disparities, namely those between the municipalities and districts within the same planning region, representing a specific issue that the regional development policy has so far failed to adequately address. Almost all of the country's regions and districts exhibit the typical contrasts of the core-periphery kind. Particularly affected in this respect are the border territories, many of the rural territories, several areas in industrial decline, as well as those with a high concentration of ethnic minorities. These are typically Bulgarian disparities that necessitate special attention since a lot of territories are in a critical condition, provoking also many negative social and social-demographic developments longterm effect of which is still uncertain.

In terms of per capita GDP, however, the differences between the individual planning regions have not been significant. This indicator was relatively higher in the South-west region, whereas in the rest of the regions it was rather evenly distributed. It should be noted that the indicator's value in certain regions (notably the North-west region as well as parts of the North-east and the South-west regions)

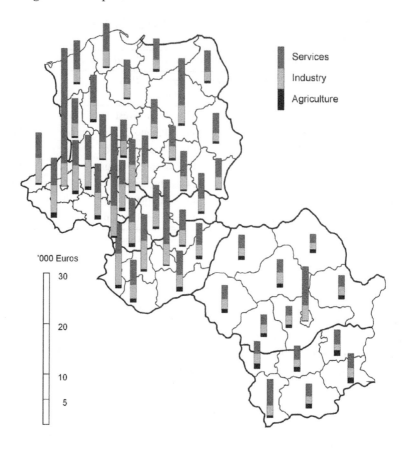

Figure 1.3 GDP per capita by region and sector in Central and Eastern Europe, 2011
Source: Designed by the author.

has been highly dependent on the actual state of local large enterprises and the population migration.

The structure of the economy in all of the country's regions showed that services had the largest share in overall output, while agriculture and forestry jointly had the lowest relative weight among economic activities. This trend appeared to be the most notable in the region exhibiting the highest GDP figure the South-west region, where the service sector accounted for 67.5 per cent of the value added in contrast to the modest 5.7 per cent share of agriculture and forestry. The share of manufacturing in GDP turned out to be the highest in the North-west region, reflecting the location of several large enterprises in its territory, whereas the service sector was relatively less developed, accounting for only 45.1 per cent of overall output. Agriculture had the largest share in the North-east region. In nominal terms, the manufacturing sector exhibited the highest GVA figure in the South-west region, while value added in agriculture was most significant in the South-central region.

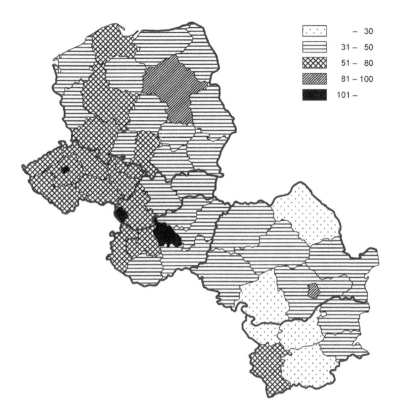

Figure 1.4 GDP per capita by region in Central and Eastern Europe, 2011, EU15=100
Source: Designed by the author.

In the Czech Republic, the Prague region is economically the most efficient one. It has created a quarter of the Czech Republic's gross domestic product for a long time. The other seven NUTS 2 regions account for the remaining 75 per cent of GDP. Their share in the economic activity of the Czech Republic is relatively balanced, ranging from 9 to 14 per cent.

With 172 per cent of the EU per capita GDP average in 2010, Prague represents a unique region, as compared not only to the other cohesion regions within the Czech Republic, but also to any other NUTS 2 region in any other candidate country. The amount of Prague's per capita GDP is even much higher than that of an overwhelming majority of the current EU regions, or higher than the value of this indicator in 13 out of the 15 EU member-states. Thus, Prague is the only cohesion region in the Czech Republic that will not ask for support under Objective 1 within the framework of the EU economic and social cohesion policy.

In terms of the interpretation of the aggregate per capita GDP indicator, the other regions represent a relatively homogenous group, fluctuating within a relatively narrow interval of 48 to 56 per cent of the EU per capita GDP average. So they

Table 1.5 Characteristics of territorial inequalities in the countries of systemic change

	Before 1990	*After 1990*
The dimension of spatial disparities	Between urban and rural areas Within settlements	Within settlements Between regions
The tendency of disparities	Decreasing inequalities between urban and rural areas Decreasing inequalities between regions Stabile inequalities between settlements	Increasing difference within settlements Increasing difference between regions Stable difference between urban and rural areas
The driving force behind the development of disparities	Industrialisation	Structural changes Services Foreign direct investment
Decision determining disparities	National level	Local level Trans-national level
Indicators expressing disparities	Demographic composition Communal and social infrastructure Social incomes connected to the use of communal and social facilities	Unemployment rate Wage level

Source: Vision Planet, p. 48.

meet the Objective 1 reference level. From this viewpoint, 99.4 per cent of the area of the Czech Republic and 88.5 per cent of the population represent the regions where development is lagging behind. As compared to the other candidate countries, the per capita GDP values in the Czech NUTS 2 regions can be considered relatively high and even close to those of a number of regions in the so-called EU cohesion countries.

Using other indicators, however, it is possible to mark some more problematic regions in the Czech Republic. The cohesion regions that are sensitive in this respect include primarily the North-west and Moravia-Silesia, which show an

Table 1.6 Level of development of NUTS 2 regions, 2010 (development regions)

Level of GDP as a percentage of EU27 average, in PPP	Number of development regions					
	Bulgaria	Czech Republic	Hungary	Poland	Romania	Slovakia
Over 150	–	1	–	–	–	1
100– 150	–	–	1	–	–	–
76–99	–	–	–	1	1	–
50–75	1	7	2	5	–	2
36–49	–	–	4	10	3	1
26–35	6	–	–	–	4	–

Source: The author's calculations on the basis of the Regions: Statistical Yearbook, 2007.

Table 1.7 Level of development of NUTS 2 regions, 2010 (population)

Level of GDP as a percentage of EU27 average	Percentage of population of the country					
	Bulgaria	Czech Republic	Hungary	Poland	Romania	Slovakia
Over 150	–	11.6	–	–	–	11.3
100–149	–	–	28.8	–	–	–
76–99	–	–	–	13.6	10.4	–
50–75	27.7	88.4	20.9	39.1	–	59.5
36–49	–	–	50.3	47.3	11.8	29.2
26–35	72.3	–	–	–	77.8	–

Source: Author, based on data from http://appsso.eurostat.ec.europa.eu.

above average rate of unemployment not only in national terms, but also in relation to the EU. Moreover, these regions are also most affected by structural unemployment, or employability, for the share of the long-term unemployed here approaches 50 per cent of the total number of the unemployed.

The Czech economy as a whole has undergone a sharp structural change in the past ten years. The shares of agriculture and industry in GDP generation have decreased (from 7.7 to 3.4 per cent and from 34.5 to 31.8 per cent, respectively) in favour of the share of the services sector (which increased from 41.8 to 49.7 per cent). A similar process took place at the level of the cohesion regions without exception; however, the intensity was different in particular cases. There has been a considerable decline in the weight of industry within overall economic activity (a major fall of the share of industry in the individual region's GDP) and simultaneously a sharp increase in the weight of service industries, or the tertiary sector within overall economic activity (a growing share of services, or the tertiary sector in the individual region's GDP) in the past ten years.

Structural changes in the individual regions were affected especially by the following factors:

- down-scaling of fuel mining, metallurgy and heavy chemistry in the North-west and Moravia-Silesia regions (nevertheless, the above-mentioned industries still remain dominant in these regions with respect to economic activity and employment);
- the process of restructuring the heavy machinery industry in the South-west region;
- high weight of the leather, textile and food industries in the North-east, Central Moravia and South-east regions;
- declining share of agriculture in the economic activity of the South-east region (mountain and sub-mountain areas).

Hungary can be characterised by significant economic, social and infrastructure differences. These are more noticeable between the capital city and the rest of the country, between individual regions, and also among micro-regions and towns and villages.

Compared with the rest of the country, the development of Budapest is striking. Seventeen per cent of the Hungarian population lives in Budapest, while it contributes 35 per cent of the GDP of the country. Its advantages result from its high population density, its function as a centre for business and financial services and as an innovation transfer centre. It has large high value added sectors, mainly business services, research and development and tourism. Twenty-eight per cent of companies are operating in Budapest: over half of the firms with foreign interests and 53 per cent of subscribed capital are concentrated here (Figure 1.5). The significant role of Budapest is further increased by its central geographical location and as the hub of the transport network. However, the large economic and social potential of Budapest has effect only in the agglomeration, but not in the more remote regions of the country.

Considering the level of economic development, household incomes and unemployment in the regions, apart from the favourable indicators of Budapest, the gap between the east and the west is large. The restructuring of the North-western and central parts of the country has been successful when compared to the remainder of the country catching up slowly.

The current dynamics of the North-western regions come primarily from the geographical position of these regions, and from the proximity to western markets. This has been the dominant factor in economic restructuring together with neighbouring Austrian provinces. In Central Hungary, Western and Central Transdanubia the well-trained labour force, its low cost compared with the average of

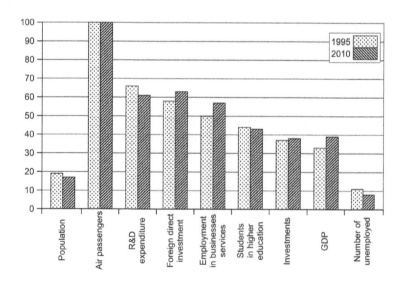

Figure 1.5 Concentration level of various activities in Budapest, 2010, per cent
Source: Designed by the author based on statistical yearbook of Hungary.

European Union, and the favourable transport network helped the influx of foreign capital and innovative, export-oriented industries. As a consequence, the unemployment rate is lowest in these areas, and income conditions are also better than the national average.

Economic performance of the rest of the regions lags far behind the three most advanced regions. The reasons for this were the inherited under-efficient industrial structure and low income generating capacity. These areas were dominated by mining, heavy industry, the agro-business, and the loss of the collapsed eastern market had a dramatic impact on them. The industrial restructuring of the 1990s had the most adverse effect in North Hungary, turning the region into a depressed area. Agriculture and the food industry were concentrated in the Great Hungarian Plain and South Transdanubia. Due to the low income generating capacity of agriculture, the proportion of backward areas is significant. In these regions the relatively low level of human resources and the high rate of inactivity limit the economic restructuring.

Diversity of the economic potential of regions in Poland is similar to that occurring in the majority of the EU member-states. The principal indicator, GDP per capita, becomes different in the proportion of 1:2.2. In the context of Poland's accession to the EU, the most important problem was not the diversity, but the low economic potential of all regions. Even the best of them did not reach, in 2000, the level of 60 per cent of the average GDP per capita index in the 15 EU countries. The weakest Polish regions are classified within the last 20 European regions.

The source of interregional differences in GDP per capita is the diverse level of labour productivity. Mainly, the sectoral structure of individual regions decides on the level of this indicator. In the sectoral system, productivity per single employee in services, industry, and construction is many times higher than in agriculture (six to seven times).

Participation of people employed in agriculture determines the average value of the labour efficiency in the region. The highest position in this respect is occupied by voivodships with structures dominated by non-agricultural activities, such as: Mazowieckie, Śląskie, Wielkopolskie, Dolnośląskie, and Pomorskie, and the lowest, Lubelskie (high percentage of labour resources in agriculture), Podlaskie, Podkarpackie, Warmińsko-Mazurskie and Świętokrzyskie.

Interregional diversity in the unemployment rate oscillates in 2011 between 7.9 per cent in the Mazowieckie voivodship and 13.3 per cent in Świętokrzyskie voivodship (in 1999 it was 9.3 in Małopolskie and 19.5 in Warminsko-Mazurskie) These differences do not overlap fully with differences in the GDP per capita level. After systemic change, unemployment was hard to estimate since in many voivodships agriculture is a kind of 'storehouse' for veiled unemployment where there is agrarian overpopulation. Despite this, in the eastern part of the country, the participation of rural population in the total number of unemployed people was the highest and varied between 55 and65 per cent limits with the country's average of 44 per cent. The highest unemployment rate was registered in 2002 in the following voivodships: Warminsko-Mazurskie (27.3 per cent), Zachodniopomorskie (26.6 per cent), Lubuskie (25.9 per cent) and Dolnosląskie (25.3 per cent). Such a situation has existed for many years as a result of the decline in the economic base in small cities and in the state owned farms in this part of the country.

Regions with the highest competitiveness and development level include the following voivodships: Małopolskie, Mazowieckie, Pomorskie, Sląskie and Wielkopolskie. Their competitive advantage results from: high efficiency of the production sector, significant human resources potential (including research centres and well prepared cadres), and a relatively well developed infrastructure. They have the greatest opportunity to participate in the European development processes (globalisation, construction of information society). Their trump cards are their capitals, big agglomerations with diverse economic structure and high participation of services in the employment sector. An essential factor limiting the quality of life in these agglomerations is the bad condition of their public transport (decline of rail transport, bus transport polluting the environment, lack of cycle lanes).

Relatively the best situation occurs in Mazowieckie voivodship, which has the biggest area and the biggest population in the country, which concentrates almost one- third of the companies registered in the country with participation of foreign capital, which has the lowest unemployment rate, the lowest number of unemployed per single job offer, the highest salaries in the country and the highest positive migration balance. The highest employment rate, the highest education level, and the lowest negative birth rate also characterise Mazowieckie voivodship. Thanks to this, all the voivodships generate the highest GDP (in absolute values and per capita). At the same time it is the voivodship with the biggest intra-regional diversity, difference in GDP per capita between Warsaw and sub-regions such as: Ostrolecki, Radomski and Siedlecki reaches 5:1.

Regions, which face serious difficulties, are the voivodships in the eastern part of Poland: Lubelskie, Podlaskie, Podkarpackie, Świętokrzyskie and Warmińsko-mazurskie. The following factors limit their development: ineffective employment structure, low productivity of agriculture, low development level of industry and services, low quality of human resources (including weak entrepreneurship), low urbanisation indices, and low involvement of foreign capital.

The situation of the Sląskie *voivod*ship is very complex. On one hand it still has a relatively high per capita level of GDP, and a low unemployment rate but, on the other hand it is currently the largest in Europe, with a concentration of traditional industries, including coal mining and steel industry. The necessary, and deep restructuring of the region's economic structure has already started. It will lead, however, to drastic employment reduction in plants, which were favoured until now, and will provoke a sharp response from traditionally, very strong trade unions.

The above-mentioned trends and phenomena show clearly that, the solution of major problems has determined the development of Polish society and economy in the last two decades. These are as follows:

• The low development rate, prevalent throughout recent years (within the limit of stagnation), may lead to an extremely low, in relation to the EU, level of income and quality of life.

- The relatively high unemployment rate and low level of social activity lowers the quality of life and threatens a large part of the population with exclusion from development processes.
- These occurrences are mutually conditioning, creating the dangerous 'impossibility syndrome' in using Poland's development opportunities in the next few decades..
- The low development rate of the economy and the necessity for it to become more competitive (increasing productivity, among other factors) are limiting demand for work, which, given its high supply (the increase in the number of people of working age in 2001–2002 amounts to over 500,000 persons), causes open and hidden unemployment.
- High unemployment rates, besides political and social problems, results in considerable public money being spent on social assistance, limiting funds for development purposes. Low income limits demand, and as a consequence reduces the level of production and services, which satisfy consumption needs.
- Analysis of the sectoral structure of human resources used and of the domestic product creation show that this problem cannot be solved without profound changes, the main direction of which will be the reduction of inefficient activities mainly in industry and agriculture, in favour of activities with the high added value, mainly market services, industry based on knowledge, and also construction.

In *Romania* there still are major differences within planning regions where heavily agricultural counties coexist with more developed areas. The phenomenon has been made even worse by the concentrated impact of economic restructuring in given areas with mono-industrial towns typically being affected by labour market shocks due to the closure of unprofitable state enterprises. Other factors with an impact on regional development traditionally include border regions and the Danube with regions bordering Moldova and Ukraine and regions along the Danube being more under-developed than the others.

One of the most striking features of Romania's economic growth over the last ten years has been the growing importance of the Bucharest area in development terms. This is in line with a well-known trend affecting all transition economies, but it is even more evident here due to the large size of the country in both population and territory. With some of 9.0 per cent of the population, Bucharest accounts or 17 per cent of the country's GDP. Twenty per cent of all SMEs are registered there and the capital has attracted 47 per cent of total foreign investment. The quite significant development of Bucharest not had any influence in neighbouring counties. Some of Romania's most under-developed counties are still to be found in the capital's immediate surroundings. The second peculiarity of regional development in Romania is the mosaic-like structure of economic development at the sub-national level. In practically all the regions, quite reasonably developed counties coexist with somewhat under-developed ones.

The main problems of regional development in Romania are as follows:

- The growing importance of Bucharest.
- Unbalanced growth between west and east of the country.
- Economic growth has followed a broad west-east direction with proximity to western markets acting as a growth spurring factor.
- Underdevelopment is concentrated in the North-east and in southern regions along the Danube.
- The urban decline of small and medium-sized towns.
- Strong negative impact of industrial restructuring in mono-industrial localities.

In Slovakia conditions that were created in the process of the transformation of the economy from a completely planned economy to a market economy have further intensified the territorial imbalance. The actual disparities are particularly evident in:

- the regional contributions to the formation of GDP;
- the unemployment rate;
- the level of entry of foreign capital in individual regions;
- the level of income of the population;
- the establishment of new firms in the regions, etc.

The evaluation of the level of regional development shows that only the region of Bratislava differs significantly. Among the other regions there are no large differences, in GDP/capita. Most significant differences obviously exist only at the county level. The region of Bratislava has a special position in comparison with the EU average. With the level of 176 per cent of the EU average (2010) it can be classified as one of the most developed regions in the EU. The other regions of Slovakia attained 50 to 70 per cent of EU average.

Districts classified as developed areas include 31.6 per cent of the population of Slovakia. Economically stable areas presenting conditions for future development comprise 25.5 per cent of population. The percentage of the population living in stagnating districts was 17.3 and the percentage of the population of economically depressed region was 25.6 per cent at the beginning of 2000 (Silvan 2000).

Slovakia is also a one-pole country. At the end of the 1990s, 51 per cent of university lectures lived in Bratislava county, 12 per cent in Western Slovakia, 15 per cent in Central Slovakia, and 22 per cent in Eastern Slovakia. The statistics for university graduates presented the same analogy (52.3 per cent in Bratislava, 13.9 per cent in Western Slovakia, 13.4 per cent in Central Slovakia, 20.4 per cent in Eastern Slovakia). Bratislava county was also the home of most of the banking sector and dominated the domestic market for savings and investments. It also reported the highest business enterprise per capita figures. Of the 100 largest non-financial business organisations in Slovakia, 34 were located in Bratislava county (Buček 1999). The predominance of the capital region did not decline after joining the EU.

Summing up, the radical transformation of the economic structure affected the different regions in different ways. The losers of transition, like in the most other European countries, where the areas were dominated by heavy industry and mining and, as a special Eastern European feature, extensive agricultural areas. The emerging market economy resulted in the strengthening of regional inequalities. Comparing the regional data of the member-states and the countries awaiting accession we find that the Central and Eastern regions are at the bottom of the European ranking, while the Czech Republic and two Hungarian regions are above the EU average, and one (West Transdanubia) is almost at that level (Tables 1.6 and 1.7).

Two key issues which influence the regional economic performance are the urbanisation level and the sectoral composition of economic activity. The following stylised classification of regions can be used for analytical purposes: agricultural, industrial and regions with services orientation (Figure 1.6). For the purpose of identifying the typical manufacturing, agricultural and service regions, the highest concentrations of employment in each sector were selected. (Criteria of

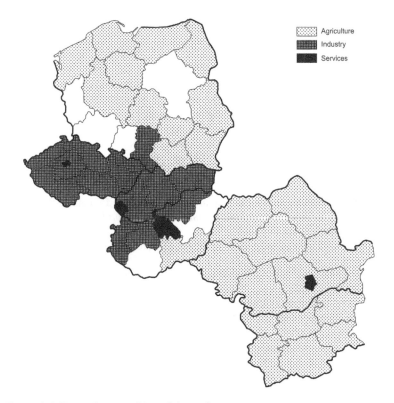

Figure 1.6 Sectoral composition of the regions
Source: Designed by the author.

designation were: percentage share of agricultural employment is more than 10 per cent; percentage share of industrial employment is more than 40 per cent and percentage share of service employment is more than 60 per cent.)

The regions depending mostly on services are clustered around capital cities. The highest concentration of services is in Prague (76.6 per cent). It is followed by the Bratislava region (Slovakia) and Central Hungary, which have similar characteristics (71–72 per cent). In contrast to the service industries, manufacturing is more closely associated with smaller cities and towns, like in EU countries, and with polycentric urban networks. Most of the top 15 manufacturing regions are in the historical core territory of Central Europe. Fourteen regions with the highest concentration of agriculture are, as it would be expected, situated in under-developed Romania and Bulgaria (all planning regions of the countries), and 11 regions in Poland and one region in Hungary. There are 24 regions where the percentage share of the agricultural employment is over 20 per cent (as against the average of 4.5 per cent for the EU as a whole).

References

Adamesku, A. (2012) *K 100-letiyu Sovieta po izucheniyu proizvoditel'nyh sil*, sops.ru/-sops/istoriya [10 November 2012].

Benedek, J. (2006) 'Urban policy and urbanisation in the transititon Romania', *Romanian Review of Regional Studies,* 1: 51–64.

Berend, T.I. and Ránki, G. (1982) *The European Periphery and Industrialization, 1780–1914,* Cambridge: Cambridge University Press.

Bihari O. (1983) *Korszerű tendenciák az államhatalom gyakorlásában* [Recent tendencies in the practice of state power], Budapest: Közgazdasági és Jogi Könyvkiadó.

Buček, M. (1999) 'Regional disparities and regional dynamics in Slovakia: a pre-accession picture', Paper presented at the RSA Congress held in Dublin. Manuscript.

Domański, R. (1973) *Gospodarka przestrzenna,* Warsaw: PWN.

Dziewoński, K. (1967) 'Teoria regionu ekonomicznego', *Przegląd Geograficzny,* 1: 33–50.

Enyedi G. (1981) *Földrajz és társadalom* [Geography and society], Budapest: Magvető Könyvkiadó.

Enyedi, G. (1989) 'Regional policy and planning in Hungary', in Berentsen, W., Danta, D.R. and Daróczy, E. (eds) *Regional Development Processes and Policies,* Pécs: Centre for Regional Studies, HAS.

Hamilton, I.F.E. (1982) 'Regional policy in Poland. A search for equity', *Geoforum,* 2: 121–132.

Horváth, G. (2008) *Regional Transformation in Russia,* Discussion Papers, 65. Pécs: Centre for Regional Studies, HAS.

Kukliński, A.R. (1966) 'Research activity of the Committee for Space Economy and Regional Planning', in Fisher, J.C. (ed.) *City and Regional Planning in Poland,* Ithaca, NY: Cornell University Press, 389–405.

Kulcsár K. (1986) *A modernizáció és a magyar társadalom* [The modernisation and the Hungarian society], Budapest: Magvető Könyvkiadó.

Lieven, D. (2000) *Empire: the Russian Empire and Its Rivals,* London: Yale University Press.

Malisz, B. (ed.) (1978) *40 lat planowania struktury przestrzennej Polski.* Warsaw: Studia Komitetu Przestrzennego Zagospodorowania Kraju. Studia, 64.

Maurel, M.-C. (2002) 'Central-European geography and the post-socialist transformation. A Western point of view', in Kaase, M., Sparschuh, V. and Wenninger, A. (eds) *The Social Science Disciplines in Central and Eastern Europe. Handbook on Economics, Political Science and Sociology,* Bonn, Berlin, Budapest: GESIS/Social Science Information Centre, Collegium Budapest Institute for Advanced Study, 578–587.

Musil, J. (1977) *Urbanization in Socialist Countries*, Prague: Svoboda.

Silvan, J. (2000) 'Slovak Republik', in Bachtler, J., Downes, R. and Gorzelak, G. (eds) *Transition, Cohesion and Regional Policy in Central and Eastern Europe,* Aldershot: Ashgate, 177–194.

Székely Kongresszus [Szekler Congress], Csíkszereda: Hargita Kiadóhivatal, 2001.

Tarkhov, S.A. (2005) 'Dinamika administrativno-territorial'nogo deleniia Rossii v XX veke', in Glezer, O.B. and Poljan, P.M. (eds) *Rossiia i ieio regioni v XX veke: territoriia – rasselenie – migracii,* Moscow: OGI, 33–75.

Treivish, A. (2002) 'Promyshlennoszt' v Rossii za 100 let', in Danilova-Danilyana, V.I. and Stepanova, S.A. (eds) *Rossiya v okruzhaiushchem mire: 2002. Analitichesky iezhegodnik,* Moscow: Izdatel'stvo Mezhdunarodnogo nezavisimogo ekologopolitologicheskogo universiteta, 1–12.

Turnock, D. (2006) *The Economy of East Central Europe, 1815–1898. Stages of Transformation in a Peripheral Region,* London: Routledge.

2 Modernisation of regional development policy

Emerging regional policy

At the beginning of the transformation period, the emerging democracies cared little about the goals, tools and institutional system of regional policy. The same applied to Hungary. Yet, the paradigm shift first began in Hungary. This was proved by the 1998 European Commission report stating that Hungary seemed the most prepared in regional policy (Regular report from the Commission on progress towards accession, Hungary). In general, this document was rather negative on the structural and cohesion policies of the Central and Eastern European countries, stating that

- the tools of regional policy are non-existent or very weak;
- the institutional system is under-developed; sectoral co-ordination in the co-financing of regional development projects is weak; the development tools of the local governments are poor and personnel lack expertise;
- the budget sector needs radical restructuring: the central funds are difficult to mobilise in the co-financing of structural programmes; the amount of co-financing resources is unclear; the efficiency of the utilisation of the resources is not guaranteed; and there is no EU-compatible monitoring.

The Commission declared that addressing these deficiencies comprised one of the tasks before accession to the EU. In most countries, significant efforts were to be made to address them, while Hungary was an exception (Table 2.1).

The above brief survey indicates that in almost all of the countries important changes have taken place, partly for internal political reasons but mainly as a response to warnings from the European Union; part of the designated tasks, at least formally, were completed by the accession countries.

Regional development acts were passed in Romania in 1998, and in Bulgaria in 1999; in the Czech Republic in 1998. Slovakia and Poland do not yet have regional development legislation. Those acts that had been passed established the frame-works of the system of goals, resources and institutions of regional policy, mostly adopting the principles of the EU's structural policy. The Hungarian regional development act differs from those of the above three countries, both in size and content. It contains a larger volume of more detailed regulation, has a more logical

Table 2.1 The European Commission's recommendations for the accession countries on regional policy

Task	Bulgaria	Czech Republic	Hungary	Poland	Romania	Slovakia
Legal regulation	X	X		X	X	X
The establishment of institutions	X	X		X	X	X
To strengthen co-ordination among existing institutions	X	X	X	X	X	X
To ensure financial resources for regional development	X	X	X	X	X	X
Co-ordination of resources	X	X	X	X	X	X
Control and monitoring	X	X		X	X	X
Regional statistics	X	X		X	X	X

Source: Enlarging the European Union. Accession Partnership. Edited by the author on the basis of the document.

structure and a wider thematic scope. It defines the directions of territorial development, the central and local tasks of assistance, and the requirements of regional decentralisation. The Hungarian ruling was more lenient, however, in the establishment of the new territorial structures. While all of the other acts defined the NUTS 2 units of structural policy, in Hungary the act was amended to mark out the planning and statistical regions only after long debates. In the other important topic of legal regulation, the institutional background of the development strategy, the general state of affairs is less favourable. Only the Hungarian parliament has approved a regional development concept. None of the other countries has a document, programme or concept to shape the spatial structure of the country. The lack of these relevant documents seriously hinders the work of the regional development institutions. It has to be noted here that over the past year Hungarian political decision makers have appeared to have ignored parliament resolution 35/1998 (III. 20.): the designation of the directions of development show a great extent of spontaneity and a dominant rural orientation.

A *regional planning and statistical system* has been established in all of the countries. In Poland and Bulgaria, the measures towards EU-compatibility were accompanied by administrative reforms. In Poland, some regional political goals were declared in the 1998 administrative reform act: regional economic policy and the preparation and implementation of development programmes play a crucial role among the tasks of the 16 new voivodships, at the middle territorial level. With the elimination of the previous, smaller voivodships, some of which were re-divided among the new administrative units, the NUTS 3 system remained without administrative basis. In Bulgaria, the reform of territorial administration was the opposite. The larger units, the nine 'oblasts', were divided into 28 smaller units, which now serve as NUTS 3 units, and six macro-regions were established. In Slovakia, eight counties comprise the NUTS 3 level as deconcentrated administrative units, while the country was divided into four NUTS 2 regions. In the Czech Republic, where the regions ordained in the constitution have not been established to this date, 14 non-administrative counties comprise the NUTS 3 level, and eight macro-regions form the NUTS 2 units. In Slovenia, owing to its small size, the designation of planning units is rather difficult; the regional development act opted for the institutionalisation of the NUTS 3 level. In the countries of this survey, with only the exception of Hungary, the capitals with their agglomerations appear independently among the NUTS 2 units. Considering the dominant territorial level of European regional policy, the NUTS 2 units, Central and Eastern Europe formally displays the same picture as the European Union (Table 2.2).

There is no unified organisational model for the *central administration of national regional policy* in Central and Eastern Europe. In all countries except Poland and Slovakia, the national regional development councils have been established and operate as inter-ministerial committees. In Romania, the council is chaired by the Prime Minister and in Bulgaria the position is held by the deputy minister of the Ministry of Regional Development and Public Works. The national regional development agency in Romania employs 120 people. Its task is to manage the regional development policy of the country and to co-ordinate the operation of the eight regional development agencies. In the Czech Republic, the National Programme and Monitoring Board for Economic and Social Cohesion carries out the tasks of the inter-ministerial co-ordination of regional development, the preparation of the programming documents required for the utilisation of structural funds, and the co-ordination of the sectoral and regional operating programmes. The board is headed by the minister of regional development.

The central administration of the regional development policy, partly as a new task, was assigned to other already existing ministries. In Poland, the Ministry for

Table 2.2 NUTS units in Central and Eastern Europe, 2011

Country	Number of NUTS units			NUTS II units	
	NUTS 1	NUTS 2	NUTS 3	Average size, '000 km²	Population, '000
Bulgaria	3	6	28	18.5	1,220
Czech Republic	–	8	14	9.9	1,310
Hungary	–	7	20	13.3	1,419
Poland	–	16	49*	19.5	2,408
Romania	–	8	42	29.8	2,525
Slovakia	–	4	8	12.2	1,348
EUR27	75	206	1,031	15.3	1,836

* The former voivodships.
Source: Statistical Regions for the Central European Countries. The author's calculations are on the basis of the document.

Regional Policy was established in 2000. In Bulgaria, although regional development is included in the name of the relevant ministry, physical planning has stronger traditional bases. The Czech Republic is the other Central and Eastern European accession country that operates a separate ministry for regional development. The qualification of the 370-strong body, however, does not yet meet the standards of the European Union.

Considering all the above facts, it is unfortunate that in Hungary the Ministry for the Environment and Regional Development, whose work was appreciated in the first country report, was, for party political reasons, abolished. It is obvious that the agricultural and rural policies belong together; regional policy, however, comprises of a much wider range of tasks than only rural developments. It is difficult to understand, therefore, why Hungary abandoned the model of a unified regional political administration, thus eroding its competitive edge in structural policy and providing ground for future criticism.

In the national regional policy the *designation of eligible areas* plays an important role. The nature and expansion of these areas have an effect on what tools have to be used in their case. They can be marked out by different methods considering different territorial units. Hungary has a complex system approved by the parliament, using the European Union's categories for eligible areas: backward areas, areas of industrial depression, rural areas and areas with high unemployment. Bulgaria has a similarly elaborated system. However, in the latter country 17.5 per cent of the population lives in problematic areas, while in Hungary this figure is at 33.5 per cent. The Czech Republic, on the basis of a few indicators (rate of industrial employment, entrepreneurial rate, unemployment rate, population density, local government tax incomes, average salary, rate of agricultural employment) recognised eight districts as structural crisis areas and 10 districts as areas of weak economy, comprising 21.8 per cent of the country's population. In Poland and Slovakia, no eligible areas have been marked out. In Romania, the regional development act assigned the designation of eligible areas to the authority of the county councils, but in 1999 the Romanian parliament passed an urgency resolution on the areas with unfavourable endowments. The 24 most backward small areas comprise 1.9 million inhabitants, or 8.4 per cent of the total population. Two-thirds of the backward areas are found in Muntenia and Moldavia (Ianoş 2000).

However, the above favourable steps in regional policy can also be regarded as merely formal improvements, as pointed out by the 1999 country reports of the European Commission (Regular report from the Commission on progress towards accession). Neither were there significant changes in the findings of the report a year later. The Commission raised the following complaints regarding the individual cases:

- Bulgaria
  - The relationship between the administrative counties (NUTS 3 units) and the planning and statistical regions is not defined.
  - Inter-ministerial co-ordination is weak. The administrative capacities required for the administration of regional development are insufficient.

- Regional development is assigned very limited resources from the central budget: there is no separate budget allocation, and the conditions of co-financing over several years have not been established.
- The Czech Republic
  - The regional development councils have a limited scope of operation.
  - There are no suitably educated regional development experts.
  - The financing of regional developments is not guaranteed.
- Poland
  - The country has no regional development legislation.
  - The country's regional political strategy has not been prepared.
  - National finance legislation regulates the principles of central support to programmes that comprise several years, but it does not include allocations for regional developments.
  - Regional development has no central responsible body; the administrative organisations of structural policy have not been established in the regions.
- Hungary
  - Despite accurate preparation, little headway has been made in the operation of the institutions for the reception of structural funds.
  - The operation of some of the county and regional development councils is not undisturbed; the establishment of eight to 10-strong regional development agencies does not indicate significant capacity improvement in regional administration.
  - The financing of regional development should be revised. In financing, the division of tasks among the ministries should be clarified; a co-ordinating mechanism should be established between the different sectoral resources. In the lack of co-ordination, and because of the poor quality of staff and poor financial resources, the preparation of development plans often stalls.
- Romania
  - The institutional system does not function yet, and the development programmes have not been prepared.
  - The financing systems of regional development have not been devised.
  - The principles of the operation of the regional development councils are unclear and the scope of their operation is very narrow.
  - The administrative capacities of regional development are very weak.
- Slovakia
  - Neither the legal nor the institutional bases of regional development have been established.
  - The country must start addressing the deficiencies urgently.

This brief summary indicates the urgent tasks that the individual countries must carry out during the accession partnership period. General deficiencies are the inadequate regional development resources, the lack of financial bases for the implementation of long-term programmes, and the poor co-ordination of resources and institutions. It is to be noted that the last report on Hungary no longer appreciates the work of the National Regional Development Council, presumably because of unfavourable experiences in its operation. In spite of all these, and considering factors not examined in the country reports, it can be stated that Hungary enjoys the most favourable position among the accession countries in the reception of the structural and cohesion funds; in this field Hungary's competitiveness is good (Table 2.3).

Although the evaluation was based on subjective judgement, Table 2.3 indicates that among the strongest countries for accession (Hungary, Poland, the Czech Republic and Slovenia) Hungary's performance in regional policy is the best. The results of Slovenia, not analysed here, are similar. The performance of Poland is remarkably poor, while that of second-round Romania is relatively good. This evaluation, however, was based on primarily formal elements, only in certain cases considering the precise factors of content and quality. In the future, however, evaluating analyses of the European Union will consider the operating experiences and results of the resource and institutional system of regional policy. The

Table 2.3 The performance of Central and Eastern European accession countries in establishing the conditions for cohesion and structural policies

Structural and cohesion task	Bulgaria	Czech Republic	Hungary	Poland	Romania	Slovakia
The legal background of development and programming	3	2	4	1	3	1
Institutionalisation of inter-ministerial co-ordination	2	3	3	1	4	1
The organisation of central administration	3	4	2	1	3	1
The NUTS 2 system	2	2	3	4	3	2
The NUTS 3 system	3	2	4	1	4	2
The administrative capacities of NUTS 2	1	1	2	4	2	1
The administrative capacities of NUTS 3	3	2	4	1	4	2
Harmony between central administration and the NUTS 2 level	2	2	2	4	2	1
Harmony between central administration and the NUTS 3 level	3	1	4	1	4	3
Designation of eligible areas	3	2	4	2	2	2
Regulation of regional development in the central budget	2	2	3	2	2	1
Co-ordination of resources	2	2	2	2	2	1

Note: 1 – Cannot be evaluated; 2 – Poor; 3 – Good; 4 – Outstanding.
Source: Compiled by the author.

preparation of comprehensive development plans has to be considered as a milestone. The judgement of the European Commission will be based upon how the community support utilisation plan will have been prepared, what it will contain, and what principles it will define.

Shortcomings of current spatial policy

Economic, social and infrastructural *inequalities are constantly growing* in the new member-states. However, the extent of spatial disparities varies from country to country. GDP per capita rates show the largest and constantly increasing disparities within core and peripheral regions (Figure 2.1). The income produced per capita shows significant changes across the countries' regions in this period. The indicators for capital city regions are currently three to four times as high as those for the least developed counties. This was characteristic of the inter-war years (the 1920s–1940s) although the gap decreased in the 1950s and 1960s. However, the gap is now continuously increasing. Such huge disparities were seen for the last time in Western Europe two to three decades ago.

The gap between the functional diversity characterising Eastern and Western European capital cities is much smaller than that between major provincial towns in Eastern Europe and Western Europe's regional centres. Business services in regional centres are weak, and most of regions do not have airports, conference and trade-fair centres, science and technology parks. National, cross-border or international functions can rarely be found.

The phenomenon of regional differentiation can be detected in the changes in the development ranking of Eastern and Central European regions (Horváth 2009). Owing to the quality of the economic structure, three Hungarian regions were among the 10 most developed regions in the mid-years of the 1990s, while in 2008 there was only one. The poorest regions have also changed their positions (Figure 2.2).

Hungarian sectoral policy, in collaboration with regional science, was the first in Eastern and Central Europe to elaborate a comprehensive regulation of regional policy in the mid-1990s. The laws on territorial development and the Parliamentary decree on the National spatial development concept were unable to manage the necessary change of direction due to the lack of reforms in other spheres of government.

A sure sign of the uncertainties surrounding spatial development is the fact that *no stable state administration frameworks* have been established for the provision of these tasks since the regime change. In Hungary, the tenth central state administrative organisation has been given the responsibility since the regime change. The reorganisation of the central government level in each new cycle generates distrust and weakens the prestige of Hungarian spatial policy in Europe. Spatial development, however, is a complex task whose execution demands regulation and organisation transcending individual portfolios and a stable institutional system. The other component of the image of central governance can be viewed as a theoretical question. This aspect is missing from the development of already existing structures. Strong regions require weaker central government positions, while weak regions require stronger centres. In Hungary neither of these models

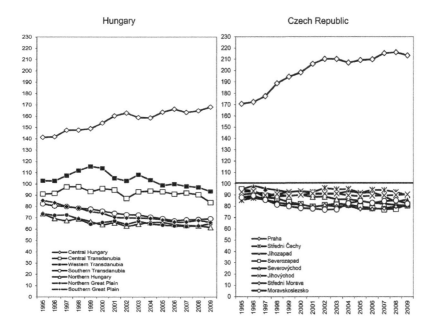

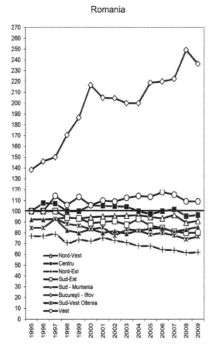

Figure 2.1 The evolution of regional GDP per capita in some countries, 1994–2009

Source: Designed by the author based on data from national statistical yearbooks.

1994   2010

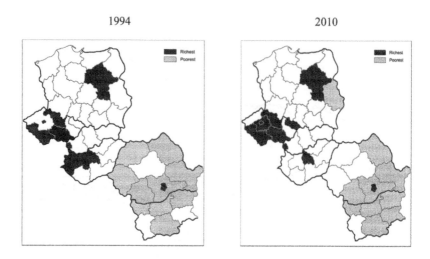

Figure 2.2 The spatial location of the ten most and least developed regions
Source: Designed by the author based on data from national statistical yearbooks.

is currently functioning. In Bulgaria, Poland, Slovakia and the Czech Republic, the same ministry has been responsible for the co-ordination of central spatial development tasks for over a decade.

Instead of gradually proceeding on the road towards Europeanisation, spatial policy of new member-states has been *caught in the stranglehold of provincialism*. This situation renders the modernisation of the countries' spatial structures even more hopeless, further hindering any growth in performance of the economies.

Resources have become fragmented and no-one regards the strategies and programmes of regions and counties as competent (Pálné 2009). Spatial development funds are the object of petty fights between micro-regional interest groups, due to expedient alliances, bargains and existential motives, and insignificant sums of development resources arrive in a haphazard fashion in a variety of places in the counties. There is no evidence that spatial development funds have launched any new processes.

Instead of the gradual gaining of power of West European type regional development policy, the survival of traditional provincialism is observed even in the newly born, EU-conforming regional development organisations, respectively.

Subsidiarity and decentralisation – the requirement of institutional capacity

The principle of subsidiarity and its practical utilisation has exerted a positive influence on the evolution of European territorial cohesion (Chantal 2003; Colombo 2012; De Pasquale 2000; Faludi 2012; Toth 1992). Those countries achieved success which regarded subsidiarity as the basic condition of the transformation of the organi-sational system of the functioning of the state and applied it in its full complexity. In other words, by the transformation of the total decision-making hierarchy, the reorganisation of the location of competencies occurred: centralised functions were redefined just as the responsibilities of lower levels were reorganised. Multiple examples prove that a system of social control can only be competitive if it clearly takes into consideration the organisational requirement according to which lower levels cannot be overburdened with tasks which they are unable to resolve, and the transfer of powers must be coupled with the transfer of sources of finance. Central and Eastern European countries may only be successful if they take these requirements into consideration, that is if they carry out fundamental state reform.

Former socialist countries used to be centralised states just like most European countries were in the past. The territorial administration had only a limited level of autonomy. After the regime change in 1990, inhabited places gained significant independence while territorial governance, county level, lost most of its previous functions. In Hungary, the law on local self-government makes no difference between various types of self-government. The county is not the administrative body that manages inhabited places in its territory and it does not co-ordinate pro-grammes for local or economic development but is a self-governing entity responsible for several institutions (high schools, social institutions, cultural associ-ations, etc.). There are big differences in the number of inhabitants of 19 counties and county populations range from 250,000 to 800,000. These population sizes are not appropriate today for the regulation of factors affecting modern territorial development. During the communist period, county political leaders wanted to obtain everything for their counties, irrespective of their actual needs. This is, for example, the reason why each county has an institution of higher education. The new, democratic Hungary has preserved its unitary character, and the system of governance remains unchanged. Central government has not devolved parts of its responsibilities to local administrations and thus Hungary has encountered a number of difficulties during the process of European integration. An excessive emphasis on county's interests can be noted while readiness for territorial co-operation is still quite weak.

The process of regionalisation had already started in Hungary in the 1970s. . During that period Europe recognised the significance of regional development. New principles in economic policy were defined and the whole range of institutions for territorial development was established. Changes in the system of public government commenced and decentralisation expanded into all the larger terri-tories. One of the consequences of economic reforms in 1968 was the launching of public regulations for territorial development. The territory of Hungary was divided into six planning-economic regions and many state institutions and public organisations (environmental protection, railroad, water management, post office, television etc.) were transferred to regional offices. However, proper regionalism, due to political structure, could not be developed and that is why positive effects of changes could not be felt. In the euphoria of regime change, a new political elite neglected the regional issues in the same way as planning issues.

The request for community planning and creation of regions can give way to surprises and misunderstanding at a certain point of the process of European integration. The law on territorial development, which was enacted in 1996, was also dealing with regions in quite a discreet way. In accordance with the EU requirements, the law was dealing with the establishment of development-statistical regions. Still, the establishment of regions was planned as an independent initiative for the association of counties and there was no definition of the counties or their number. The inconsistency of such a concept was soon noted. Changes and amendments to the law in 1999 defined seven development-statistical regions and also listed the counties belonging to each region. These regions have become territorial units for the drafting of national development plans. In 2006 the Hungarian government tried to organise regions as administration units but the opposition parties (Alliance of Young Democrats-FIDESZ and the Christian Democrats) did not support the draft law even though they had announced the reform of regional administration in their 1998 pre-election programmes.

The new right-wing government which was elected with a two-thirds majority in 2010 reorganised the state system of Hungary focusing on centralisation. The new local government act prevented local government from operating in the following administrative areas: education, health and disaster protection would be wholly the responsibility of the central government. Most local state administration services of were merged into county-level administration (headed by a government representative and appointed by the prime minister). Earlier authorities in the regions (de-concentrated organs of central ministries, development agencies) have largely disappeared. Counties are subjects of the new territorial development policy, which does not have a competent organ (ministry or national office) at central level. János Kornai, the famous economist, drew attention to dangers of centralisation:

> The government has attained its real goal: it has seized power violently; by strengthening centralisation and extending the power of the state it has gained the means of exerting unlimited power. But autocratic rule, unbridled centralisation and excessive expansion of state activity are incompatible with the healthy running of a modern capitalist market economy out of the trap, out of the stagnation and onto a path of sustainable growth.
>
> (Kornai 2012)

As several examples from Western European countries demonstrate, regions will exist in Central and Eastern Europe only *if economic actors initiate and force their creation*. The activity of economic and entrepreneurial alliances is needed. The speed of their decision illustrates the economic potential of the economy. A new opening for the institutionalisation of regions depends on them.

The modification of factors shaping spatial development necessitates the transformation of the *system of objectives, instruments and institutions of regional policy* all across Europe. The long-term trends of European spatial development require the development of the most heterogeneous institutionalised forms of decentralisation in the countries with different traditions in the continent. The new Central and Eastern European member-states are able to meet the cohesion requirements of the European Union only with decentralised institutions. This is not solely a question of public administration, but also the precondition of the efficiency of research and development in with the aim of improving competitiveness. The predominance of regionalism may result in the modernisation of the spatial structures. In decentralised countries, the spatial diffusion of the knowledge intensive economy is faster than in centralised countries.

The need for *polycentric regional development* will also transform the power structure of countries in transformtion. Regions as the subnational level of the power structure are territorial units endowed with local governmental powers serving sustainable economic growth and the modernisation of the spatial structure. They have access to their own sources of finance and pursue an autonomous development policy. Regions become the areas of innovative development, the regional embeddedness of innovation producing basic institutions will be strong. The Lisbon criteria will not be realisable in the unitary states of Europe where there have been few attempts at decentralisation, which include Hungary.

The new member-states must first and foremost prove that regional institutions are able to guarantee the efficient absorption of structural funds promoting European cohesion. Without autonomous regional development policy, the realisation of the priorities of the new European cohesion policy will encounter serious obstacles. If the incoming and hopefully optimal amount of EU funding absorbed in the current dominant sectoral structure, the diminution of marked interregional disparities will be impossible. Without hopefully strengthening the economic performance of countries, the results of the EU cohesion policy will remain limited. Decentralised and regionalised development policy may be the only solution for Eastern and Central Europe in conformity with the EU. This requires a totally new spatial development paradigm. Since the late 1990s, every measure was directed at the creation of the system of objectives, instruments and institutions of central regional policy. During the coming decade the guarantees of the individual policy-making of regions would have to be established through legislation and the problem of the financing their operation will have to be resolved.

Development planning for the period between 2007 and 2013

With the elaboration of national development plans of EU member-states for the periods between 2004–2006 and 2007–2013, a new era began in determining development directions of the Eastern and Central European regions. National development plans were made using EU planning methodology (Stead and Nadin 2011).

The number and nomination of operational programmes of national development plans vary from country to country. National programmes are divided into five large groups of activities in harmony with EU requirements. The Economic Competitiveness Operational Programme covers the development of small and medium-sized enterprises, support for R&D and investment in technology. The

Environmental Protection and Infrastructure Operational Programme focuses on the development of a healthy domestic environment through the creation of environmental infrastructure, the improvement of environmental safety and aims to develop a transport infrastructure. The objectives of the Human Resources Development Operational Programme are to raise the standard of training and education, to improve the competitiveness of the workforce and to promote social inclusion. The Agricultural and Rural Development Operational Programme focuses on the modernisation and increased efficiency of agricultural production on the one hand, partly through the development of production technologies and food processing; and on the other, on the development of rural areas, the creation of alternative income opportunities for the population. Regional Operational Programmes cover developments under the responsibility of development regions.

A negative phenomenon is that the process of accession to the European Union has had a centralising effect on all new member-states. National development plans reflected a top-down approach. The central government had an almost exclusive role in the elaboration of programmes. The development regions, not being administrative units, could only partially enforce their interests and development ideas and their role was mostly limited to the collection of projects. National development plans denominate mostly sectoral development tasks. Regional operational programmes were not based on the development ideas of regions; instead, tasks omitted from sectoral operational programmes were regarded as of regional significance. A sign of the undervaluation of the regions is that the rate of development resources allocated to regional operational programmes does not reach 25 per cent of the development resources in any country (Table 2.4).

EU-financed developments will be mainly infrastructure-related (roads, sewage system construction, etc.) and in environmental protection (48 per cent of the expenditure in Romania, 45 per cent in Slovakia), which can temporarily improve the conditions for local entrepreneurs involved in these construction works and develop the local environment and improve accessibility and living standards, but

Table 2.4 EU support for operational programmes, 2007–2013

	Hungary		Romania		Slovakia	
	Million Euros	%	Million Euros	%	Million Euros	%
Competitive economy	2,810	11.3	2,724	14.2	2,975	26.4
Environment and infrastructure	10,905	43.8	9,286	48.3	5,007	44.5
Human resources development	5,430	21.8	3,476	18.1	1,750	15.5
Regional development	5,771	23.1	3,726	19.4	1,532	13.6
Total	24,916	100.0	19,212	100.0	11,264	100.0

Source: Eligible areas under the Convergence Objective and the Regional Competitiveness and Employment Objective (http://ec.europa.eu/regional_policy/atlas2007 [2009. 04.19.]).

they do not provide adequate resources for sustainable growth. Romanian development policy allocates far fewer resources to the development of a competitive economy and to regional programmes than required. Therefore, other methods should be used for the reinforcement of economic bases. The methods and techniques of the market-based development of the economy (which means the production of internationally marketable products and services) can and must be mastered. This is necessary, because fundamental changes are expected in the support policy of the EU from 2014 onwards. It is important to be prepared for this and Hungarian communities should be involved in this preparation work. It is still a false conception, even in Hungary, that the creation of a competitive society can be based on EU support. However, healthy communities do not require socio-political control of society.

The result of the strong dependence on the central government is that local and regional synergies are neglected. The experiences of concluded or still effective national development plans indicate that the mechanism of centralised decision-making does not support the reduction of spatial disparities but their increase. Regional financial resources are not capable of investments in cross-border cooperation since they are primarily allocated to tasks related to settlement regeneration, education, culture and tourism development. The results of an international research project conducted in the Hungarian-Romanian frontier area warns that the efficiency of centrally controlled programmes for the development of peripheries is low. Central administration offices located in frontier areas are insensitive to local peculiarities and the bureaucratic nature of the organisation disables co-operation among the actors of spatial development policies.

References

Chantal, M.D. (2003) *Il principio di sussidiarietà*, Rome: Giuffrè editore.

Colombo, A. (ed.) (2012) *Subsidiarity Governance. Theoretical and Empirical Models*, New York: Palgrave Macmillan.

De Pasquale, P. (2000) *Il principio di sussidiarietà nella comunità europea*, Naples: Editoriale Scientifica.

Faludi, A. (2012) 'Territorial cohesion and subsidiarity under the European Union treaties: a critique of the "territorialism" underlying', *Regional Studies*, 1: 1–13.

Horváth, G. (2009) *Cohesion Deficiencies in Eastern and Central Europe – Inequalities of Regional Research Area*, Discussion Papers, 72. Pécs: Centre for Regional Studies, HAS.

Ianoş, I. (2000) 'Less-favoured areas and regional development in Romania', in Horváth, G. (ed.) *Regions and Cities in the Global World*, Pécs: Centre for Regional Studies, HAS, 176–191.

Kornai, J. (2012) 'Központosítás és kapitalista piacgazdaság' [Centralization and the capitalist market economy], *Népszabadság*, Január 28. 1: 6–9.

Pálné Kovács, I. (2009) 'Regionalization in Hungary: options and scenarios on the "road to Europe"', in Scott, W.J. (ed.) *De-Coding New Regionalism. Shifting Socio-Political Contexts in Central Europe and Latin America*, London: Routledge, 199–214.

'Regular Reports from the Commission on Progress Towards Accession.Various Countries', Brussels: European Commission, 1998–2003.

Stead, D. and Nadin, V. (2011) 'Shifts in territorial governance and the Europanization of spatial planning in Central and Eastern Europe', in Adams, N., Cotella, G. and Nunes, R. (eds) *Territorial Development, Cohesion and Spatial Planning. Knowledge and Policy Development in an Enlarged EU,* London: Routledge.

Toth, A.G. (1992) 'The principle of subsidiarity in the Maastricht Treaty', *Common Market Law Review,* 29: 1079–1105.

3 Regions as frameworks of power

Intermediate-level regional development tasks

Regional and community development is one of the tasks of the subnational level in all modern states. The new economic paradigm of the past decade made its effects felt also in the development of regional policy. Changes have taken place in the traditional relations between central governments and regional communities. Traditional regional policy instruments (significant government presence in regional developments, the top-down incentive system, etc.) have lost their economic and political motivation and new regional strategies have emerged.

Unlike the centrally managed regional development policies, a basic feature of the new models is that they attribute decisive importance to endogenous features as opposed to external factors in the development of regions. Centrally directed policies were realised primarily in sectoral development programmes, which the regionally installed bodies of central authorities could co-ordinate only in the technical sense and proved to be unable to mobilise local resources. The new development policies, however, put emphasis on democratic decision-making procedures, the complex utilisation of resources and innovation.

The development models of the Western European regions show a multitude of peculiar features but also a number of common characteristics. The majority of region-specific features stems from the difference of national regional policies and the social and economic positions of the regions within the country.

The new regional policy which could be called innovation-oriented or local initiative development policy, focuses on the establishment of marketable products, industrial processes and services and the regular, programmed renewal of these. This model therefore clearly serves to develop the ability of the regions to adapt. Local and community decisions are not influenced by central norms any more but appropriate local and regional economic decisions based on market and prosperity indications prompt the attainment of performance required for the change. The clearly delineated common goals of these strategies are the following:

- seeking out new development resources, compilation of these in a system, creation of the institutional background required to operate this system;
- establishment of regional and local corporate co-operation networks (these goals were most perfectly attained by the industrial zones in Italian regions

where traditional corporate co-operation was combined with breaking down production into phases moved to separate locations);
- institutionalisation of information, innovation and enterprise promotion transfers (setting-up industrial parks, business-innovation centres, R&D consortia);
- organisation of local and regional development coalitions of various interest groups, harmonisation of rigid local hierarchies, construction of flexible decision-making systems;
- transforming the quality and cultural-scientific atmosphere of the living environment into a determining factor for economic growth and tuning the complex community supply into a capital-attracting feature.

European regions which were able to formulate, obtain acceptance of and apply a development strategy which fits their own demands have stabilised in a relatively short while and their new structures have started to grow.

On the other hand, regions unable to set up their own programmes (often due to their inherent traits) could expect to be regenerated via central support. Structural changes driven from the centre, along the lines of the traditional regional development, however, resulted only in a temporary stabilisation. The economic structure of these areas has been preserved and their growth potential and competitiveness remained weak. They still encounter obstacles in trying to integrate into the international regional division of labour.

The transformation of regional policy, with unchanged goals, demanded changes also in the organisation of central public administration and the financing of the objectives. Central governments on the one hand strive to make the central direction of regional policy the competence of a single high authority, and, on the other, the participation of regional governments in formulating regional policy priorities in the medium term (5–10 years) is guaranteed by supplementary laws. In-depth changes occur also in the regional planning system. The planning organisation which regulates the tasks and financing between the central government and the regional body, and the thorough conciliation of regional components of sectoral plans with the regional bodies concerned, as in the French model, is gaining recognition.

Promoting and organising international co-operation became an important element in the development policies of Western European regions. The enhancement of co-operation was also spurred by the European Community's norms on creating the internal market. Uniform customs and tariff rules and the Western European line infrastructure network meant intensifying cross-border relationships as well.

Inter-regional co-operation stepped beyond the limits of formal relations when market players have also set up their own co-operation networks. Collaboration between market organisations of different types became institutional, creating their own playing field without requesting co-ordination from the administrative agencies. Cities which hold fairs and exhibitions, chambers of commerce and economy, business-enterprise and technological centres today maintain contact based on their own programmes. One of the reasons for the integration difficulties of the Eastern European periphery is that these institutions, the recipients of co-operation offers are lacking (or are extremely under-developed) . Europe, therefore, has a unique dichotomy: while the driving force behind co-operation in the Western regions is provided today by market organisations, in the Eastern regions, this is still is still executed by various (mainly central) administration bodies.

The conclusion, therefore, is that public administration in regional integration is generally co-ordinated and carries out political tasks. The dense web of co-operation networks can only be created by direct co-operation (or by way of associations) between market players.

The general task of regional administration in Western Europe is to represent and defend the notion of co-operation before central government agencies. No European regional co-operation arrangements were free of tension between central and regional agencies. Owing to the constitutional traits of the internal organisation of the state, federal states have the widest leeway. Medium-level units of the regionalised and unitary states, however, extended their powers to establish international contacts through lengthy, and not yet concluded, constitutional debates.

Constitutional disputes flared up especially after 1980, when the European Framework Convention on Trans-frontier Co-operation between Territorial Communities or Authorities (Madrid Convention) of the Council of Europe declared the need for decentralised organisation of cross-border co-operation (Scott 2000; Stumm and Gabbe 2001). This convention requires that the regions be free to select the form of cross-border co-operation, while containing guarantees that the central government may use supervisory and control instruments to maintain the sovereignty of the state. Though the framework convention did not oblige the ratifying states to transform their internal law, it was still instrumental in allowing the emergence of organisational and legal institutions for regional co-operation and preventing the regions' autonomous efforts from being considered unconstitutional. After ratification of this convention, additional national laws were created: for example, the 1987 resolution of the Constitutional Court of Italy extends the basic rules set out in the framework convention not only to border regions but also to distant ones (La Pergola 1987). In the course of preparing the constitutional reform in Austria, it was set out clearly that the *Länder* should be allowed to conclude international agreements on matters falling under their separate jurisdictions (Kicker 1988).

Notwithstanding these legal achievements and the incomparably more extensive powers, positions and financial assets of regional medium-level authorities compared to Eastern Europe's, there continues to be conflict between central government and the regions.

Regionalism, the regional decentralisation of power and the distribution of labour among the different forms of local government, is now in the crossfire in the unitary states of Eastern and Central Europe. The change of the political system, the process of connecting to the globalising European economy, the construction of a local governmental structure using the concepts of civic democracy, all shed new light on the mutual connections of central and regional local power, the harmonisation of settlement independence and meso-level public administration functions. In almost all of the former socialist countries the central issue has become that of the economic, political, and functional transformation of the basic levels of local government. The earlier subnational levels disappeared (as in the successor states of the former Czechoslovakia). Their functions to a large extent decreased (as in Hungary), changed (as in Poland), or, alternatively, new regional meso-levels were created (as in Croatia) or are being created (as in Slovenia).

The construction of regions in the countries of Eastern and Central Europe became one of the important debate topics for preparation for EU membership (Illner 1997; Keating and Hughes 2003; Marcou 2002; Rose and Traut 2002; Sturm and Dieringer 2005). However, the application of EU structural policy relates to appropriate size in terms of the population potential of subnational development units and their economic capacities. In view of the concepts of economies of scale, and, during the preparation of the EU pre-accession programmes, planning-statistical regions had to be created in all countries. From a formal point of view, completing this task did not create any particular problem. The government of each country listed the regional public administration units as meso-level development regions, and, on the basis of EU recommendations, the formal organisational structures (regional development councils, development directorates, and agencies) were also created.

In parallel with the creation of the organisational framework of an EU-compatible development policy, an intensive debate on issues of content began in most countries. In these debates, numerous issues (which had earlier received less attention among the topics relating to the change of regime) were raised: What functions should the development regions have? How can they become public administration units serving the decentralisation of the centralised state system? What criteria should they have to fulfil the development programmes? Which city in the region should become the regional centre?

EU accession opened up a Pandora's box in the countries of Eastern and Central Europe. The fundamental issue of how unitarily structured states can be set on a decentralised path became the centre of debate. This present study searches for an explanation of the reasons for the difficulties of Eastern and Central Europe in regional construction; it summarises the administrative and political development prerequisites of the transition to a regional outline of the possible advantages of a regional institutional system in the creation of the cohesion policy ensuring a decrease in regional differences.

The formal change in regional administration

The new nation-states in Eastern and Central Europe established in the aftermath of World War I had to face two difficulties, from the point of view of their future regional development. One of the issues to be addressed was how to create a unified structure for those (new) parts of the country that earlier had been developed in different economic areas, in order to link their infrastructural systems. The other was to create a new system of regional organisation of central government power. The heavily centralised state powers created their own regional bodies partly on their former administration basis, but, after completing those tasks, they needed to create the new, unified state territory that was most effectively assisted by the low number of administrative units involved. Following World War II, the Soviet-style regional administration was organised differently, based upon different power considerations. The Communist states, in accordance with their political interests, heavily changed the countries' regional administration on several occasions, sometimes organising smaller regional units and sometimes larger ones. Hungary can be considered as an exception to this, in that, in the twentieth century (apart from some underpopulated counties being combined) the number of subnational units in the country has not changed (Table 3.1).

In Central and Eastern Europe a hierarchical planning organisational system, with a fairly powerful central planning office at the top in each country, had previously been the decisive organisational form of regional development. Regional development based on central large-scale investment and state social policy did not require a multiparticipant institutional system operating in horizontal co-operation. In addition, the state's interest in redistribution, together with the central policy, was carried out most effectively by vertically subordinated organisations. This philosophy of state organisation also defined the regional administration system.

Although public administration under socialism did not differ significantly from that of the developed democracies in respect of form and certain operational concepts, it produced an unusual administrative organisation, despite the dominant organisational concept of the (so called) 'democratic centralism' and the omnipotence of the Communist Party. The local organs of power to a very large extent (and especially in the first three decades of extensive industrialisation and settlement development) imposed the central will by diktat, ignoring any kind of potential advantage that a region might have in development terms. However, as the strongly centralised state system in countries such as Poland and Hungary gradually softened. Local initiatives were given greater opportunities, and, due to this, in these countries in the 1980s, civic values in respect of settlement development, such as improvements in services and private house construction, made their appearance.

Table 3.1 Changes in the number of regional administrative units in Eastern and Central European countries

Country	Pre-WW II	1950s	1960s	1970s	1980s	2012
Bulgaria	9	13	28	28	9	28[1999]
Czech Republic	2	13	8	8	8	14[2001]
Hungary	25	20	20	20	20	20
Poland	14	22	22	49	49	16[1999]
Romania	9	18	18	40	41	42
Slovakia	2	6	4	4	4	8[1996]

Source: The author's own chart.

Following the change of regime, the organisational framework of Eastern and Central European states underwent important conceptual changes. A local government structure has replaced the hierarchical, executive council system, and the related legislation has created the constitutional basis for decentralised exercise of power (Horváth M. 2000) By now, in fact, local authorities have been equipped with constitutional guarantees of their organisational and decision-making independence, and very significant changes have been introduced into local government financing. In formal terms, public administration in Romania and Hungary has remained unchanged, although in Bulgaria the previous multicounty system was restored. At the same time, both the Czech Republic and Slovakia (as in the period between 1949 and 1960) created counties relatively small in size. Only Poland established large 'voivodships' and here the reform of the country's public administration has been an important milestone in the process of preparing for EU accession (Kowalczik 2000; Stasiak 1999; Yoder 2003).

The other country to be devoted to regionalisation is Hungary. Hungarian meso-level units, if we look retrospectively over several centuries, partly because of their actual size and partly because of their greatly weakened positions after the change of regime (a counter reaction to the political role that they played in the planned economy) are simply not competent to undertake large-scale development tasks. In the twentieth century, several attempts to modernise public adminis-tration in this strongly mono-centred country were made, but, one after the other, all of the plans failed, due to their rejection by central government and due to a lack of agreement among the regional political elites. In 2006, the government, within the framework of the general reform of public administration, submitted a legislative programme to parliament for the reorganisation of regional adminis-tration. The parliamentary opposition, however, has not supported the legislative programme (to amend the Hungarian Local Government Act, a two-thirds majority in parliament is required, but the government coalition parties fall well short of this).

It is, therefore, quite evident that the question of the public administration units (meso-level) positioned between central government and the settlements will continue to be an open issue, and also extremely important from the point of view of regional policy. It is, in fact, a general phenomenon in Eastern and Central Europe that these levels, as a reaction to the mainly negative role that they played under the previous system and their extremely strong political and redistributive functions, have very few local administration rights.

In recent decades, important differences can be seen between Western and Eastern Europe in the operation of the regional administration system and its changes of function. In the EU member-states, after the Single European Act was ratified, the role of the subnational level became more important, partly, since it resulted in the extension of the new general organisational concept of the European Communities, that is, subsidiarity, (following the amendment of the original concept). However, the level below that of central government was also handed a key role from the (Common European) Regional Policy point of view. The new structural and supportive policy laid down, as a basic concept, co-operation with the local regional authority (these having weak structures and deteriorating economies) and co-ordination between regional and national economic development strategies.

The realisation of the market economy and the structural reorganisation of the economy, made it clear relatively quickly that regional tensions cannot be reduced. Regional political aims (as set out in most of the countries) cannot be fulfilled and regional programmes cannot be elaborated without a radical reform of the functions of the regional meso-levels. Consequently, it was no accident that the review of meso-level functions evoked in each country the issue of the institutionalisation of regionalisation, the creation of a low number of regional units, similar in size and armed with similar powers as the regional meso-levels in the West European regional and decentralised states.

The unitary states of Europe, consequent upon the globalisation and internationalisation of the economy and the increased sophistication of European integration, can relatively soon move toward a new order of state structure. The factors supporting the further development and rethinking of meso-level public administration in Eastern and Central Europe are as follows:

1 The phenomena of disintegration experienced in the local government sphere indicate that the links between legal and specific interest issues are lacking, with the consequence that the notion of the model as working exclusively and voluntarily on a 'bottom-up' basis seems to be both misleading and unrealistic.

2 Due to the (basically, single-level) system of local government, regional development responsibilities are left uncontrolled, and attempts are made to plug this gap by the, now deconcentrated, state organs, with one part of the (deconcentrated) administration filling the vacuum left at meso-level, but undertaking tasks foreign to the organisation and with its segmented structure resulting in a hiatus in the process of co-ordination and information, as well as in the reconciliation of interests.

3 The disintegration of local government and the dysfunction of deconcentrated public administration gave new life to central governmental trials, and in regional public administration units a model with state and local government in competition with each other began to appear.

4 The tendency toward nationalisation at the meso-level is, of course, in direct opposition to the EU's integration process, but this contradiction can be resolved by the creation of a local government meso-level.

5 An important future responsibility for regional public administration can be to represent and defend the concept of inter-regional co-operation against the organs of central government, and it should be remembered that 'the Europe of the Regions' – as one of the key concepts of European integration – can be conceived of only with the co-operation of regional units of relatively similar competencies and complexity.

The development planning regions

A prerequisite for Eastern and Central European countries to join the EU or to benefit from support from the Structural Fund was the creation of large regions (NUTS-Nomenclature of Territorial Units for Statistics 2 units). On this basis, the most effective development concepts and the programmes serving their realisation, could best be drawn up. The 206 NUTS 2 regions established in the 15 member-states of the EU are very different from the point of view of their public law and administration situation and their physical size and population numbers. Basically, we are looking at units nationally determined, in which, at the same time as the NUTS 2 system of each country should meet common requirements, they operate as statistical (calculating, analysing, planning, programming, coordinating) and developing (support policy, decentralising) units. In the 10 associated East European countries the number of meso-level administration units at the end of 1999 was 357, and it was clear that the EU's support policy could not supervise such a high number of regional units. In consequence, it became essential to create larger regional development and statistical units.

Defining boundaries within the NUTS system is, from the EU's point of view, an internal affair, which means that, apart from size, there are no absolute EU requirements in terms of the creation of the regions: the decision lies within the scope of national governments. However, on the basis of experience with creating regions, the various concepts and likely impacts can be expressed in a way that makes the definition of the region relatively straightforward:

1   a history of regional co-operation and, hence, the chances of regional cohesion;
2   relative size status from the point of view of the national regional structure;
3   relative spatial homogeneity in terms of the basic aims of regional policy;
4   an effective internal structure (centre, subcentres, skills, and the ability to co-operate, etc.) and the observance of public administration borders;
5   the existing (or demanded) 'geo-political' similarity of the units united in a region and the degree of identity of the definitive, long-term, international orientations;
6   the costs of creating and operating the regions (decision preparing, decision-making and professional administrative background institutions, organising the information, planning, managing, and monitoring activities, the institutional system of decentralised financing, etc.), the economies of scale from a functional point of view;
7   the existence of a multifunctional, major urban regional centre.

The NUTS 2 regions are listed in the Regional Development Acts or Government Decrees of each country. However, the Regional Development Act adopted in Hungary in 1996 was quite cautious, indicating merely that the counties could create regions in order to carry out common tasks. It did not, however, define the development regions of the country; and this imprecise regulation had, as a consequence, the fact that counties amalgamated widely differing regions purely for fund-raising purposes, and there were counties that participated in three or four regional alliances. However, the amendment to the act in 1999 defined seven development-statistical regions and divided the counties into regions. In fact, a Government Decree listing, in an itemised form, the theoretical concepts defining development regions was created only in Bulgaria (Geshev 2001). The Bulgarian government defined the aspects of the creation of the regions in 1999 as follows:

1 The number of regions should be relatively low and they should be defined on the basis of their size and natural resource potential; their economic and social capacities should be able to undertake large-scale programmes.
2 The regions should not be too large to be manageable, and the number of counties comprising a region should be optimal in order to be able to be organise their co-operation.
3 There should be a common development problem in the region, which could be experienced in any part of the region and which motivates the regional development actors to co-operate.
4 Natural geographical units and historical traditions should be taken into consideration.
5 The region should have a relatively developed urban network and several growth-poles.
6 The planning region should comprise complete public administration units.

In the other countries, and after long debate, a compromise decision was reached in terms of the creation of NUTS 2 regions, and these (more or less) matched the above basic concepts. As regards size, they parallel very closely the average of the older EU member-states (Table 3.2). Individual countries, however, did not come to define their central regions in the same way. In Bulgaria, Poland, Hungary, and Romania, for example, the capitals, together with their surrounding agglomerations, made up one NUTS 2 unit, while, in the Czech Republic and Slovakia, the

Table 3.2 The most significant data of NUTS 2 units in Eastern and Central Europe

Country	NUTS 2 regions		
	Number	*Average area* *('000 km²)*	*Average population* *('000s)*
Bulgaria	6	18.5	1,407
Czech Republic	8	9.9	1,290
Hungary	7	13.3	1,463
Poland	16	19.5	2,411
Romania	8	29.8	2,851
Slovakia	4	12.2	1,319
Total	49	14.7	1,910
Total EU15	206	15.3	1,830

Source: The author's own calculations on the basis of Regions: *Statistical Yearbook 2010.*

capitals alone constitute one single region. As demonstrated in Eastern and Central Europe that general pattern of spatial economy in which the larger region surrounding a country's most developed growth-pole can show weaker performance (a consequence of the 'filtering-down' effect), this solution generated strong debate in Hungary. The overall performance of the Central Hungary Region (due to Budapest's high gross domestic product (GDP) per capita) is as much as 98 per cent of the average of the EU-15 and cannot, therefore, be included in the target group for convergence. Support, therefore, will be more modest (Budapest itself produces 125 per cent of the EU average, while the region's remaining unit, Pest county, produced just 53 per cent in 2003). Similar problems can be noted in the other three countries as well.

At the time when the development-statistical regions in Eastern and Central Europe were being planned, those ethno-cultural factors used in the organisation of West European regions were not applied. In Romania, the three counties comprising the historic Székler territory were incorporated into the Central region, in which half of the Hungarian population living in Romania (730,000 people) live. The three counties together could themselves have made up a separate development region with their population of 1.1 million people, but in this case the proportion of Hungarians in the population of the region would have been 59.2 per cent. Romanian governmental pressures and political factors blocked the Székler territory from becoming an independent region, and a region with a population of 2.6 million was created, in which Hungarians make up less than one-third. The debates surrounding the creation of an individual Székler region have simply fuelled today's ethnic conflicts in Romania (Bakk and Szász 2010).

In Slovakia, the neglect of ethno-cultural factors was already detectable during the establishment of the new regional administrative system. The overwhelming majority of the Hungarian population live in the southern areas of the country bordering Hungary. However, the borders of the new counties were drawn in such a way that large areas inhabited by Slovaks were attached to clusters of Hungarians, with the result that in none of the counties of Slovakia could the Hungarian population be the majority.

The organisational system of the development-statistical regions was introduced in each country on the basis of a scheme recommended by the European Union. Under this, development councils and development agencies operate in the regions, and these organisations are managed by the central regional development body. Their responsibilities are essentially restricted to simple co-ordination, to accumulating projects, and to assembling development plans. Their operative bodies, the development agencies, or directorates, work with 20 to 40 people, and their powers lie within a narrow framework. It can be seen as a general problem for member-states that those favoured under the programmes were the central state administration bodies. In the central bodies of regional development, staff numbers were increased to several hundreds, while in the regions only a fraction of this number was possible. The weak position of the regions is also indicated by the fact that, in the programming period 2004–2006, only 17–30 per cent of EU support was devoted to regional operative programmes.

Since the regulations defining the composition of regions contained nothing about regional centres (a task which, in any case, should not be handled within the framework of spatial development regulation) conflicts between towns and cities have broken out in individual regions for the privilege of becoming the seat of a particular regional development institution.

The dilemma of the regional centres

Those larger towns or cities can be called regional centres which, on the basis of their size and geographical location, fulfil the role of administrative, industrial and transport centre of a large area which has between one and 3 million inhabitants. These stand out from their surroundings and enjoy a higher proportion of the resources of their region than would be justified by their population.

Due to the influence of urban development processes, the regional centres of Western Europe built up their position over centuries, and their functional accumulation of wealth and growth of resources are closely connected with their region. In their development, the restructuring of the economy and the quality change in their transport and service sectors also played a major role. The settling and gradual expansion of the leading positions of central and local government administration, naturally, played their part also, in that more favourable conditions were created in these cities to enable them to accept the new economic growth-driving forces, although, in the development of their performance capacity, administrative factors can only be seen as secondary resources. Their dynamism was basically generated by the role of industry and services affecting both their regional and their wider markets. It is, therefore, no accident that, when the institutionalisation of regionalism, in particular countries in different development phases, led to changes in public administration, the choice of headquarters for a region seemed quite obvious in each West European country: the largest city, the richest in functional terms, the most outstanding in economic potential became the centre of public administration for the region.

In many countries, the decentralising trends of national regional policies, and especially the growth-pole concepts, played an important role in the development of the regional centres (Hall and Hay 1980; van Kempen *et al.* 2005). The essence of the use of the growth-pole strategy was that those innovations given regional development support were directed only to a limited number of locations (mainly as a part of the planned concept targeting the modification of the regional spatial structure), attempting to support economic activity to raise the level of welfare within the region. The creation of the growth-pole was, first of all, motivated by complex industrial development, by the dominant new (or modernised) economic sectors and developed services. Using the principles of the French spatial economics school in economic policy resulted in an essential strengthening of connections in the economic space among companies and sectors.

Similar strategies were also followed in Western European countries. The programmes serving the structural strengthening of the major urban centres, albeit after some time, reached beyond the urban administration borders, and more and more attention was drawn towards the urban regions (Meijers, E. J. 2007; Parr 2004) The starting point for this concept was the activation of the growth-pole. In the background to this, two quite different theories can be detected. One of these is rooted in the recognition that development in the regional economy has a 'cause and effect' connection – as a result of the extension of concentration and polarisation. To support this, there was an array of historical reasons. A later theory asserted that investments which found their way to a limited number of centres, and with a relative degree of concentration, in fact do generate effective development. The other theory essentially approached the planned growth-pole from a sectoral point of view, holding that the development of the region was linked to the large-company sector and starting with the premise that this sector is the one which initiates the development of the connecting industrial sectors within the pole and/or motivates the spill-over of growth within its sphere. However, in using the growth-pole concept, it is clear that the experience acquired during several decades will contain many contradictions.

Paralleling the clear results achieved in the development of those major urban centres which are treated as poles, the consequences in terms of the effect as experienced on regional transformation are less favourable. It is not in every country that growth-poles have been developed as the driving forces of regional development, and especially in those countries where the spatial-political, politico-economic and the political strategies involved in public administration could not be framed within a unified system, the results of the use of this paradigm are spoken of with some scepticism. The elaboration and fulfilment of their (incomplete) policies were not embedded in a unified decentralised concept, but appeared as separate, disjointed steps or attempts to reform, and they were ineffective – especially since the underperformance of the synergies produced some undesired results.

As a consequence of the multi-coloured administrative structure of European countries, we can speak of regional centres in a variety of ways. In countries with a federalised and regionalised system, the public administration centres work at the meso-level as real regional centres, whereas, in decentralised, unitary countries the centres of the NUTS 2 units have more limited (planning and organising) functions.

In the development of regional centres in each country, many identical and numerous specific factors played a role. However, the general trend seems clear, in that, in the great majority of European regions, the largest town or city is the centre of the region. However, as a result of European urbanisation development processes, the density of the large cities in the countries across the continent differs, and the proportion of the population living in towns or cities with more than 100,000 inhabitants varies from country to country. Eight to 34 per cent of the population of the EU-15 member-states live in cities with populations above 100,000. (In defining the population proportions we did not take the population of capital cities into account.)

In terms of the number of towns or cities, Germany is at the top of the ranking. Germany, in fact, has 83 towns exceeding this 100,000 figure; then comes the UK with 65, Spain 55, Italy 49 and France 35. Regarding the proportion of the national population which this represents, the order is: Spain, Germany, Italy, Sweden and the Netherlands.

The picture is more intricate if we look at the populations of the regional centres. A total of 150 out of the 343 towns or cities which comprised the 'big city' network of the earlier EU-15 have region-related functions. The number of regional centres in the federalised and regionalised countries (Spain, Germany, Italy, Belgium France and Austria) is 64, while in the countries which do not have public administration regions but which have managed to build up relatively well-established regional institutional systems (the UK and Portugal), the number of regional centres is 18. In the other countries, the criteria defining regional centres are less relevant. Despite this, we can see the establishment of de-concentrated state offices and region-related institutions (universities, conference centres, specific health institutions, technology parks, etc). This also happened even in the unitary Scandinavian states, first of all in 17 major cities.

The differences in size detected in the 'big city' network are also coupled with different structural specifications. In Spain, with its expansive big city network, there are 22 cities with a population exceeding 200,000, and there the spatial spread shows great disparities. There are regions with large populations (for example, Andalusia, Catalonia, Valencia and the Basque Country) in which six to eight major cities are situation, one-half or one-third of them having a population of over 200,000. In the under-developed regions, however, there is only one big city heading the urban hierarchy. For example, the capital of the Aragon region, Zaragoza, with a population of 645,000, is followed by a provincial capital (Huesca), which has a mere 48,000 inhabitants. In such cases, designating the administrative centre of a region presented no problem. It is also the case that in Spain the general West European pattern applies, in that the regional centres are the largest towns of the region. The Basque Country can be considered as an exception to the rule, since the capital of the region, Vitoria-Gasteiz (at 226,000 inhabitants) is smaller in population terms than the actual economic and financial centre of the region, Bilbao (with 353,000 inhabitants). At the same time, however, the Basque Parliament and Government, and numerous other institutions of the region, established their centre in Bilbao.

In the other Iberian country, Portugal, we find a totally different situation: the city network of the country is extremely polarised. One pole is represented by the two major agglomeration belts (Lisbon and Porto) which comprise over half of the country's total population. At the bottom of the urban hierarchy there are 42 small towns with 10,000–20,000 inhabitants. The 13 medium-sized towns, with 40,000–50,000 inhabitants, are concentrated along the coast, and altogether, only one town (Braga) has a population a little over 100,000, although, on the basis of the population of the urban belts, the city of Coimbra in the centre of Portugal is considered by Portuguese statistics as a settlement of more than 100,000 inhabitants. One of the reasons for the slowness of the Portuguese regional organisation process is a lack of functionally rich regional centres.

Austria is the archetypal example of the third type of large urban area structure. The centres of the regions (*Länder*) (excluding the capital city) can be split into three groups. The big cities (Graz with 266,000 inhabitants, Linz with 191,000, Salzburg with 146,000 and Innsbruck with 121,000) are part of a *Land*. In the second group, there are two middle-sized towns (Klagenfurt with 95,000 inhabitants and St Pölten with 52,000), while the third group consists of two, the capital of the Vorarlberg (Bregenz, with 28,000 inhabitants) and the capital of the Burgenland (Eisenstadt, with 13,000). The Austrian medium-sized city network is quite weak: the country altogether has only a few towns in the 40–60,000 population bracket. In the process of selecting the regional centres, these cities with their historically important spatial organisation functions did not need to compete with rivals.

Table 3.3 shows the range in terms of size of the regional centres of the EU member-states with NUTS 2-level public administration units. The data clearly support our earlier statement to the effect that, in each country the largest cities are the regional centres. For an explanation of Germany's specific situation, we have to go back to the Four-Power Control Policy which followed World War II. In the case of two German provinces (*Länder*) the allied powers did not wish to give provincial capital status and functions to those cities which had played a leading role in the Third Reich. For this reason, Wiesbaden (with 272,000 inhabitants in 2012) became the capital of Hesse, instead of Frankfurt – which currently has a population of 688,000. Likewise, Cologne (with the highest population in 2012 of 1,024,000) is not the capital of North Rhine-Westphalia capital, but the smaller city of Dusseldorf (572,000). After re-unification, in two of the five new East German *Länder* the largest city did not become the regional capital. There are very minor differences in size between the capital of Saxony (Sachsen) which is Dresden (529,000 inhabitants) and Leipzig, which is slightly larger at 531,000. The same can be said of the capital of Saxony-Anhalt, which is Magdeburg (232,000), not Halle (233,000). In the UK, Scotland provides the only example of this anomaly, in that the historical capital of the country, Edinburgh, with 495,000 inhabitants has a lower population than Glasgow, which, as the economic and financial centre, has the largest population of 598,000.

Table 3.3 Situation in selected European countries regarding size of regional centres

Country	Regional centres		Total number of regional centres
	Largest town	Not the largest town	
Austria	9	–	9
Belgium	3	–	3
United Kingdom[1]	10	1	11
France	22	–	33
Germany	11	4	15
Italy	20	–	20
Spain	16	1	17

Note: Centres for regional government offices.
Source: Author's own construction.

The big city network in Central and Eastern Europe, except for Romania and Poland, is thin. In the whole area, 97 towns or cities have a population of over 100,000, and two-thirds of these are in Poland and Romania. Slovakia has only one major city, apart from the capital (Figure 3.3). In these two countries the number of regions is much lower than the number of cities but the largest cities are evenly distributed over the whole area and can be become potential regional centres. For this reason, therefore, designating a regional centre could be much easier. In most of the Eastern and Central European countries the debates over the designation of regional centres became more intense as the EU accession process progressed.

In Poland, after the introduction of the new 'voivodship' public administration, the leading major cities became the centres of the new regions. The only exception is the Kujawsko-Pomorske voivodship where the regional centre is not Bydgoszcz, the industrial centre with 357,000 inhabitants, but Toruń, with its historical traditions and a population of 205,000. In the other countries the competition among towns or cities goes on almost exclusively in respect of setting-up of the labour organisations of the development agencies and changing the number of the NUTS 2 regions.

The latter is especially at the centre of debate in Romania. Several cities with traditionally strong regional organising functions in the country, such as Arad, Oradea, Sibiu, and Târgu-Mureş) lost their potential regional centre role. These demand a change of the national regional system. The dissatisfaction in the counties belonging to the planning-statistical regions is shown by the fact that the headquarters of the regional development councils in several cases in Romania were set up in smaller county centres.

There were also examples of neglect of the role of the leading cities in Bulgaria. As a result of the public administration reform undertaken in the 1970s, in which, instead of small spatial units, six large 'oblasts' were created, the leading major city was replaced, and a smaller-sized town in the geographical centre of the region became the regional centre.

Is Eastern and Central Europe unitary or decentralised?

Should it be thought desirable to give an important future role to the meso-level units in regional policy in Eastern and Central Europe, this would clearly bring the current meso-level system into sharp focus. Both the size and economic potential of the counties in their current form are too small for them to become the basic units of decentralised regional policy, and it is to be expected that, in the future, regionalism will become stronger in more and more countries, and that this will lend weight to redefining distribution of labour between the centre and the provinces. There will be a serious opportunity to establish inter-regional co-operation operating on the basis of economic conformity and to increase cohesion in Eastern and Central Europe, but, even then, only if the tasks now accumulating (a genuine regional decentralisation of power and the creation of a regional development strategy conforming to the market economy) could be carried out, would it be possible that regionalism in its West European meaning could take root in this area. Today, the driving forces of growth are concentrated in the core areas of individual countries, something that indicates, over the long term, the maintenance of the differences between the national regional units, or even their increase.

The changes occurring during the last decade indicate that the political scope of activity within regional policy at the beginning of the new century, over and above the self-determination of economic development, are defined by two major factors: the first of these is the EU's organisational, operational, and financial reform together with Eastern enlargement, while the second (to no small extent influenced by the first) is the establishment of a new distribution of labour within government in the nation-states, in other words, decentralisation.

Decentralisation, as proved most clearly by the processes of previous decades, is now regarded in Europe as a perfectly normal phenomenon. In 1950, a quarter of the population of the continent lived in federalised or regionalised states, a figure which, by the mid-1990s had risen to 60 per cent. My forecast at the end of the last century was, that by the end of the first decade of the twenty-first century, without taking into account the successor states of the former Soviet Union, more than three-quarters of the population of Europe would live in countries where the state would not influence the factors of economic growth, but subnational local adminis-trations would play the defining role. This quantitative change, according to our current knowledge, would have been the result of the creation of new regional administrations in two countries with a high population, the UK and Poland. But the UK Labour government (1997–2010) after having established a regional parliament in Scotland and regional assemblies in Wales and Northern Ireland failed to institutionalise devolution strategy in England, and unitary character of the state philosophy did not change.

The basic interest of the nation-state in the future will be to attempt to use its power to determine economic policy within its borders to counterbalance the effects of external pressure from globalisation and integration, by increasing the ability of the regions to defend their interests in a regulated fashion (Keating 1988, 1998). It is already the case that the traditional regional development practice of Keynesian economic policy cannot be used successfully in the new paradigm, and the state's regional policy will be substituted by the region's own policy. This paradigm exchange, however, cannot occur automatically, because the interests of the regions are being developed to different levels. In the institutionalisation of regionalism, important differences are to be seen. The poorest regions can hope for improvement through outside (national and international) help, as in the past, their motivations depending more on traditional support systems than on what might be gained through the autonomy (in its wider sense) of a 'Europe of the Regions.' The devoted fans of regional decentralisation come from the group of developed regions that will clearly be the beneficiaries of the single market and of economic and monetary union. It is not by chance that, today, Europe's most efficient regional co-operation network (not even connected territorially) comprises: Baden-Württemberg, Lombardy, Rhône-Alpes, and Catalonia, who created such a network under the name 'Europe's Four Engines' (Amin and Tomaney 1995; Späth 1989).

The general spread of regionalism, however, still faces large barriers, and national governments will continue in the future to play an important role in the connections between the regions and the EU Commission. The poorest regions of Europe can realise their interests least of all in the integration decisions, as the poorer countries have fewer representatives in the EU bodies. The competition policy of the EU also reinforces the effects of centralisation, and community regional policy, but is less capable of counterbalancing the differences emanating from varying competitive abilities. Federal Germany is the best example of this; the regional regionalism and the decrease of spatial differences can also be matched at central government level.

In parallel with the irreversible intensification of European integration, the key functions of the national government are still retained, at least in three areas. One of the most important tasks of the state is to regulate capitalism in public companies, and industrial development, even in the future, cannot be imagined without effective national financial systems. The safest starting point for corporate strategies will be the domestic market and the regulation environment too. The other important central government task remains the co-ordination of national innovation and technical development programmes. Finally, the third national level priority can be considered to be the labour market and industry-political functions. Success in fulfilling these two latter national functions depends on how effectively subnational public administration can fulfil numerous partial tasks. Consequently, regionalisation is, at the same time, a prerequisite for the successful operation of the nation-state, since macropolitical aims cannot be fulfilled without competent human resources, education, training, and enterprise development; nor can well-balanced market competition take place without the co-operation of the social partners. The solution of these, however, is the most optimal at regional level (Keating and Loughlin 1997).

In Eastern and Central Europe today, the future of the division of power between state and region still seems uncertain. The prospects for decentralisation depend on the success of economic efficiency and the results of the 'top to bottom' managed change of regime, but the preconditions at regional level for setting-up power are unfavourable. In the former planned economies, the organisational framework derived from strong centralisation has remained, even if the substance of central power has changed a great deal. Even in the most favourable cases, the process of decentralisation is likely to be long (Keating and Hughes 2003).

Three possible ways of decentralisation can be envisaged in Eastern and Central Europe, and each of these differs from the others in terms of the extent and quality of the division of power. The choice of way, naturally not an arbitrary one, the historical traditions of an individual country, the nature of the economic transformation, the establishment of institutions of the market economy, political power relations, and the degree of sophistication of the spatial structure all influence the decline of power concentrated at the centre. The pressure to decentralise that falls on the central state administration is obviously stronger in those countries where the dynamic, regional major urban centres (for example, in Poland) wish to initiate their autonomous development, their structuring into the European regional division of labour, with the help of (possibly, most liberalised) their internal resources and post-industrial development factors. However, the legitimisation of bottom-up initiatives meets greater resistance in those countries (for example, in Hungary) where the central region (capital city) has a dominant, even a strengthening, position in the factors of production, thus increasing competitiveness. Although the example of these two countries is effective in demonstrating that the existence of regional centres capable of being made effective is no more than a potential advantage, the 'suction effect' toward decentralisation originating from the political legitimacy of Hungarian regional local authorities and the legal regulation of regional development can somehow counterbalance the lack of strong regional centres of appropriate European size.

In the first possible decentralisation model, the division of labour between central and regional bodies is organised under clear, precise rules, and the development tasks for which the two types of body are responsible differ simply in respect of which regional unit these tasks affect. To solve these problems, regional authorities even have their own income resources and have wide-ranging rights in respect of planning, and the development of local authorities that are part of their own circle can be subsidised from these (regional) funds. Depending on the economic development level of the region, 'its own' and 'shared' income can be supplemented by transfers from central government funds. This strategy provides the most comprehensive form of decentralisation, and, in the long term, this is the most effective solution. However, to create this, numerous (political, constitutional, public administrative, and economic) preconditions are necessary, and, even today, the progress of regional self-government in Eastern and Central Europe does not seem a realistic prospect.

The gist of the second decentralisation strategy model is that only certain functions (planning, development, executive, authorisation, and financing) are transferred from the centre to the regions, with the remaining regional, political tasks continuing under the aegis of central government. The expansion of the redistribution of power depends on the tasks that are to be decentralised, the institutional system that is to take them over, and the tools that will be at the regions' disposal. This version is the best in the short term for those countries with a unitary system, since the preparations for transferring power need less effort, there being no need for a complete transformation of the public administration system, since the actual influence of the central bodies does not change (which is the most important consideration), and, as the management of regional development through deconcentrated state organisation will be more complex, perhaps their efficiency will increase.

In the third option, the new division of responsibility between central and regional organs is based upon their handling of specific, occasional tasks. They create a common managing body for developing the peripheral, backward regions, and the state provides part of its financial resources to this decision-making forum, while the execution of the development programmes is delegated to the spatial units. This version represents the weakest form of decentralisation, but, since there is no need to change the established power structure, it is not surprising that most Eastern and Central European countries have started to elaborate their spatial development programmes on this basis. Central governments consider this solution as the easiest way to solve the problem: they do not need to put their hands into a hornet's nest and the vertical and horizontal power relations remain untouched.

References

Amin, A. and Tomaney, J. (1995) 'The regional dilemma in a neo-liberal Europe', *European Urban and Regional Studies,* 2: 171–188.

Bakk, M. and Szász A.Z. (2010) 'Conflict and convergence: regionalisation plans and autonomy movements in Romania', *Acta Universitatis Sapientiae. European and Regional Studies,* 1: 19–32.

Geshev, G. (2001) 'The role of regions of South-Eastern space in the enlarging European Union', in Gál, Z. (ed.) *Role of the Regions in the Enlarging European Union,* Discussion Papers, Special. Pécs: Centre for Regional Studies, HAS, 81–100.

Hall, P. and Hay, D. (1980) *Growth Centres in the European Urban System,* London: Heinemann.

Horváth, T.M. (ed.) (2000) *Decentralization: Experiments and Reforms, Volume 1,* Budapest: Local Government and Public Sector Reform Initiative.

Illner, M. (1997) 'The territorial dimension of public administration reforms in East-Central Europe', *Polish Sociological Review,* 1: 23–45.

Keating, M. (1988) *State and Regional Nationalism. Territorial Politics and the European State,* London: Harvester-Wheatsheaf.

Keating, M. (1998) 'What's wrong with asymmetrical government?' *Regional and Federal Studies,* 1: 195–218.

Keating, M. and Loughlin, J. (eds) (1997) *The Political Economy of Regionalism,* London: Frank Cass.

Keating, M. and Hughes, J. (eds) (2003) *The Regional Challenge in Central and Eastern Europe. Territorial Restructuring and European Integration,* Brussels: Peter Lang.

Kicker, R. (1988) 'Föderalismus in der österreichischen Aussenpolitik. Initiativen der Bundesländer', *Österreichische Zeitschrift für Politikwissenschaft,* 2: 133–144.

Kowalczik, A. (2000) 'Local government in Poland', *Decentralization: Experiments and Reforms,* 1: 217–253.

La Pergola, A. (1987) *Tecniche costituzionali e problemi delle autonomie garantite: riflessioni comparatistiche sul Federalismo Regionalismo,* Padua: Cedam.

Marcou, G. (ed.) (2002) *Regionalization for Development and Accession to the European Union: A Comparative Perspective,* Budapest: Open Society Institute.

Meijers, E.J. (2007) *Synergy in Polycentric Urban Regions,* Delft: Delft University Press.

Parr, J. (2004) 'The polycentric urban region: a closer inspection', *Regional Studies,* 3: 231–240.

Rose, J. and Traut, J. (eds) (2002) *Federalism and Decentralization: Perspectives for the Transformation Process in Eastern and Central Europe,* New York: Palgrave Macmillan.

Scott, J.W. 2000: 'Euroregions, governance, and transborder co-operation within the EU', in Van Der Velde, M. and Van Houtum, H. (eds) *Borders, Regions and People,* London: Pion, 104–115.

Späth, L. (1989) *1992: Der Traum von Europa.* Stuttgart: Dt. Verlag-Anst.

Stasiak, A. (1999): 'The new administrative division of Poland', in Duró, A. (ed.) *Spatial Research in Support of the European Integration,* Pécs: Centre for Regional Studies, HAS, 31–42.

Stumm, T. and Gabbe, J. (2001) *The Status Quo of Transeuropean Co-operation between Territorial Authorities and Future Steps that Contribute to Realise a New Model of European Governance,* Gronau: Association of European Border Regions.

Sturm, R. and Dieringer, J. (2005) 'The Europeanization of regions in Eastern and Western Europe', *Regional and Federal Studies,* 3: 279–194.

van Kempen, R., Vermeulen, M. and Baan, A. (eds) (2005) *Urban Issues and Urban Policy in the New EU Countries,* Aldershot: Ashgate.

Yoder, J.A. (2003) 'Decentralisation and regionalisation after communism: administrative and territorial reform in Poland and the Czech Republic', *Europe-Asia Studies,* 2: 263–286.

4 Towards a knowledge based regional development

Intellectual potential and regional development

One reason for Europe's diminishing role in the world economy is the fact that the development of research capacity and of the human factor lags behind that of their US counterparts. A programme aiming to correct these deficiencies was drawn up in the European Union's Lisbon Strategy.

Europe's further development depends on the way in which growth factors are spread across its regions, and one reason for the lower level of competitiveness is major regional differences in R&D. Weak regional cohesion and an exaggerated spatial concentration of modern regional development factors clearly have a negative effect on European competitiveness today. Activities with high value added are concentrated within the London-Paris-Milan-Berlin-Amsterdam pentagon, but the distribution of innovative industries differs even in the developed countries. The role of national core areas is vital to R&D capacity, high-technology industries and to advanced services, but, again, the situation is very similar in the Eastern and Central European countries, where the level of concentration, in fact, increased after the change of regime in 1989—1990.

The establishment and distribution of institutions of economic and social innovation have played an important role in European development since medieval times, and the first universities on the continent had close contact with the actors in both their nearer and more distant regions. The 'universities' in the early Christian Irish monasteries were the innovation centres of their time. They gathered and codified cultural, technological and professional information from all over Europe and disseminated this through their networks to what was tantamount to the production level. Owing to this, Ireland was Europe's most important innovation centre in the second and third centuries, in spite of its peripheral position (Joyce 1907; Ó Drisceoil 1993; Pounds 1990).

The geographical deconcentration of the development of universities was typical of the Middle Ages. The central areas of the Italian Peninsula became the principal development centre in the twelfth centuries, and, by the 1400s, 13 of Europe's 30 universities were based there. At that time universities were quite common in Western Europe, and, at the beginning of the sixteenth century, Europe's total of 70 universities were spread evenly across Spain, Germany, France and Italy. The regional contacts of these universities were limited to financial matters, and one prominent responsibility of these institutions, maintained as they were, by urban capital, was the spread of humanist culture across the regions. Economic contacts were less important, although the hugely significant role of German universities in the development of the printing industry is unquestionable.

In the eighteenth and nineteenth centuries the centralised states deliberately, through financing and by exercising foundation and endowment rights – attempted to draw universities away from regional influences. The Prussian and French education systems were able to achieve this, but Switzerland has, even today, still not managed to establish a federally operated university. Moreover, in (both unitary and centralised) Great Britain, regional influence remained strong in the creation of universities during the nineteenth century. Only in extreme cases did some universities manage to extricate themselves from centralisation, and, following the French annexation of the Netherlands in 1802, the University of Groningen was able to survive, but only because the northern region was geographically isolated. Meanwhile, most Dutch universities had either been closed or reconstituted as a lower level institution (Florax 1992).

With the passage of some 150 years, the growing importance of geographical decentralisation and regional stimuli had become a major motivation force in European academic development, and, in the meantime, the social role of the university and of the economic and political environment had also changed. The demand for innovation in economic development was growing fast and this inspired the development of new institutions which focused only on research and development. The Kaiser Wilhelm Institute, established in Germany in 1911, was the name given to 29 institutions between World War I and World War II, mainly in the German provinces. There were 12 in Berlin (Macrakis 1993).

After World War II, institutions of higher education (higher education) were characterised by strong centralisation. First, education and research were concentrated in relatively few institutions, with central government having direct control over universities, while, second, in almost every country the universities were located in the most developed cities, some of these, especially the capitals, having an overwhelming position.

The 1950s, however, were a period of extensive development in higher education, in that its higher levels were largely replaced by forms of mass education, which met the needs of society and the economy as a whole. Between 1960 and 1970, the number of university students rose from 1.8 to 4.8 million. For example, the number of Norwegian students quintupled, while the number of British, Italian and Swedish students quadrupled. The order of the leading countries also changed in the European ranking order.

Around the beginning of the 1960s, institutions of higher education diversified as a result of decentralisation and the monopoly of the universities ended in many countries. Specialised colleges were founded, the independence of individual institutions grew and education became much broader.

Functional decentralisation not only meant the establishment of new institutions (comprehensive universities in Germany, polytechnics in the UK, high schools in the Netherlands and regional institutes of technology in Ireland), but also the reorganisation of the fragmented higher education structure targeting economies of scale. In Sweden 100 smaller colleges were reorganised into 33 new units and the 385 (newly established) colleges in the Netherlands were consolidated into 85 institutions (Neave 1979).

The academic network broadened and regional economic development came to play a decisive role in the funding of new universities. In the UK, the development concept had been elaborated by the British Higher Education Commission, which was founded in 1961. This gave priority to increasing student numbers and eradicating regional differences. In the UK the 1960s saw the founding of 22 new universities,such as the Robbins universities of Sussex, East Anglia, and Warwick. King's College, Durham University became the University of Newcastle-upon-Tyne and the women's colleges of London University admitted male undergraduates. Nowadays one-third of British university students study at newly established universities (Commonwealth Universities Yearbook 2003). This was because a total of 41 new universities were created in– almost all in 92 with a few in 1993, 1994 and 1995. Thirty-eight were former polytechnics. The previous total was 47, although this did include London University as a single entity even though this federal institution comprises several 'colleges' which are practically universities in their own right both in terms of quality and size, but the University of London awards the degrees.

In 1970 the West German Federal Parliament (the Bundestag) enacted a law to improve the structure of higher education in West Germany. The law specified new regions for university establishment but did not initiate any significant expansion of the traditional historical university centres. Regional development issues featured prominently in relation to location, with the Ruhr (in a state of structural crisis) and the rural areas of Bavaria being allocated more new institutions (Lömker 1986). Regional considerations also prevailed in the operation of the Max Planck Institutions which had been developed from the institutional base of the Kaiser Wilhelm Society but had been compromised during the National Socialist era. Today, there are 12,000 researchers and 9,000 doctoral students and research fellows working at no fewer than 80 institutions. Berlin and Bonn (the former capital of West Germany) do not feature very strongly. The similar multidisciplinary Fraunhofer Society is research organisation with 58 institutes spread throughout Germany, each focusing on different fields of applied science. It employs over 12,500 researchers, with an annual research budget of about €1.2 billion.

In Sweden, universities were concentrated in five southern cities in the 1960s. The regional concept, drawn up to develop the northern regions, led tothe founding of Uppsala and Umeå universities at the end of the 1960s, with the first northern university being established in 1971 in Luleå. Regional concerns also had priority in the expansion of the Swedish higher education system. The training structure of the new universities and colleges was geared to the needs of regional economies, and so faculties of technology, economics and administration were given priority. Technical universities, faculties and colleges of technology became regional innovation centres and developed strong connections with regional authorities and local economies. The increasing international competitiveness of Swedish industry can be attributed to the new regional higher education system (Hjern 1990). Similar regional structural anomalies were eliminated in a similar manner by the Finnish government. Fourteen new universities were established in the 1960s, consistent with the country's regional development policy principles, alongside the traditional university cities of Helsinki, Turku and Tampere.

As a result of geographical decentralisation, the importance of the central regions and capitals of countries declined. Even though these were still able to preserve their leading position in many cases, the general tendency was for some of the larger regional centres of higher education and research to strengthen gradually.

Higher education has an effect on internal regional development, not only due to its role in the R&D sector, but also because of its dominant position in the training of specialists who organise, produce and sell technologically developed products and competitive services. In parallel with technological change, industries and companies who produce competitive products choose their location according to quality criteria. higher education has an important role among these, its power to attract capital being influenced not only by any advantages of the labour market generated by itself, but also by the innovation capacity concentrated there. Throughout Europe, influence on major technological systems was primarily in the hands of the R&D department of metropolitan or agglomeration-based companies. However, higher education institutions were dominant in the technological renewal of SMEs and in organising local and regional technological co-operation networks. The driving force of such regional institutions can be shown by the growth of industrial areas in Central and North-east Italy and the regional development of Bavaria, Northieast France and the Netherlands, and so on (Bennett and Krebs 1991; Ciciotti 1993; Cooke *and* Piccaluga 2007).

A higher education network must meet at least four criteria in order to fulfil its function and be able to carry out *integration tasks* as part of the innovation system:

1   Research has to be qualified as a core function of higher education, and this has to be taken into account financially and in the operation of universities and colleges.
2   National technology policy and regional institutions must support organised co-operation between higher education and the economy with appropriate stimuli.
3   The structure of higher education must be able to generate technological and economic innovation.
4   HE must be geographically decentralised, and its institutional measures must reach the critical mass needed to fulfil these functions. This produces equality with the institutions of the central region concerning research funding and distribution of international research and development.

Autonomy and independence are essential to public universities in stimulating good teaching, training and research. Research must be a major and permanent part of university activity, but it needs critical evaluation to ensure that only high-quality work is funded. The place of higher education in the socialist societies of Eastern and Central Europe was entirely defined by its societal function. Therefore, goals, structures and content of higher education were dominated by the political monopoly and ideological monism of the state (Mitter 1996).

The organisation of scientific institutions in Central and Eastern Europe, 1950–1990

The different levels of development of the two halves of Europe are particularly evident in relation to science, and the roots of this reach back several centuries. The university foundation period of the Middle Ages, in fact, had very little influence in Eastern Europe. Four universities were founded in this region (which played a prominent role until today). These were the universities Prague (1347), Krakow (1364), Vienna (1365) and Pécs (1367). Higher education appeared in other parts of Europe only several centuries later. For example, Bulgaria's first university was founded in Sofia in 1888 (after many years of Turkish rule) but newer universities in the country appeared only after 1970. The first universities of Romania were founded in Bucharest in the 1850s and in Iaşi (Moldavia) in the 1860s. In some major cities, a university network, primarily in Transylvania, developed between the two World Wars, and in the communist era many new universities were founded in major cities or industrial centres, including the underdeveloped parts of the country.

Developments in many Eastern European countries were relatively uniform. The basis of higher education and research appeared only after the World War I and the number of institutions was very small. Only four universities were operating in Hungary between the two World Wars, the number of students being 14,000 out of a population of 9 million in 1938.

Due to regional development issues, and from the viewpoint of sectoral education, few adjustments were made after the Second World War. The University of Heavy Industry in Miskolc and the University of the Chemical Industry in Veszprém were founded in 1949, at the beginning of the communist era.

The foundation of *national academies of sciences* was crucial for the scientific systems of the countries of Eastern Europe, and all these academies had been founded by the beginning of the 1950s. The academies were not only the coordinating institutions for science in their respective country, but had an extensive research network, typically embracing some 40–70 institutions. The consequence of centralised government was that these academic research institutions were, with few exceptions, located in the capital cities.

The modest changes in over-centralisation introduced in some countries have some influence in the deconcentration of the institutions. For example, the government in Hungary issued a decree reforming science policy within the economic reform programme started in 1968, and the communist party document issued in 1969 also asserted the need for science to be decentralised. The decree reflected the negative aspects of the excessive concentration of research in

Budapest and proposed to decrease the differences between the disciplines and to develop the social sciences. The enactment of the decree, however, was only partially successful. At the beginning of the 1970s, science developed noticeably in regional centres, and the Hungarian Academy of Sciences organised a Biological Research Centre in Szeged, which was the most highly developed in Central Europe. The Faculty of Business and Economics began to operate at the University of Pécs, only the second institution of education in economics in the country, and the academic research institutions of Pécs acquired a new profile, that of regional science. However, the relocation of research and higher education institutions away from Budapest was not successful. A decision had been made to move the Faculty of Veterinary Science from Budapest to Debrecen, the centre of Hungarian agriculture, in eastern Hungary –, but, due to obdurate opposition (for personal interests) by the university's officers, the plan failed.

Although the Communist Party's policy for science had different characteristics in individual countries, as in other spheres of the economy and society, we can detect some characteristics common to all:

1   Science enjoyed a privileged position in the socialist era, a typical feature of the Soviet model. The favoured groups of people in the sciences (academicians, principal researchers) received higher incomes and enjoyed a variety of social benefits.

2   Intensive state intervention and government control were accompanied by continuous and adequate budgetary resources, although these varied in the different branches of science. Of the national income, 2 per cent was spent on R&D in the Eastern European countries in the 1970–1980s. This high rate of expenditure was due in part to research in the armaments industry, and a further explanation is that many industrial products (in telecommunications and computer technology) were produced on the basis of domestic research because of restrictions on importing Western European technology.

3   The state established research institutes in technology and the natural sciences in the 1950s, a period of extensive development and promotion of science, but the social sciences remained in an inferior position for decades, due to the dominance of Marxist ideology. The new branches of science (sociology, political and regional sciences) developed relatively late, and they were only incorporated into the higher education system with difficulty. The ratio of researchers employed in the social sciences amounted to less than one-fifth of that in several countries.

4   Academic research networks, sectoral research institutes controlled by the ministries and corporate research units were dominant in the institutional structure of research. For example, in Hungary in 1985, corporate research units absorbed 48 per cent of all R&D expenditure. Universities were primarily institutions of education and research expenditure within universities was marginal. In Hungary, in 1985, higher education institutions accounted for no more than 12 per cent.

Until the late 1980s, the supranational features of R&D systems in the socialist bloc were ultimately the decisive determinants, rather than the particular interest and features of individual countries. This began to change with the remarkable political events of 1989–1990. The state renounced responsibility for research and development through the abolition of state planning, the dissolution of ministries and other bodies formerly responsible for R&D. Autonomy was granted to universities and academies of sciences. In all cases, this was associated with a substantial reduction in state funding. In most countries, these reductions far exceeded the general level of economic downturn, in reaction to the earlier emphasis on science (Meske 2004; Schiermeier and Ockenden 2001).

The impact of the systemic change on the regional structure of R&D

The systemic change at the beginning of the 1990s produced a significant restructuring of the scientific potential of Eastern and Central European countries. One characteristic common to all was a considerable reduction in scientific capacity. Two fields of research capacity shrank dramatically, one of these being the sectoral research institute network. The majority of research institutes funded by national bodies (such as ministries) were closed and the number of employees in academic research institutes declined just as dramatically. As a direct consequence, the percentage of GDP allocated to R&D was greatly reduced, to one-third or even one-fifth. We show this in terms of GERD/GDP in Table 4.1 (*g*ross *e*xpenditure on *r*esearch and *d*evelopment as a percentage of gross domestic product).

After the systemic change, R&D underwent a substantial restructuring. The reorganisation of the higher education system was the starting-point of a range of positive changes. In East European countries, the number of undergraduates doubled or even tripled. New colleges and universities were established and R&D was given an important role. One part of the major, state-owned research institutes closed (apart from the academic networks) and the other was privatised. Certain groups of companies started to increase their R&D activity, including several multinational companies established in Eastern and Central Europe. The structure

Table 4.1 Changes in R&D main indicators in Eastern and Central Europe, 1980–2005

Name	Bulgaria		Czechoslovakia		Poland		Hungary		Romania	
	1980	2005	1980	2005	1980	2005	1980	2005	1980	2005
GERD/GDP	2.5	0.5	3.9	1.4[1] 0.5[2]	2.2	0.6	3.2	1.0	No data	0.44
Number of researchers, in thousands	31.6	21.6	39.6	37.5[1] 17.5[2]	96.3	55.0	31.4	23.0	71.1	33.4

Source: Horváth (2010: 122).
Note: [1]Czech Republic, [2]Slovakia.

of expenditure changed perceptibly, with spending on state- or community-financed research continually decreasing and that on corporate research rising.

There are, however, considerable differences between the countries of Eastern and Central Europe. In the Czech Republic, expenditure on business research locations accounts for nearly two-thirds of all GERD, data similar to the EU-27 average. The ratio of business financed research is the lowest in Bulgaria where government finance is still of great importance. In two countries, Hungary and Poland, the influence of higher education institutions in financing research exceeds the EU average, and in all countries government-supported research institutes have a notably higher share of GERD than the EU average due to the maintenance of a network of Academies of Sciences (Table 4.2).

The sectoral transformation of research institutions was followed in none of the countries by a positive change in regional structure, and it remained typical of the spatial structure of research centres that they were still mainly concentrated in the capitals. In the 1990s, however, the spatial structure of R&D changed in several countries. The central or core areas declined in importance, and the major results of decentralisation are evident in the regionalised and federalised countries. The relative weight of Vienna in Austria decreased by 15 percentage points and, in Spain, that of Madrid by 12. There was a slight decrease, or even no movement at all, in the unitary states of Hungary and Greece. In the latter, the Attica region even increased its share in the national GERD (Figure 4.1).

In Eastern and Central Europe, the capitals and metropolitan regions are the bastions of research and science, the weight of the metropolitan region being greatest in Bulgaria. Four-fifths of the country's research potential is concentrated in Sofia and its vicinity, and two-thirds of Hungary's GERD is found in the central Hungarian (NUTS 2 development) region which consists of Budapest and Pest county). The research capacities of the Czech Republic, Poland, and Slovakia reveal a slightly more balanced picture, the metropolitan proportion in these countries being under 50 per cent (Table 4.3).

Most of the important R&D indicators in the core areas of CEE countries are below the EU average, and in no more than two (Czech) regions of the 49 NUTS 2 regions of the six do CEE countries exceed the EU average for the GERD/GDP

Table 4.2 Distribution of GERD by sectors, 2011, per cent

Name	Business	Government	Higher education
Bulgaria	50.0	33.3	16.7
Czech Republic	56.2	18.8	25.0
Hungary	67.5	15.4	23.1
Poland	25.0	37.5	37.5
Romania	40.0	34.1	17.9
Slovakia	40.0	40.0	20.0
EU-27	62.9	12.7	23.4

Source: http://appsso.eurostat.ec.europa.eu/nui/submitViewTableAction.do.

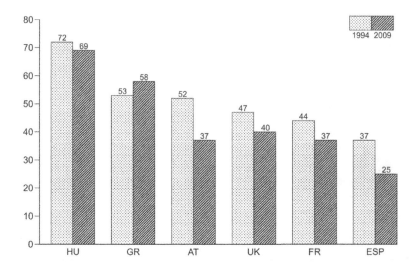

Figure 4.1 Share of the core areas in GERD, 1994–2009, per cent
Source: Horváth (2010: 123).

ratio. In eight regions, the GERD/GDP level is between 1.0 and 1.9 per cent, and in 39 regions the level does not reach one per cent. In 20 regions it is even below 0.3 per cent (Figure 4.2).

If we look at the regional spread of R&D activity, we would draw a similar conclusion. In most countries, the most highly concentrated R&D activity is corporate-financed, and foreign joint ventures' target locations for establishing R&D units in CEE countries were almost solely capital cities.

The location of the academic institutions, the leading basic researchers, is no more positive. Most of the institutes of academies of sciences are located in national capitals and no more than seven (19 per cent) of the 37 research institutes

Table 4.3 Weight of capital regions in national R&D, 2011

Country	Core region	Percentage share in R&D expenditure	Percentage share in R&D employees
Bulgaria	South-west	83.4	71.6
Czech Republic	Prague	37.5	40.4
Hungary	Central Hungary	68.8	63.4
Poland	Mazowieckie	42.5	32.6
Romania	Bucharest-Ilfov	59.3	60.9
Slovakia	Bratislava district	47.6	49.8

Source: Compiled by the author on the basis of http://epp.eurostat.ec.europa.eu.

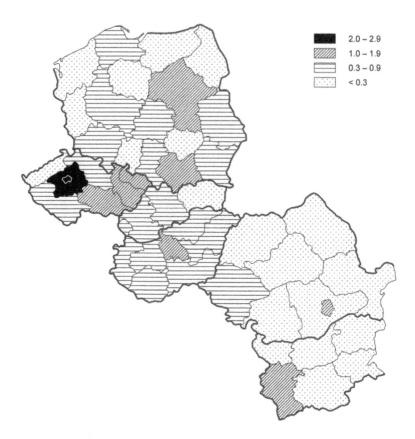

Figure 4.2 GERD as per cent of GDP in CEE regions, 2009
Source: Horváth (2010: 125).

of the Hungarian Academy of Sciences operate outside Budapest. This means that only 15 per cent of the Academy's employees, some 4,000 in number, work in these institutes. By contrast, 38 per cent of the Polish Academy's employees work in institutes outside Warsaw. It is important to emphasise that, in federal states, the spread of academies is very different from the above. There are a remarkable number of research centres in the federal states of Austria and Germany (Figure 4.3).

Great expectations followed the change of regime in terms of the modernisation of the regional structure of higher education. In almost every country, the total number of students tripled or quadrupled, although this increase was spatially unbalanced. The dynamic of higher education in the capital is as strong as the increase in the number of students outside the capital. The developments were discursive in that no regional policy concepts were applied and, moreover, spatial development planning was undeveloped. The unfavourable spatial structure of higher education was preserved, with some 30–40 per cent of students still

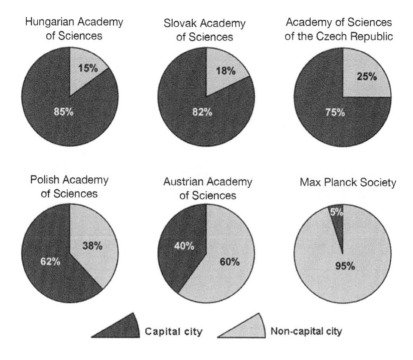

Figure 4.3 Employers of state institutes of science outside the capital citys in specific
European countries, 2010

Source: Horváth (2010: 126).

concentrated in the capital (Table 4.4). A further characteristic of rapid change was
the significant increase in the incidence of the social sciences in the higher
education system of most countries, important in terms of establishing the
economic bases of regional development. The weight of social sciences in higher
education is higher in CEE countries than in other member states of the EU, but,
at the same time, the importance of natural sciences and technology in higher
education is lower (Table 4.5).

At the beginning of the 1990s a faculty of social sciences was founded in many
cities by the former political elite. The establishment of university faculties or
colleges in regional public administration centres was a result of political change,
and the former official buildings and education centres of the Communist Party
offered an adequate infrastructure for higher education. The Ministry of Education
accepted implicitly the relatively cheap and extensive developments in social
science education. As a result of the demand for specialists required to work in the
market economy, there was a noticeable increase in economics education.

The slight decrease in the regional distribution of R&D was generated by the
fact that research and development was given an important role in university
functions. In the analysis of the R&D investment structure, we have already

Table 4.4 The distribution of students in higher education in central areas, 2006

Country	Number of students ('000s)	National (%)
Bulgaria	114	47.1
Czech Republic	125	37.0
Poland	445	20.7
Hungary	187	42.6
Romania	294	35.2
Slovakia	65	32.8

Source: Compiled by the author based on http://epp.eurostat.ec.europa.eu data.

Table 4.5 Students in higher education by field, 2006, per cent

Country	Students ('000s)	Social sciences[1]	Technology sciences[2] and natural	Other fields[3]
Bulgaria	243	43.5	35.2	21.3
Czech Republic	337	27.6	38.7	33.7
Poland	2,145	40.9	30.1	29.0
Hungary	439	41.5	28.6	29.9
Romania	835	50.0	31.5	18.5
Slovakia	198	28.3	43.9	28.3
Austria	253	34.9	35.1	30.0
Finland	309	22.4	52.8	24.8
Netherlands	572	38.0	32.1	29.9
Ireland	186	23.1	36.0	40.9

Note: [1]Business, psychological behaviour, law and other social sciences; [2]Biological and physical natural sciences; [3]Teacher training, liberal arts, personal and security services, environmental protection,

Source: Compiled by the author based on http://epp.eurostat.ec.europa.eu

mentioned the different distribution of higher education in different CEE countries, and we saw that in Poland and Hungary expenditure on R&D higher education is considerably above the European average, There is no other type of research organisation outside higher education in any of the CEE countries in this study: the role of corporate research is well-nigh invisible and the number of regional development planning institutions and research centres of many West European countries are somewhat thin on the ground.

Regional inequalities of intellectual resources in the Western Balkans

The future development of the Western Balkans will be greatly determined by the mental condition of the population and the research and development potential. The Balkan countries still occupy the bottom positions in tEuropean competitiveness ranking. As regards the two factors of global competitiveness demonstrating intellectual resources (higher education, training and innovations), a more significant variance can be detected in the position of countries. Four countries occupymiddle third of the international ranking of the quality of intellectual resources. Albania and Bosnia-Hercegovina are in the middle to end of the last third of the 139 examined states (Table 4.6). The problems arising from the scarcity and insufficient quality of human resources and R&D capacities necessary to maintain long-term economic growth are aggravated by the uneven spatial distribution of these factors within the respective countries.

In order to create a new economic structure necessary for the amelioration of the currently rather low income producing capacities, highly qualified professionals, industrial and service companies producing high added values and insitutions capable of creating innovations are required in the respective regions of these countries. A small proportion of the working-age population were university or college graduates in the Western Balkan countries (6 per cent in Albania, 15 per cent in Croatia, 14 per cent in Serbia). The number of regions with large populations where the share of highly qualified individuals does not even attain 4 per cent is considerable. During the past two decades, the number of students enrolled in higher education institutions in these countries has not increased with the same speed as in Central and Eastern Europe. The number of students per 100,000 inhabitants (2,571 in 2008) is two-thirds of the EU average.

Among the laws related to the functioning of the democratic political system and the market economy in the Balkan countries, we can also find legal documents regulating the new norms and institutions of higher education, training and research and development. However, the normative dispositions focusing on the moderation of regional inequalities of these two main domains of activities is absent from them.

The Balkan countries' system of higher education underwent a significant quantitative development simultaneous with the development of the market economy (Figure 4.4). Student numbers increased and university structures were

Table 4.6 The position of Western Balkan countries in the global competitiveness index ranking of countries

	Global competitiveness index		Higher education and training		Innovation		Quality of scientific research institutions	
	Rank	*Score*	*Rank*	*Score*	*Rank*	*Score*	*Rank*	*Score*
Albania	88	3.94	84	3.86	121	2.57	128	2.47
Bosnia-Herzegovina	102	3.70	88	3.80	120	2.59	104	2.97
Croatia	77	4.04	76	3.97	70	3.08	51	4.01
Macedonia	79	4.02	72	4.04	97	2.88	71	3.52
Montenegro	49	4.36	52	4.51	45	3.48	36	4.39
Serbia	96	3.84	74	4.01	88	2.93	56	3.89

Source: Author's own calculation based on The Global Competitivness Report, 2010–2011.

transformed, leading to a growing number of faculties. New disciplines appeared in higher education institutions. Despite a significant quantitative development still lagging behind the Eastern European average, the quality and competitiveness of higher education are considerably insufficient.

The low enrolment ratio, the large spatial concentration, the non-uniform system of higher education, the unfavourable disciplinary structure, the weak infrastructure and the lack of financial resources are among the most crucial problems in the higher education system of the Balkans (Table 4.7). The evolution of student numbers in the Balkan states was much more modest than in Eastern European countries. Even though the Albanian system of higher education experienced the largest growth (200 per cent), this country has the lowest proportion of students enrolled in higher education among the college-age population. The training structure of universities and colleges shows large disparities. The number of students studying technical and scientific subjects is low. Serbia is the only exception, where the numbers in of technical training is almost equivalent to the EU average.

The spatial structure of higher education is characterised by the outstanding dominance of capital cities. More than 50 per cent of the students are concentrated in the largest cities, two-thirds in Albania and Macedonia. In Montenegro, a country with a small population, only the capital has a higher education institution (although the University of Podgorica has established faculties in several cities).

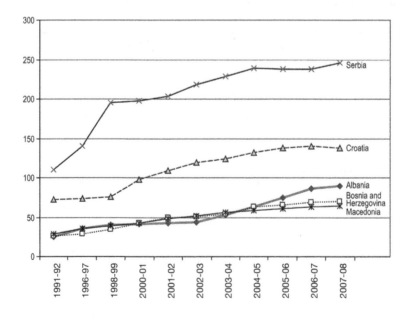

Figure 4.4 Development of student numbers in the Western Balkan countries, 1991–2008, in thousands

Source: Author's elaboration on national statistical data.

Table 4.7 Some important indices of higher education in countries of the Balkans, 2007

Country	Student numbers, ('000s)			Distribution of student numbers between the main disciplines (%)				Weight of the capital (%)	Percentage of students in college age pop. (%)
	1999	*2007*	*Change, (%)*	*Arts*	*Social sciences*	*Natural sciences*	*Technical sciences*		
Albania	38.5	80.7	209	5	29	2	4	65.8	19
Bosnia-Herzegovina	–	68.3	–	16	37	4	10	48.8	34
Croatia	95.9	140.0	146	8	38	7	12	52.7	47
Montenegro	–	–	–	–	–	–	–	100.0	–
Macedonia	–	–	–	11	32	7	11	67.0	36
Serbia	194.2	238.7	123	10	39	8	21	51.5	48

Source: Author's own estimations based on UNESCO Institute for Statistics sources.

Such a great concentration in the development of human resources is seldom found in European countries. The concentration of higher education is twice or three times as high as the share of the capital in the country's population. (Zagreb concentrates 17.4 per cent of the population of Croatia, Belgrade 21.5 per cent of the population of Serbia and 18.0 per cent of Albania's population lives in Tirana.)

The fragmentation of Yugoslavia, the collapse of the system of self-management and the transition to market economy transformed *the research and technological map* of the Western Balkans. The weakening industrial and production linkages between former parts of the country had a negative effect on research and development capacities. The Yugoslav system of innovation showed a higher level of development than in other Eastern European communist countries. The developed Yugoslav industry accustomed to applying modern Western technologies operated a large number of research units as well. In the constituent Yugoslav republics with developed industries, 2–3 per cent of the GDP was assigned to R&D purposes. The institutional system of Yugoslav science was decentralised; scientific academies of member republics established their own institutional networks, and sectoral research institutions were subordinated to the control of the republic. The federal government was responsible for the harmonisation of research and development.

Following the break-up of Yugoslavia, the former research and development bases also collapsed. In contrast with higher education, there was extensive job loss in the R&D sector in the Balkan countries after regime change. A large number of institutions were dissolved and the number of researchers declined severely. Several thousands of researchers migrated to Western Europe and the United States.

Large-scale industry and the innovation network with developed Western European links collapsed and the financial resources of R&D decreased due to the emerging economic and political crisis. In more developed republics (Serbia and Croatia), the decrease was between 15–30 per cent (Meske 2004). Serbia's network of research institutions diminished considerably. There were 375 research institutes in Serbia in 1980 and their number fell to 163 by 2005. The number of business research and development organisations fell by one-third. The number of researchers was 35,000 at the end of the 1980s, and after a continuous decline reached its lowest point in 2001 with 19,000 researchers employed in Serbia (Kutlača 2006). There then followed a phase of slow growth and a new phase of decline began in 2007.

Similar tendencies could be detected in the rest of the countries. During the last years of the former Yugoslavia, the tendency of researchers to migrate abroad was already strong and further increased due to the war and the economic crisis. In Albania, the consequences of outward migration of professionals from the country were also severe. The University of Tirana lost 40 per cent of its lecturers in the 1990s, the majority of whom were young professionals under the age of 40 (Uvalić 2006).

The share of research in the national GDP was reduced to a minimum level in several republics. In Bosnia-Herzegovina, the share of R&D in GDP fell to 0.03 per cent in 2007 from 1.5 per cent in 1990. A major cause of the decline was the dissolution of Elektroinvest in Sarajevo, the flagship company of Yugoslav industry with large export capacities and scientific potential. In 1990, 30 per cent of Bosnian industrial export consisted of products developed in Bosnian research units. This value is considerably lower today (UNESCO Science Report, 2005).

R&D indices of Western Balkan countries present an unfavourable picture, both in terms of research expenditure and research employment data compared with average European performances (Table 4.8). Despite lagging behind in several areas, Croatia's research system shows the strongest resemblance to development trends in the European research area.

Weak innovation potential is a major reason for the low indices of competitiveness in Western Balkan countries. Based on the analysis of pillars of global competitiveness (health care, primary education, macroeconomic stability, higher education and training, development of the business sector, market efficiency, institutions, infrastructure, technological readiness, innovation performance), Balkan countries show a heterogeneous picture. The largest disproportions can be detected in the development level of infrastructure. Albania and Macedonia perform badly in each sector of infrastructure, and infrastructural networks of the previously relatively developed Bosnia-Herzegovina were destroyed during the war. Among the factors of competitiveness, innovation and technological receptiveness reveal the lowest values. Factors related to institutions of the market economy show a higher performance and continuous development. The tendency of Europeanisation is visible. Even though this leads to the permanent amelioration of external conditions of research and development, no such favourable changes have occurred in the private sector that would stimulate demand for new technologies.

Due to the weak absorption capacities of the economy, the great bulk of research is financed by public funds in all of the countries except Croatia. Higher education is regarded as the most prominent research sector in each country. Three-quarters of research expenditure in Albania, and over 50 per cent in Serbia is related to

Table 4.8 Some important R&D indices in Western Balkan countries, 2007

	Albania	Bosnia-Herzegovina	Croatia	Macedonia	Montenegro	Serbia	EU27
Researchers per million inhabitants	609	197	1,384	–	1,143	1,190	2,728
R&D expenditure in percentage of GDP	0.18	0.03	0.93	0.18	0.24	0.34	1.9
Distribution of R&D expenditure, percentage	100,0	–	100.0	100.0	100.0	100.0	100.0
Business sector	1.0	–	23.5	11.0	5.5	1.7	64.0
Governmental sector	25.1	–	32.9	24.0	15.7	39.8	13.4
Higher education	73.9	–	43.6	65.0	78.8	58.5	22.6

Source: UNESCO. Institute for Statistics (http://stats.uis.unesco.org/unesco/TableViewer/chart View.aspx [2010. 05.14.]).

universities. Universities have always fulfilled an important role in different phases of economic development in the area. For this reason, technical, technological and engineering faculties operate with a large number of students in all of the important regional university centres. However, the necessary conditions for establishing strong linkages between industrial companies and universities are still lacking in Balkan countries.

To rebuild Balkan economies, international community plans for the stabilisation of political conditions have highlighted the importance of the modernisation of training and higher education and the reorganisation of research and development. UNESCO provides permanent counselling in the area. Several large international companies elaborated strategies to keep qualified workforce in the area and to organise innovative training programmes at local universities. Every Balkan country has joined the research framework programme of the European Union. European standards appear formally in the regulation of national institutions. In the mid-2000s new laws on higher education, research and development and innovation were implemented in all of the countries. The development of the institutional system of research management has begun. International counselling organisations have supported the elaboration of the first national scientific and research strategies. In Albania, Croatia and Serbia, medium-term research and development plans were accepted by the governments. Unfortunately, national policies do not pay attention to the large disproportions in the spatial location of R&D units.

The presence of large spatial disparities hindering the development process characterises the organisational system of research as well. As a result of the concentration of higher education in the capital and the implantation of research units in higher education institutions, inner regions of the Balkan countries do not carry out research and development activities. Several elements of the innovation chain are missing and endogenous resources of structural transformation of the economy are modest. The spatial location of research units in the different countries is shown in Figure 4.5.

Research capacities in Macedonia and Montenegro show the biggest concentration. With one exception, all of the research units in Montenegro are located in the capital. Eighty-seven per cent of Macedonia's researchers are concentrated in the capital. The second most important research centre is Bitola, which, thanks to its university, provides 7 per cent of the country's researchers. The rest of the research centres have only a 2–3 per cent share.

In Balkan states with large populations, regional disparities in research and development are somewhat lower than in the former countries, yet compared to EU standards, they are still considerable. In terms of the number of research units, the weight of capital cities is two to three times higher than their share of the

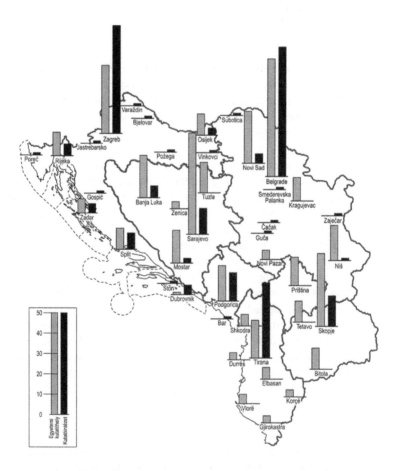

Figure 4.5 Regional distribution of research units in countries of the Balkans

Source: Author's own work based on accessing and disseminating scientific information in South-eastern Europe and various internet sites and national sources.

country's population, exceeding 50 per cent. Croatia is the only exception, where the degree of concentration in the capital is below 50 per cent. This is due to the presence of large universities outside the capital, technological and innovation centres six provincial towns and research institutes and regional centres of the Croatian Academy of Sciences and Arts.

In the Balkan countries, similar to Eastern European states, the academies of sciences founded by the state have fulfilled an important role in science and the organisation of research. The Yugoslav Academy of Sciences and Arts (whose legal successor is the Serbian Academy) established local-regional academies in the former constituent republics in 1972. The Albanian Academy of Sciences was established in the same period. At present, the legal successors of these organisations operate as a combination of scientific societies and institutions fulfilling scientific management functions. Several academies operate their own research institutes. They are quite scarce and the number of their employees is low: 400 researchers are employed in 29 institutes and nine regional centres of the Croatian Academy of Sciences and Arts. The Serbian Academy has 10 research institutes and 250 researchers. The majority of academic institutions are engaged in social sciences (mostly humanities) and their research activities focus on the analysis of national specificities.

References

Bennett, R.J. and Krebs, G. (1991) *Local Economic Development: Public-Private Partnership Initiatives in Britain and Germany,* London: Belhaven Press.

Ciciotti, E. (1993) *Competività e territorio, l'economia regionale nei paesi industrializzati,* Rome: La Nuova Italia Scientifica.

Commonwealth Universities Yearbook, 2003 London: The Association of Commonwealth Universities, 2003.

Cooke, P. and Piccaluga, A. (eds) (2007) *Regional Development in the Knowledge Economy,* London and New York: Routledge.

Florax, R. (1992) *The University: A Regional Booster?* Aldershot: Avebury.

Hjern, B. (1990) 'Improvement of regional qualification structures as a task of regional economic policy', in Ewers, H.-J. and Allesch, J. (eds) *Innovation and Regional Development, Strategies, Instruments and Policy Co-ordination,* Berlin: Walter de Gruyter, 207–224.

Horváth, G. (2010) 'Inequalities in the Central and Eastern European research area. Challenges of regional decentralisation', in Pálné Kovács, I. and Kutsar, D. (eds) *Internationalisation of Social Sciences in Central and Eastern Europe. The 'Catching up' – a Myth or a Strategy?* London: Routledge, 115–130.

Joyce, P.W. (1907) *Ancient Ireland: a Smaller Social History of Ancient Ireland,* New York: Longmans, Green & Co.

Kutlača, Đ. (2006) 'Science and technology system in Serbia: between survival and restructuring', in Nechifor, I. and Radosević, S. (eds) *Why Invest in Science in South Eastern Europe? Proceedings of the International Conference and High Level Round Table,* Paris: UNESCO, 131–139.

Lömker, K. (1986) 'Regionalization in the sector of tertiary education institutions development in the Federal Republic of Germany', *Higher Education in Europe,* 3: 44–49.

Macrakis, K. (1993) *Surviving the Swastika: Scientific Research in Nazi Germany,* New York: Oxford University Press.

Meske, W. (2004) 'The reorganization of R&T systems in CEECs during the 1990s', in Meske, W. (ed.) *From System Transformation to European Integration. Science and Technology in Central and Eastern Europe at the Beginning of the 21st Century*, London, Hamburg: Lit Verlag, 357–380.

Mitter, W. (1996) 'Higher education in Central and Eastern Europe. An approach to comparative analysis', in Burgen, A. (ed.) *Goals and Purposes of Higher Education in the 21st Century*, London: Jessica Kingsley, 167–191.

Neave, G. (1979) 'Higher education and regional development', *Higher Education Review,* 11: 10–26.

Ó Drisceoil, P. (ed.) (1993) *Culture in Ireland – Regions: Identity and Power,* Belfast: The Institute of Irish Studies, The Queen's University of Belfast.

Pounds, N.J.G. (1990) *A Historical Geography of Europe,* Cambridge, New York: Cambridge University Press.

Schiermeier, Q. and Ockenden, J. (eds) (2001) *Perspectives of Sciences in Central and Eastern Europe – Emerging Directions from the Past Ten Years,* Amsterdam: IOS Press.

UNESCO Science Report, 2005. Paris: UNESCO, 2006.

Uvalić, M. (2006) 'Science and economic development in SEE', in Nechifor, I. and Radosević, S. (eds) *Why Invest in Science in South Eastern Europe? Proceedings of the International Conference and High Level Round Table,* Paris: UNESCO, 53–60.

Part II

National characteristics of regional development and policy

Country case studies

5 From a country to regions?

The natural history of East German regional development

The German Mezzogiorno?

Every country in the world is characterised by a heterogeneous spatial structure and the existence of regional disparities, and the aim of regional policy is to moderate these inequalities in the spatial development of economic activities. There are certain countries where spatial disparities are extremely large and areas lagging behind belong to one specific geographic area featuring a dual economic structure. There are, specifically, two large areas amongst the developed countries of the European Union whose economic performance lags behind the EU average and the development paths of which are unique in many ways. An investigation into the unique development specifics of these two large, but coherent, territories, the regions of Southern Italy (the Mezzogiorno) and Eastern Germany, has attracted the interest of regional scientists for a long time.

Today, the name 'Mezzogiorno' is synonymous with long-term underdevelopment, while the other large area in question was reintegrated into the 'mother country' after half a century of separation. Underdevelopment can be detected in almost all elements of the economy, the infrastructure and living conditions (Table 5.1). These regions are among the main beneficiaries of EU support, but, in addition to the enormous amount of EU funding, the national budget continuously assists development programmes with financial subsidies. We can ask with some justification whether these huge financial subsidies contribute seriously to reducing developmental disparities in a positive way and whether these areas are then enabled to achieve higher positions in the economic and social development rankings (Burda 2005; Desmet and Ortín 2007; Hall and Ludwig 1993; *Lentz* 2010; Trigilia 1994).

In the literature, we can find several cases where development difficulties in the Eastern provinces are explained by means of the 'Mezzogiorno phenomenon', and occasionally they refer to the Southern Italian failures, that is, fruitless efforts linked to continuous financial investment, as a negative example in the elaboration of development paths (Hallett and Ma 1993; Page 2002; Sinn and Westermann 2000).

The underlying reasons for the low performance are many and varied. A partial or total absence of driving forces of classical, developed capitalism characterises the development of the Italian macro-region even today (Cafiero 2000; Cannari

Table 5.1 Main indices in the two large regions, 2008

	Population, thousands 2009	GDP, € millions	GDP per capita (PPP), € thousands	GDP per capita (PPP), EU27 =100	Percentage of people with higher education, aged 25–64
East Germany	16,461	360,430	22.0	88	–
Berlin	3,432	84,540	25.7	103	35.7
Brandenburg	2,522	51,886	21.7	85	30.3
Mecklenburg-West Pomerania	1,664	34,066	21.2	85	27.0
Saxony	4,193	90,589	22.4	90	32.3
Saxony-Anhalt	2,382	51,269	22.3	89	25.0
Thuringia	2,268	48,080	22.0	88	28.2
Southern Italy	20,858	360,117	17.3	69	–
Abruzzo	1,335	28,454	21.6	86	16.3
Molise	321	6,447	20.3	81	14.9
Campania	5,813	95,428	16.6	66	12.8
Puglia	4,080	68,901	17.1	68	11.6
Basilicata	591	11,302	19.3	77	12.6
Calabria	2,009	32,956	16.6	66	13.9
Sicily	5,038	83,754	16.8	67	12.3
Sardinia	1,671	32,875	19.9	79	12.3

Source: Eurostat.

2010; Villari 1979). Agriculture was the main activity in Southern Italy during the first half of the twentieth century, the sector having a 56 per cent share of total employment in 1936 and regional incomes remaining below 60 per cent of average values in the North. In present-day East Germany, on the other hand, agricultural employment represented 22 per cent in the inter-war period, when income per capita levels exceeded the West German average by 27 per cent. The majority of the East German provinces belonged to the most dynamically developing regions of Europe at that time, with their internationally renowned engineering, optical, chemical and vehicle production companies being among the most competitive on the continent.

Post-World War II, political constraints forced the German states to strike out along new paths. Five East German *Länder* and East Berlin were under Soviet occupation, and the planned economy of the German Democratic Republic created in 1949 gave rise to specific patterns of socio-economic development. Governmental instruments were used to ameliorate the situation in under-developed Southern Italy and the 'Mezzogiorno programme' facilitated a (slow) catching-up process in these eight regions. In the meantime, the development rate of the previously advanced German provinces was considerably slower in the newly formed state than in West

Germany, and in the year of German re-unification, labour productivity indices of East German areas were one-third of the West German average, while indices for the Italian South were 60 per cent lower than in the country's developed areas. Nevertheless, in the first years of the present century, the East German *Länder* showed more rapid convergence with the developed regions' average values than the Southern Italian regions (Sinn and Westermann 2000).

The weight of the two regions in terms of the economic and human sectors has remained smaller than their share of the population. In spite of large-scale emigration, the population of the Southern provinces of the country's total (35.5 per cent in 1936 and 34.5 per cent in 2007) has shown only a slight decrease due to higher reproduction rates and the immigration of foreigners. In the meantime, due to wartime damage, the proportion of the population of East Germany decreased by 10 per cent compared to the 1930s. The decline is much more significant in terms of employment and industrial production (Table 5.2).

This chapter aims to explore how various eras have left their mark on the recent regional development of East German *Länder*, what kinds of spatial transformation have occurred, what factors can be detected behind these changes and how spatial disparities have evolved in this vast, but backward, area in developed Europe.

Historical pre-conditions – partial structure of the German Empire

After the unification of Germany in 1871, the dozens of provinces and free states showed a very heterogeneous picture. Large disparities were evident in the sectoral structure of their economy, in the manner and extent to which they were able to integrate modern European development trends and in their population and settlement networks alike.

The 26 provinces comprising the constitutional monarchy, duchies, principalities and free city states, show enormous disparities in terms of their respective population size. The average population of a political unit was 1.6 million, but the difference in terms of the population numbers between the largest and the smallest formerly independent entity was over seven-hundredfold. In the closing years of the nineteenth century the population in seven political units (e.g. Schaumburg-Lippe, Waldeck, Schwarzburg-Sonderhausen) remained below 100 thousand. In contrast, the Kingdom of Prussia had 30 million inhabitants, Bavaria 5.6 million

Table 5.2 The weight of the Eastern *Länder* in Germany, 1939–2009 (as percentage share in the total Federal Republic)

	1939	1950	1960	1989	1991	2009
Surface area	30.4	30.4	30.4	30.4	30.4	30.4
Population	29.2	26.9	23.5	20.9	19.7	20.0
Employed persons	27.7	27.4	25.0	26.1	21.2	19.8
Employed in production	30.4	29.5	31.6	48.7	18.9	17.8
Industrial output	29.4	28.6	22.5	15.2	4.0	12.9

Source: Statistical yearbooks, various years.

and Saxony 3.6 million. The population of Prussia, the largest state of the unified Germany was 60 per cent of the country's total population.

Rural inhabitants made up 64 per cent of the total in the 1870s, but accelerated industrial development was accompanied by a rapid increase in the urban population. The dominance of the latter was clear by 1910, its share rising to 60 per cent. Berlin stood at the top of the urban hierarchy with 2 million inhabitants and 20 cities formed the metropolitan area network with over 200 thousand inhabitants each. Macro-regions which served as political and economic hubs were powerful administrative centres (Table 5.3). The cities with a population above 100,000 constituted 5 per cent of the population of the German Empire in 1871, 21 per cent by 1910 and, due to a massive wave of urbanisation, 32 per cent by 1939.

The dominance of Prussia resulted in the rapid growth of Berlin. The population of the city was 198,000 in 1818, 702,000 in 1871 and 2,071,000 in 1910. The central function of Berlin was obviously a result of the presence of political institutions, with 25 per cent of all employees working in public administration (Urwin 1982). At the same time, the specific feature of German state organisation was that the centres

Table 5.3 Changes in the population of large cities, 1850–1910, in thousands

	1850	1871	1910	Growth, 1871–1910, 1871=100
Berlin	412	826	2071	251
Hamburg	175	826	931	321
Leipzig	63	107	679	635
Munich	107	169	596	352
Dresden	97	177	548	309
Cologne	97	129	517	400
Breslau (Wrocław)	111	208	512	246
Frankfurt on Main	65	91	415	456
Düsseldorf	27	69	359	520
Nuremburg	54	83	333	401
Hanover	28	88	302	343
Essen	9	52	295	567
Chemnitz	34	68	288	425
Stuttgart	47	92	286	311
Magdeburg	52	84	280	333
Bremen	53	83	247	298
Königsberg (Kaliningrad)	73	112	246	219
Stettin (Szczecin)	47	76	236	310
Duisburg	9	32	229	715
Dortmund	11	44	214	486
Kiel	16	32	212	663

Source: Reulecke 1978 (24–26).

of political units were also given a significant role in state-building, which inevitably resulted in the continuous strengthening of polycentrism. For this reason, Berlin was not able to exert such a powerful influence on state organisation as for example, Paris or London.

The Central German metropolitan political units (Leipzig, Dresden, Magdeburg and Chemnitz) developed in the most heavily industrialised areas. The development energies of centres in Silesia, West and East Prussia (Breslau, Stettin and Königsberg respectively) were primarily administrative and political in nature.

The evolution of wages also shows significant territorial disparities. As a result of the obsolete sectoral structure of the economy and the low standard of qualification in Eastern regions, average wages remained below the national average. The national average wage of a qualified metal industry worker was 90.1 Pfennig, 102.2 in Berlin, 79.0 in Breslau, 76.7 in Königsberg (Bessel 1978). Low income levels had a negative impact on the living standards of the population. The housing conditions in East Prussia were much worse than elsewhere and the health of the population and the provision by all areas of the social infrastructure were below the national average.

Germany lost a part of its national territory after WWI, and the country's population decreased by 13 per cent. However, the losses were much more severe in heavy industry sectors, with 44 per cent of pig iron production, 38 per cent of steel production and 26 per cent of coal-mining capacity now located outside the country's borders. The more industrialised Eastern parts of the country were ceded to Poland with the detachment of one-third of Upper Silesia. The changes taking place in the economic structure of the Eastern regions were unfavourable. The weight industry decreased and agriculture resumed its dominance. Fourteen per cent of the country's population was concentrated in these areas which produced only 10 per cent of GNI and 23 per cent of German agricultural products were produced by) regions east of the River Elbe.

Successive inter-war governments elaborated various programmes and measures to support the East Prussian provinces. The objectives behind spatial development concepts were manifold. The basic aim of the nationalist approach to the support of peripherial border areas was to ensure protection against Poland. Concepts with economic objectives sought to counterbalance the unfavourable position of Eastern areas, and the influence of special interest groups reliant on reaping the benefits of public aid programmes was not insignificant either (Buchta 1959; Fiedor 1971). Finally it was the nationalist approach which undertook to resolve the Eastern problem. Support for the National Socialist Party increased even among Protestant farming communities. While the Party gained only 6.2 per cent of the national vote during the parliamentary elections of 1924, in 1930, the figure was already 22.5 per cent in East Prussia (Bessel 1978).

Present-day East German territories (then a part of Central Prussia) were classified as intermediate regions. North Brandenburg, Mecklenburg-Schwerin and West Pomeraniawere agricultural areas. Industrial development in the Southern areas (Saxony, smaller and larger principalities and duchies) was launched by the construction of the Leipzig-Dresden railway line (the second railway line in

Germany), and, besides light industry, the chemical, energy, glass and machine-building industries (based on lignite mining in Upper Saxony and East Brandenburg) constituted the main forces of spatial development.

War preparations were the priority of the *Third Reich's* economic policy and were based on autarky. This philosophy had no significant impact on the country's spatial structure but traditional industrial centres became the primary beneficiaries, although the four-year plan adopted in 1936 considered the decentralisation of production as a basic principle of industrial development.

Military preparations for defence left their mark on the spatial structure of industry also. To defend the country from external attack, some of the factories in densely industrialised border areas of the Ruhr, Upper Silesia and Saxony were reelocated to the Hanover-Magdeburg-Halle triangle in Central Germany (Hardach 1976). Vast rural areas of the province of Mecklenburg were still excluded from mainstream development policy. Only city of Rostock was included in military developments where new munitions companies were established. The proportion of agricultural workers was 65–70 per cent in the Northern regions in 1925, and this did not fall below 60 per cent even at the outbreak of World War II. Meanwhile, in the Southern regions the corresponding figure was only 14–30 per cent.

Most industrial indices of Central German provinces (Saxony, Saxony-Anhalt, Brandenburg and Thuringia) led the development rankings, even though the last two were not part of the developed regions. In terms of per capita industrial output, the index of Central Germany (excluding Berlin) was 725 marks, 609 marks in Western parts of the country and 249 marks in the Eastern provinces, as opposed to the German average of 600 marks. Berlin stood first in the ranking list with 855 marks (Hardach, 1976). The weight of the Central German provinces – with 29 per cent of the population – in various economic sectors exceeded their share of the total population. Forty-three per cent of the German textile industrial output originated from these areas as well as 39 per cent of machinery and vehicle construction and 34 per cent of electrical products.

In the aftermath of the Great Economic Depression, provinces introduced job-creation schemes to remedy large-scale unemployment (Conze and Raupach 1967). Public works programmes were launched. Thousands of the urban unemployed were employed in rural areas in soil improvement works. Some provinces organised agencies to recruit young workers for large industrial centres, and labour retraining centres were established in several cities.

The most significant job-creation undertaking of Hitler's Germany was the development of the military and vehicle industries and the motorway network. More than 1 million new jobs were created in the transport sector (the automobile industry, the public road network and related activities) by 1938 (Overy 1995). The total extent of motorways exceeded 3,000 kms by 1939, and most large German cities were linked to the network (Figure 5.1).

The Sovietisation of Central Germany

The four-power treaty concluding World War II placed the Central German *Länder*

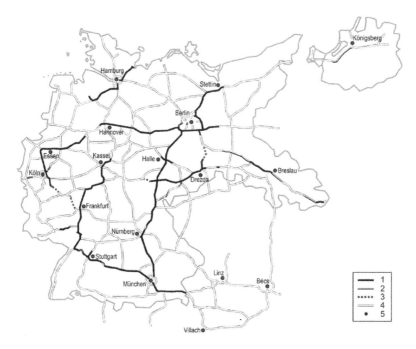

Figure 5.1 Germany's motorway network in 1939

Source: Author's own construction based on Zeller (2006: 58).

under Soviet control. Former Eastern territories were either ceded to Poland (Lower and Upper Silesia, Pomerania, West Prussia and southern East Prussia) or to the USSR (northern East Prussia). The Soviet belt was completed by East Germany respecting the new German state boundaries. The basic principles of the victorious powers in the reorganisation of Germany (demilitarisation, denazification, political decentralisation and economic deconcentration) were designed to prevent the strongly centralised state machinery, the major industrialists, the 'Junker' land-owners and the military elite from ever regaining power, although these basic principles were not adopted in the Soviet zone. The Communist German Demo-cratic Republic was established in 1949.

Institutions for a planned economy were created and a system of state adminis-tration was reorganised following the Soviet pattern. Districts (*Bezirke*) replaced states (*Länder*) as new basic units of territorial public administration (Figure 5.2). These new territorial units followed the borders of earlier states. Due to its special status, East Berlin was originally not counted as a *Bezirk* but it was recognised as the "capital city of the GDR' (though legally, it was not even fully part of the GDR's territory). In 1961, after the construction of the Berlin Wall, East Berlin came to be recognised in GDR administration as the Berlin *Bezirk*. The *Bezirke* (with the exception of Berlin, which consisted of a single municipality) were again divided into rural districts (*Landkreise*) and urban districts (*Stadtkreise*).

1949–1952   1952–1989

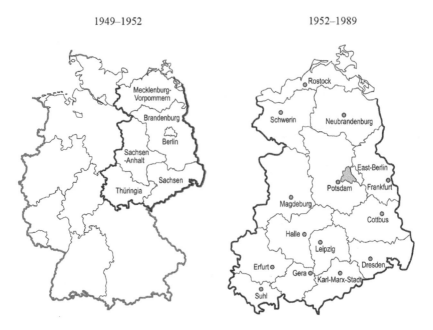

Figure 5.2 Territorial administrative units of East Germany

The State Planning Commission designed basic units of long-term spatial planning according to the former *Länder*. This system had two formal specifics: on one hand, they refrained from using historical names, and, instead, they divided the country into Northern, Central, Southern and South-western regions according to their geographical position. Berlin and Magdeburg were integrated into the Central region, while Saxony and part of Saxony-Anhalt (Halle *Bezirk*) constituted the Southern region.

As a result of the damage caused by the War (the destruction of half of the industrial facilities and a 70 per cent loss in the high-technology sectors) and the reparations paid to the USSR (in which framework 1,700 factories were relocatedto Russia), the national production volume at the end of the 1940s remained below 60 per cent of the 1936 value. Economic recovery in East Germany advanced faster: industrial production in the Eastern provinces in 1948 reached 71 per cent of the 1936 volume, but only 60 per cent in Western provinces. However, this temporary lead disappeared after a couple of years and the economic performance of Western areas showed continuous improvement. The East German economy under total state control was unable to perform well under competition (Herrigel 1996). Besides restrictions imposed by the planned economy, economic performance further decreased due to massive emigration from the East Germany. At the outbreak of World War II, Central German states had 16.7 million inhabitants, but due to the large number of refugees from the East, this number had risen to 18.65 million by 1946. Three million left the country between 1950 and 1961, 60 per cent of them active wage-earners, the majority qualified skilled workers and highly qualified intellectuals (Hardach 1976).

The foundations of the regional structure of the new East Germany were defined by historical heritage. The demographic and economic centres of gravity were located in Southern (Halle, Leipzig, Dresden and Chemnitz districts) and South-western (Erfurt, Gera, Suhl districts) regions. Thirty-eight point four per cent of the country's territory held 55.7 per cent of the East German population. These areas provided 70.4 per cent of industrial output and 76.2 per cent of the total export volume of the country. The weight of the capital city, East Berlin in terms of population was 6.4 per cent, 5.0 per cent in industrial production and 5.7 per cent in exports (Ostwald 1989).

The capital was much stronger in the R&D sector, with institutions in Berlin employing 17.2 per cent of R&D staff. Historical structures again influenced the spatial location of science, in that the number of R&D staff employed by industrial firms, universities and academic institutions in Dresden, Leipzig, Jena, Halle, Magdeburg, Rostock and Potsdam reached 10-20 thousand (Figure 5.3). A significant factor in the education policy of communist governments was the foundation of new, primarily technical, institutes of higher education.

The main objective of the German planned economy in the period from the 1950s to the 1970s was to stimulate traditionally less developed branches of industry, develop high- technology sectors in the larger industrial centres, create industrial centres in former agricultural areas and, the elimination of significant differences between urban and rural areas. (One of the best examples of these aims is the construction of the Eisenhüttenkombinat started in 1950 in 100 km southeast of Berlin.)

The spread of industrial-scale agriculture also facilitated the structural transformation of under-industrialised agricultural areas. A slow but evident change was witnessed in the evolution of territorial disparities in industrial development (Berentsen 1981; Mohs and Grimm 1984; Nemes Nagy 1979).

Northern and Central German regions showed a small percentage increase in industrial production, but there was a decrease between 1955 and 1980 in the Southern region and East Berlin (Figure 5.4). A specific feature of East German economic governance was the operation of large industrial conglomerations (Combines). The industry Ministries were responsible for 156 combines, and Regional Economic Councils directed 96 large companies. More than half of the headquarters of combines were located in industrial agglomerations, where half of the member companies and three-quarters of the R&D sector were situated.

The impacts of the structural transformation of the economy were also felt in the evolution of the spatial structure of migration. In the 1950s and the following decade, the higher fertility indices of northern agricultural areas transformed the territorial structure of the population also. Extensive industrial development resulted in a positive migration balance to Eastern (Cottbus, Frankfurt on Oder) and Northern (Rostock, Schwerin) districts and East Berlin, while Southern industrialised areas recorded a negative migration balance.

The change in the power system and the economic restructuring of the country left their mark on the urban network. East Germany was one of the most urbanised countries in Europe. In the middle of the 1970s, 75.3 per cent of the country's population lived in cities. At the peak of the settlement hierarchy, the order of cities by size (Berlin, Leipzig, Dresden, Chemnitz, Magdeburg) had shown remarkable

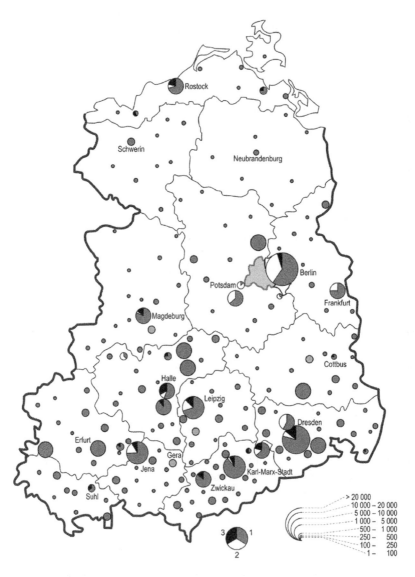

Figure 5.3 Territorial structure of R&D in the GDR, 1987

Key: 1 Private research units. 2 Academic research institutes of the National Academy of Sciences of the GDR. 3 Colleges, universities.

Source: Ostwald (1989: 62).

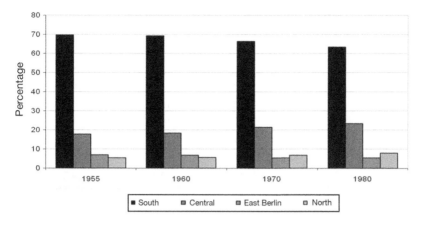

Figure 5.4 The macro-regional distribution of industrial output, 1955–1980
Source: Author's own design based on Mohs.Grimm (1984: 10).

stability since the beginning of the twentieth century. A small number of seats of new territorial-administrative units and industrial centres, the so-called socialist towns, advanced in the ranking of cities. Neubrandenburg, for instance had 22,000 inhabitants in 1950, but after becoming a district seat and an important industrial location, its population had increased to 91,000 by 1990, and rose from eighty-sixth in ranking to nineteenth. The population of Eisenhüttenstadt, the main metallurgical centre of the GDR, increased from 12,000 to 52,000 and the population of Schwedt, the capital of petroleum refining, increased from 7,000 to 53,000 over 40 years. A period of stability followed the changes taking place at intermediate level in the settlement network. Massive population movements benefited certain towns in the Northern and Eastern regions, while small- and medium-sized towns in Southern metropolitan areas experienced a slow but gradual population decline.

The operational resources of the East German economy and society had been exhausted by the 1980s. The driving forces of spatial development had weakened and, simultaneously, international and domestic political events leading to German re-unification had accelerated. In 1990, a reunified Germany was faced with an unprecedented problem: what policy to pursue in relation to the less-advanced part of the country which constituted one-third of the national territory and 22 per cent of the population (Table 5.4).

In the year of re-unification, GDP per capita in East Germany was only 49.7 per cent of the German average of €20,000. Obsolete industrial and low-quality agricultural products, an outdated production infrastructure, an unmotivated labour force and the collapse of foreign economic relations foreshadowed the fear that, in order to integrate this part of the country into the German and European economic area, considerable financial support would be required. Such large-scale development tasks in Europe had been necessary in the Italian Mezzogiorno.

Table 5.4 Major data of German macro-regions, 1992

Macro-region	Area		Population		GDP1995	
	'000km²	*%*	*millions*	*%*	*€ billions*	*%*
North	64.2	18.0	12.5	15.5	255.2	16.6
North Rhine-Westphalia	34.1	9.6	17.5	22.6	349.0	22.6
Central-West	43.5	12.2	10.7	13.4	224.1	14.5
Baden-Württemberg	35.8	10.0	10.0	12.5	217.8	14.1
Bavaria	70.6	19.8	11.6	14.4	254.5	16.5
East Germany	108.8	30.4	18.0	22.4	241.4	15.7
Germany total	357.0	100.0	80.3	100.0	1542.0	100.0

Source: Eurostat, Regional Statistics.

The regional impacts of the collapse of the GDR

Following the re-unification of Germany in 1990, East Germany was transformed from the most developed territory of the former COMECON area into the least developed part of the newly formed state. The building of the market economy and the transformation of the political system significantly changed the development possibilities of East Germany which had never been able to boast its strength. The mechanisms and institutions of the planned economy were eliminated. The economic structure underwent massive transformation, and unfavourable migration trends began to emerge. The unification of the two parts of Germany produced an immediate and drastic reduction of formerly huge transportation costs, and the impacts of this transformation activated processes of differentiation in the new states of this part of the country (Heimpold 2010).

Re-unification produced the most serious economic consequences in the *industrial sector.* The low level of competitiveness of the bulk of Eastern industrial companies became evident during the transition from a centralised system, the planned economy, to the market economy. Weak industrial performance was due to a combination of factors: outdated capital stock, the collapse of the former COMECON markets, an obsolete product structure and low productivity.

The sectoral structure of employment was also deeply transformed. While industry contributed 40.1 per cent to GDP in 1989, this had fallen to below 20 per cent by 1994 due to rapid de-industrialisation (Volkswirtschaftliche Gesamtrechnungen der Länder). The number of workers and staff employed in the industrial sector of the GDR was 3.2 million in 1987, but the number of workers employed in manufacturing in 1992 was only 2.1 million in the new *Länder* (including Berlin). This decline in employment by one-third was not only a consequence of closing of production units, but also a consequence of the integration many of the old functions of the major companies (health, education and culture) into the domain of community or private services.

Large firms were totally eradicated from East German industrial statistics. In 1988, the GDR had 46 large firms employing from 5,000-10,000 workers, 72 employing 10,000–30,000, 18 employing 30,000–50,000 and 9 employing over 50,000 workers; while today this category is represented by a mere four firms employing 5,000–10,000 thousand and one employing 10,000–30,000 thousand workers (Lentz 2010).

The percentage of *agricultural* workers fell from 10.2 per cent to 3.8 per cent during the 1989–1994 period, while those in market services (finance, consultancy, insurance, property, etc.) rose from 6.4 per cent to 20 per cent. The transformation of the employment structure showed a heterogeneous picture in each economic sector and there were significant regional disparities also. In the category of developed services, the R&D sector showed significant deterioration, in contrast to general trends. Research units were closed with the disappearance of the large industrial firms and the institutional network of East German Academies of Science was also eliminated. The R&D sector (employing 86,000 in 1989 had lost half its workers by 1991, and only 32,000 R&D employees were recorded in 1993 (Krull 1991).

The decrease in the number of *employees* was fairly similar in each *Land*, about 20 per cent. The largest decline was experienced in agriculture and heavy industry. The most moderate initial recession in East Germany was experienced in Saxony, which was home to the most modern base for mechanical engineering. In fact, the number of employees in manufacturing industry rose by one-fifth in this *Land*. The changes in Brandenburg were even more favourable. Its central position near to Berlin made it an attractive investment site, and the number of employees in manufacturing industries rose by one-third. The most striking growth occurred in the banking and financial services sectors, where the number of employees within the territory of the former GDR doubled. On the other hand, there was a remarkably weak transformation to a market economy in the large rural areas of Mecklenburg-West Pomerania.

Unemployment rates rose constantly in line with the economic restructuring. At the end of the first phase, the rate of unemployment was between 12 per cent and 16 per cent, increasing to 16 per cent to 20 per cent during the following decade. It started to decrease gradually from 2005, varying between 12 per cent and 14 per cent from province to province. The highest unemployment rates were recorded in Saxony-Anhalt and Mecklenburg-West Pomerania during each phase.

The changes did not leave the *spatial structure of the population* in the new states undisturbed. The unfavourable trends emerging in the 1980s in the demographic structure of the GDR gradually worsened, and new phenomena affected the settlement structure. The opening of borders resulted in a massive movement of the population from the Eastern *Länder* to West Germany, beginning in 1989. It reached its peak in 1991, when 240 thousand East German inhabitants (1.6 per cent of the population) migrated to Western *Länder*, primarily to North-Rhine-Westphalia, Bavaria and Baden-Württemberg. The number of migrants coming from Western to Eastern states was considerably lower, 64,000. Migration gradually decreased during the following years, and the annual average number of migrants was below 50,000 by the end of the 1990s. With the exception of Berlin and Brandenburg, the Eastern *Länder* suffered a considerable loss of population during the first post-re-unification decade (Table 5.5). Between 1989 and 2001, 7.5 per cent of the East German population had moved to Western *Länder* (Brücker and Trübswetter 2007).

The migration behaviour of the East German generations of young adults constitutes a specific phenomenon. One determining factor is the attractiveness of cities with universities, while another is the tendency of qualified young adults to prefer places offering higher quality employment such as Baden-Württemberg, Bavaria, Hesse, Bremen and Hamburg, the cities of Dresden, Leipzig and Erfurt in the East and Berlin (Herfert and Lentz 2010). The annual migration loss in these age groups in several East German large and medium-sized cities and towns (Jena, Gera, Halle, Cottbus, Rostock, Frankfurt on Oder) ranges from 2 per cent to 8 per cent.

One further factor behind the changes in the *settlement structure* is related to suburbanisation. East German metropolitan areas were affected by marked suburbanisation during the 1990s. The reasons behind this are many and various. On one hand, the opening of the housing market and the growing number of private cars facilitated the movement of inhabitants from central urban districts to the outer-suburbs. During the early 1990s, suburban settlements in the proximity of large cities with a population below 2,000 showed dynamic growth, while the population of core cities decreased. However, this tendency reversed in the early 2000s, due to various measures and the development of inner residential districts became permanent. In the third phase of spatial mobility following east to west migration and the development of suburbs we can witness the flow of the upper classes to large cities.

The transformation of the metropolitan network did not result in significant changes in the ranking of cities. The population of metropolises with over 100,000 inhabitants did, in fact, decline, but almost all retained their former ranking position. The higher-ranking multifunctional cities with strong economies (Berlin, Dresden, Leipzig, Erfurt) were able to maintain or increase population numbers during the two decades following re-unification (Table 5.6).

Table 5.5 Population changes in the East German *Länder*, 1990–2008

	1990	1995	2000	2008	Change, 1990–2008, 1990=100
Berlin	3,400,426	3,472,009	3,386,667	3,416,255	100.5
Brandenburg	2,641,152	2,536,747	2,601,207	2,535,737	96.0
Mecklenburg-West Pomerania	1,963,909	1,832,298	1,789,322	1,679,682	85.5
Saxony	4,900,675	4,584,345	4,459,686	4,220,200	86.1
Saxony-Anhalt	2,964,971	2,759,213	2,648,737	2,412,472	81.4
Thuringia	2,683,877	2,517,776	2,449,082	2,289,219	85.3
Total	18,555,010	17,702,388	17,334,701	16,553,565	89.2

Source: http://epp.eurostat.ec.europa.eu.

Table 5.6 Evolution of population numbers in East German metropolises, 1989–2009, in thousands

	1989	Rank, 1989	1995	2001	2005	2009	Rank, 2009	Population change, 1989–2009, 1989=100
Berlin	3,438	1	3,471	3,388	3,395	3,442	1	100.1
Leipzig	530	2	520	502	502	514	3	96.9
Dresden	501	3	501	495	495	517	2	103.2
Chemnitz	302	4	302	256	247	243	4	80.5
Halle	300	5	283	243	237	232	5	77.3
Magdeburg	288	6	259	230	229	230	6	80.0
Rostock	253	7	227	199	199	201	8	79.4
Erfurt	217	8	211	200	203	204	7	94.0
Potsdam	141	9	141	142	148	155	9	110.0
Gera	132	10	124	110	104	100	12	75.8
Schwerin	130	11	114	100	97	95	13	73.0
Cottbus	129	12	125	111	105	101	11	78.2
Zwickau	119	13	111	102	98	94	14	79.0
Jena	106	14	101	101	103	104	10	98.1
Dessau	101	15	107	97	92	88	15	97.1

Source: www.citypopulation.de [August 7, 2011].

Based on the development trends, the settlement network of East Germany can be classified into three regional types (Herfert and Lentz 2010). The first category consists of dynamic metropolitan areas (Berlin, Leipzig, Dresden and the so-called Thuringian string of towns located between Jena and Eisenach). The second group consists of conurbations with population losses considerably exceeding the avarage in Saxony-Anhalt (Magdeburg, Halle, Dessau), East Thuringia (Gera, Greiz), Saxony (Zwickau, Chemnitz), the Polish borderland areas (Görlitz, Frankfurt on Oder) and the Baltic coastal towns (e.g. Greifswald). The third type is constituted by towns remote from main centres. The medium-sized towns in the state of Mecklenburg-West Pomerania and Brandenburg fall into this category.

The first post-re-unification decade brought radical changes to the economic and settlement structure of the East German federal states. The economic growth stemming from infrastructural investment, privatisation and the revival of small enterprises at the beginning of the 1990s came to a halt by the middle of the decade and stabilised at the West German average level during the whole of the decade that followed. Factors influencing economic growth in the long-term show a high level of spatial concentration. Berlin, Potsdam, Dresden, Leipzig, Chemnitz, Halle (Saale), Jena and Erfurt can be regarded as the growth centres of the Eastern *Länder*. The favourable economic structure of these towns is characterised by a high level of labour productivity, state-of-the-art and satisfactory levels of qualified employees, a large export potential and a high level of R&D activities, and the existence of agglomeration effects.

The price and impacts of reintegration

An extremely short time was needed to achieve the formal reintegration of the new east German *Länder* into the unified German state. The building of market economy institutions and the creation of the democratic political system did not take long since it was a matter of adopting the West German legal system. The transformation was assisted by considerable public funding, and most of the political decisions supporting the region's integration were derived from the concept of the social state. Public transfers granted to the new *Länder* are considered by certain authors to be among the final consequences of World War II and as compensation for the sacrifices born by the Eastern territories (Eltges and Strubelt 2010). Without enormous capital injection, the (collapsed) East German economy would not have been able to achieve any growth. Investments (two and a half times greater than in Western Germany) were for initial state infrastructural developments, and there were incentives for the privatisation of state property and for encouraging the wide-scale distribution of small- and medium-sized enterprises to replace the former large combines.

Unit labour costs in the manufacturing sector remained higher in Eastern areas than in Western Germany until the end of the 1990s, and this necessitated enormous and intense investment in capital stock. Twenty-four billion euros were spent on investment funding between 1991 and 2004 in East Germany, involving 58,000 separate investments. The volume of investment reached €122 billion and approximately 776,000 jobs were created. Meanwhile, the per capita labour cost dropped below the West German average in every Eastern state. The decrease in per capita wage costs not only raised the international competitiveness of East German industry, but produced other disadvantages too. The significant decrease was supported by growing productivity, which, of course, automatically contributes to a reduction in the required labour force. In the first decade of the 2000s, the growth of added value was no longer a clear trend in the East. Growth rates in the different provinces showed wide variations around the national average. The biggest growth dynamics were witnessed in 2006 when the growth rate was 4.5 per cent in Saxony, 3.7 per cent in Mecklenburg–West Pomerania and 3.6 per cent in Thuringia as opposed to the 3.5 per cent national average. In 2009, in contrast with the minus 5.5 per cent average rate of German recession, the added value decreased by 1.1 per cent in Berlin, 2.2 per cent in Mecklenburg-West Pomerania and 5.6 per cent in Saxony-Anhalt.

Large financial resources have been spent by the German state and society to encourage development of the new East German *Länder*. Article 72 of the German constitution establishing the traditional fundamental principles of the social market economy states:

> The Federal Government shall have the right to legislate on these matters if and to the extent that the establishment of equal living conditions throughout

the Federal territory or the maintenance of legal or economic unity renders Federal regulation necessary at national level.

The German legislature applied this constitutional doctrine in legal materials on the reduction of spatial disparities. Article 1 of the Law on Spatial Planning (Raumordnungsgesetz) declares that the entire territory of the Federal Republic has to be developed, a specific spatial policy has to be designed and co-ordination between plans and development programmes with spatial impacts has to be achieved.

The German state wishes to create equal living conditions for citizens over the entire territory of the country and to moderate regional disparities. Another objective of Federal spatial policy is to encourage the exploitation of development potentials in structurally weak rural areas, to enhance employment opportunities, to co-operate in the organisation of the housing market, to develop the infrastructure and urban functions and to actively participate in environmental protection.

The need for powerful public intervention in order to reduce spatial inequalities is unquestionable. The region, despite its incontestably significant progress, showed severe backwardness in comparison with Western states in 2009 (Figure 5.5). The disparities in the income-producing capacities of the Eastern states are relatively significant. GDP per capita in Berlin only reaches 85 per cent of the German average, followed by Southern provinces with their 73–74 per cent values, and the Brandenburg (71 per cent) and Mecklenburg-West Pomerania (70 per cent) indices do not also lag behind the other provinces. GDP by purchasing power parity (PPP) in the Eastern states and in Germany show a deteriorating performance in terms of European comparison. Berlin was above the national average in 1995 in respect of this index, but in the following years its position deteriorated in relation to the EU average.

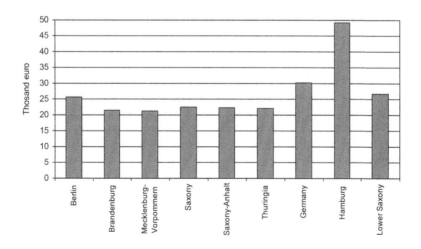

Figure 5.5 GDP per capita in some German *Länder*, 2008, PPP

Source: Author's construction based on http://epp.eurostat.ec.europa.eu.

East German *Länder* occupy the last six positions in the development ranking of the 16 German *Länder*. The West *German Land* with the weakest performance (Lower Saxony) shows a lower GDP value than Berlin, the most developed Eastern *Land*. The per capita performance in the capital was only half of the most developed *Land*, Hamburg. We obtain a somewhat more different picture if we examine per capita GDP values in smaller territorial units, namely NUTS 3 areas. In East German areas, performances below the national average show an even spatial distribution. Of the 102 NUTS 3 areas (metropolises, urban townships and districts) only eight had GDP values above the national average (€30,200), while GDP in 41 NUTS 3 areas remained below two-thirds of the national average (€20,000). With the exception of Saxony-Anhalt, we can find at least two high performing regions in each state. In 41 out of the 327 West German NUTS 3 areas, GDP by PPP does not reach €20,000, but in 104 areas it exceeds €30,000. Forty per cent of NUTS 3 areas in East Germany and 12 per cent if these areas in West can be regarded as low-performing. Two-thirds of the under-developed areas are in the provinces of Mecklenburg- West Pomerania, Saxony, Lower Saxony, the Rhineland-Palatinate and Bavaria.

Regional subsidies

Most of the backward areas receiving economic structural support in the framework of regional policy are located in the Eastern *Länder* (Figure 5.6). Twenty-one billion euros were invested in restructuring programmes as a result of constitutional regulation post-re-unification (between 1991 and 2010). In Germany, 79 per cent of the funds were absorbed by the manufacturing industry (Deutscher Bundestag, 2009). Some 80–90 per cent of the funds were allocated to the economic development of the new East German provinces. The amount of support which these regions received annually exceeded €1 billion from 1992 to 2001 (peaking in 1993 at €2.02 billion in support). Distribution among the provinces is very much in line with their population size (Figure 5.7).

The financial contributions for creating equal living standards for the population are regulated by Articles 106–107 of the German Constitution. In the light of these articles, 75 per cent of the revenues from personal income tax is to be distributed among the *Länder* according to their share of the country's population and Federal law allocates 25 per cent of the revenues to *Länder* with lower tax capacities under Federal law. Further, the Federal government maintains special funds for supporting under-developed spatial communities with low tax incomes. Article 91a of the Constitution states:

> In the following areas the Federation shall participate in the discharge of responsibilities of the Länder, provided that such responsibilities are important to society as a whole and that federal participation is necessary for the improvement of living conditions (joint tasks): 1) improvement of regional economic structures, 2) improvement of the agrarian structure and coastal preservation.
>
> (Basic Law for the Federal Republic: 80)

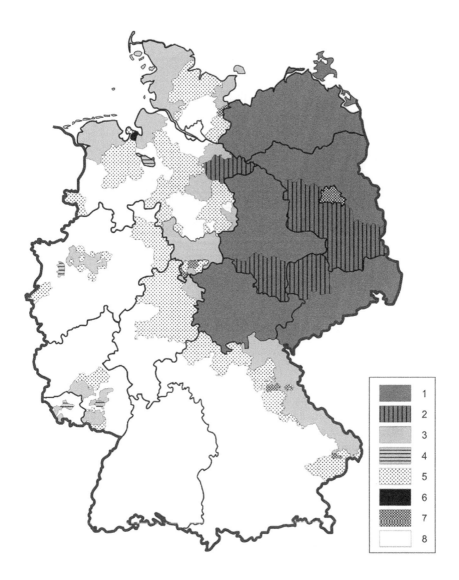

Figure 5.6 Areas eligible for support for the improvement of Regional Economic Structures, 2007-2013

Key: 1 – Eligible area type 'A', regions with the lowest economic performance; 2 – Regions listed among eligible area type 'A' due to their statistical features; 3 – Eligible area type 'C', economically weak regions with a higher performance than type 'A' (in old provinces); 4 –Small-sized (urban/micro-regional) areas in category 'C'; 5 – Eligible area type 'D', rural areas receiving limited support (in old provinces); 6 –Small-sized (urban/micro-regional) areas in category 'D'; 7 – Eligible area under category 'C', and 'D'; 8 – non-eligible areas.

Source: Deutscher Bundestag 2009. p. 173.

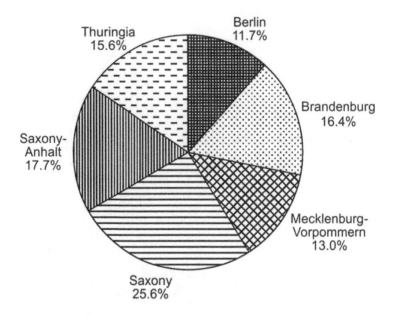

Figure 5.7 The regional distribution of support for economic restructuring in the new
        Länder, 1991–2010, per cent

°Source: Author's construction based on data from Deutscher Bundestag, 2009.

The other major group of financial instruments supporting the reorganisation of the
East German territory contains those of the EU's Cohesion and Structural Funds.
Seventy per cent of the near-€20 billion of Structural Funds (€13.6bn) allocated to
Germany during the programming period 1994–1999 were absorbed by the new
Länder. Similar rates are seen in the two planning periods which follow. The rate
of EU support granted to the East German *Länder* during the programming period
2007–2013 declined by almost one-third compared to the previous period. This is
due to the fact that the income and development possibilities of several NUTS2
regions in three provinces (Brandenburg, Saxony and Saxony-Anhalt) showed
significant improvement and fell into a category featuring a phased reduction in
funding. The weight of financial aid received by the new provinces decreased
slightly, but it still represented two-thirds of the total amount.

Financial resources transferred to the Eastern *Länder* by the German government and the European Union are primarily in the domain of social welfare and
health-care services and are targeted at raising wages and pensions and improving
the overall income position of the population. In the GDR, wage costs in the
manufacturing industry constituted 7 per cent of the West German average at the
end of the 1980s reaching already 70 per cent by the end of the post-unification
decade. Over 60 per cent of the funding was allocated to causes with a direct impact
on living standards. In light of the Eastern solidarity contract the annual contribution of the federation to the budget of the provinces is €25 billion. Besides direct

subventions, various examples of tax relief are used to foster the development of infrastructure. Eastern provinces received approximately €750 billion euros support during the post-unification decade. This transfer of an annual €80 billion euros contributes to the East German GDP with 30 per cent and amounts to nearly 4 per cent of the GDP of Western *Länder* (Blum *et al.* 2009).

It is becoming increasingly evident that other activities promoting the augmentation of regional income levels will be required in the future utilisation of financial transfers. Regarding the spatial distribution and quantity of modern forces of spatial development, the Eastern part of the country still shows a rather unfavourable picture compared with the former provinces. With respect to two significant factors of the new European growth path, modern industry and research and development, this region shows considerable backwardness.

Two driving forces of sustainable development: industry and R&D

Industry was affected most severely by the economic transformation of the highly industrialised East Germany. Its weight decreased significantly both in terms of the labour market and income generation. There were fundamental changes both in the size of companies and in their ownership. In 1989, the proportion of employment in industry was above 45 per cent in Saxony-Anhalt, Saxony and Thuringia. In 2009, however, this index was above 30 per cent only in Saxony and Thuringia. The role of industry in the income-generating capacity of regions, in strengthening competitiveness and in spreading technological innovation is still hugely decisive. In their absence, growth is considerably slower in under-industrialised regions and the opportunities for convergence are much less favourable. The privatisation of East German enterprises was undertaken by the German Property Agency (Treuhand). By the end of 1994, 6,400 companies had been bought by private investors and 1,600 were re-privatised. Three-hundred companies had become the property of the local community and 3,700 firms were closed down (Stack 1997). The era of reindustrialisation began in 1994 in the new *Länder*. The main driving forces of the process were West German investors and foreign direct capital. The West German business world did not show much interest, only one-tenth of East German companies being set up by West German firms. Certain parts of the old, large companies were privatised, and SMEs were established. There is no large company sector lacking, and only 4 per cent of German firms employing over 1,000 employees (30 firms) are located in the East (Ragnitz 2005).

Sister companies almost exclusively perform production tasks, activities with a high added value remaining with the parent companies. Applying this periphery model has hindered the growth of productivity from the very beginning since the manufacture of new products and the use of the latest technological processes has remained solidly with companies in the West. Furthermore, the location of industry has had a negative impact on the professional structure of labour, with there being much less demand for highly qualified manufacturing experts (Ragnitz 2009). At the same time, it is worth noting that, with respect to employment in high-technology sectors, Eastern and Western *Länder* do not show many serious differences. Thuringia led the ranking order of German states in 2007 (11.7 per cent), followed by Hesse (10.2 per cent) and Saxony (10.0 per cent).

Clearly the the effects of economic stabilisation on industry is a highly positive factor. During the 12 years following the development of the new East German industrial structure from 1996, the added value of industry rose by 17–38 per cent in three Southern provinces with a traditional industrial structure (Saxony, Saxony-Anhalt and Thuringia), while it stagnated in Brandenburg and declined in Berlin and Mecklenburg-West Pomerania (Figure 5.8). In provinces with an adequate industrial base, production rates increased by an annual 2.5–3.5 per cent until 2007.

Despite the unarguably positive evolution of income generation and labour productivity, serious structural weaknesses prevail in East German industry. Its structure is incompatible with the requirements of sustainable development. Industry in the new *Länder* mainly is mainly labour-intensive sectors, and production functions dominate. Technology-intensive sectors with higher development potential are under-represented in these regions. Their export potential lags behind that of West German industry and R&D capacities (Heimpold 2010).

The quantity, structure and spatial distribution of *research and development* capacities constitutes the other major element of sustainable development, and by the end of the 1980s, the number of employees in R&D stood at almost 100,00 The large companies also operated research institutions. Twenty-four thousand employees were employed in the 59 research institutes of the Academy of Sciences of the GDR and a significant number of research institutes operated under the control of ministries. The role of the higher education sector in the GDR was much

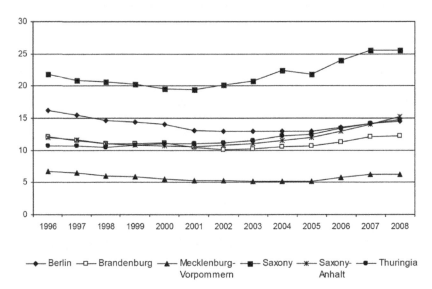

Figure 5.8 The evolution of industrial added value in East German provinces, 1996–2008, million euros, current prices

Source: Author's construction based on http://epp.eurostat.ec.europa.eu.

more modest, with the nine universities and a small number of colleges of technology carrying out research. Higher education in East Germany in the pre-1990 era did not consider research to be among its priorities and the size structure of higher education also posed obstacles to research: in 22 out of the 45 specialist institutions, the student population was under 1,000 (Hüfner 2002).

Re-unification produced substantial changes in the East German higher education system and the research network. The number of higher education institutions doubled and universities increased fivefold, resulting in 43 universities in the higher education system of Eastern *Länder.* One part of the institutional network of the Academy of Sciences was closed and the remainder placed under the control of a new research management body, while most company research units disappeared. Research became a priority in higher education (Krull 1991; Bundesministerium für Bildung und Forschung, 2011). As a result of this reorganisation, the number of R&D employees decreased by one-third. Currently, East German R&D indices lag considerably behind the national average (Table 5.7). The dominance of Berlin is due to the simple fact that Berlin once more became the capital of the whole re-united country, and so it no longer makes sense to look at the concentration of functions in Berlin as part of the Eastern territory of the country.

The operation of the new research network is the responsibility of four research associations and societies (the Fraunhofer-Gesellschaft, the Max Planck-Gesellschaft, the Leibniz Gemeinschaft and the Helmholz Gemeinschaft). These four research organisations maintain altogether 89 research institutes employing 18,600 people in the East German *Länder*. Even though this figure is only three-quarters of that of the former Academy of Sciences, the number of institutes shows a significant increase. The majority of these (38) are operated by the Leibniz Gemeinschaft, 42 per cent of whose research staff are located in the East German federal states. The other three institutions control lower numbers (19 per cent, 21 per cent and 14 per cent respectively).

Table 5.7 Major R&D indices in the East German *Länder*, 2010

	R&D expenditure as % of GDP	Sectoral distribution of R&D expenditure, %			Number of employees, thousands
		Business	Government	Higher education	
Berlin	3.5	1.4	1.2	0.9	30.2
Brandenburg	1.2	0.4	0.8	0.3	8.9
Mecklenburg-West Pomerania	1.8	0.6	0.8	0.4	6.2
Saxony	2.8	1.2	0.9	0.7	25.8
Saxony-Anhalt	1.4	0.4	0.5	0.5	7.3
Thuringia	2.2	1.1	0.5	0.6	10.8
Germany	2.8	1.8	0.4	0.5	574.7

Source: Author's construction based on http://epp.eurostat.ec.europa.eu.

The changes, however, had a negative impact on the spatial structure of higher education, with the weight of Berlin increasing (due to the re-emergence of Berlin as national capital). Currently, 32 per cent of the higher education institutions and 35 per cent of the employees in non-university research establishments are concentrated in the capital (Figure 5.9). The second most important research centre in

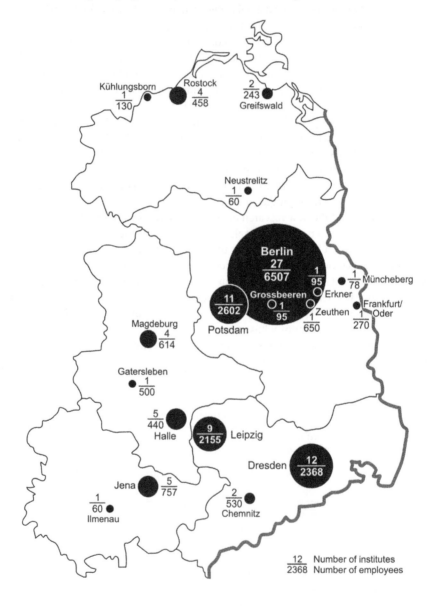

Figure 5.9 Regional distribution of research institutes supported by the government, 2010

Source: Author's design based on web pages of the Fraunhofer-Gesellschaft, the Max Planck-Gesellschaft, the Leibniz Gemeinschaft and the Helmholz Gemeinschaft.

East Germany is Potsdam, where 2,600 researchers are employed in 11 institutes. Dresden ranks third with 2,400 employees in 12 establishments.

Per capita R&D expenditure in East Germany showed a gradual increase from the mid-1990s until 2001, after which it declined somewhat and then stagnated. In 1991 the amount was only €200, but by 2007 it showed a 2.5-fold increase, reaching €458. For the sake of comparison, former Western *Länder* showed a 50 per cent growth rate during this period. In 1991, per capita R&D expenditure was already €814 and by 2007 it had reached €1,223. Research intensity in the business sector was much higher in Western Germany than in the Eastern areas, but this is due to structural differences. The Eastern *Länder* were mainly home to SMEs and to large companies with headquarters located elsewhere. In the latter cases, R&D of any strategic significance was carried out at company headquarters.

East German economic restructuring and cohesion were characterised by a high degree of the exploitation of innovation. Innovative activities won new markets in both East and West Germany, although the innovative propensity of the private sector is significantly lower in the new provinces than in West Germany. An examination of data from the individual states reveals that the expenditure of the business sector reached 50 per cent of whole R&D expenditure in Saxony and Thuringia. This implies that the development of R&D activities in the business sector is in harmony with the development of the public research infrastructure which was successful in stabilising the research potential in the new *Länder*. This evolution can be seen in the gradual rise in the number of researchers. Technological innovation would contribute to the cohesion of East Germany by providing new and permanent positions for companies in regional and international markets.

References

Basic Law for the Federal Republic of Germany. www.iuscomp.org/gla/statutes/ htm#72 [2012. May 15.].

Berentsen, W.H. (1981) 'Regional change in the German Democratic Republic', *Annals of the Association of American Geographers,* 1: 50–60.

Bessel, R. (1978) 'Eastern Germany as a structural problem in the Weimar Republic', *Social History,* 2: 199–218.

Blum, U., Ragnitz, J., Freye, S., Scharle, S. and Schneider, L. (2009) *Regionalisierung öffentlicher Ausgaben und Einnahmen. Eine Untersuchung am Beispiel der Neuen Länder,* 4. Sonderheft. Halle: Institut für Wirtschaftsforschung Halle.

Brücker, H. and Trübswetter, P. (2007) 'Do the best go west? An analysis of the self-selection of employed east-west migrants in Germany', *Empirica,* 4: 371–395.

Buchta, B. (1959) *Die Junker und die Weimarer Republik. Charakter und Bedeutung der Osthilfe in den Jahren 1928-1933,* Berlin: Verlag der Wissenschaften.

Bundesministerium für Bildung und Forschung (2011) *Bildung und Forschung in Zahlen. Ausgewählte Fakten aus dem Daten-Portal des BMBF,* Bonn and Berlin.

Burda, M.C. (2005) 'What kind of shock was it? Regional integration of Eastern Germany after unification', Paper presented at the Annual Meetings of the American Economic Assocation, Boston.

Cafiero, S. (2000) *Storia dell'intervento itraordinario nel Mezzogiorno (1950–1993),* Rome: Manduria.

Cannari, L. (2010) 'Mezzogiorno e politiche regionali', *Rivista dell'Associazione Rossi-Doria*, 1: 76–97.

Conze, W. and Raupach, H. (eds) (1967) *Die Staats- und Wirtschaftskrise des Deutschen Reiches 1929/33,* Stuttgart: Klett.

Desmet, K. and Ortín, I.O. (2007) 'Rational underdevelopment', *Scandinavian Journal of Economics,* 1: 1–24.

Eltges, M. and Strubelt, W. (2010) 'Equal living conditions and their fiscal basis', in Lentz, S. (ed.) *Restructuring Eastern Germany.* German Annual of Spatial Research and Policy, Berlin and Heidelberg: Springer, 57–77.

Fiedor, K. (1971) 'The character of the state assistance to the German Eastern provinces in the years 1918-1933', *Polish Western Affairs,* 2: 309-326.

Hall, J. and Ludwig, U. (1993) 'Creating Germany's Mezzogiorno?' *Challenge,* July–August: 38–44.

Hallett, H. and Ma, Y. (1993) 'East Germany, West Germany and their Mezzogiorno problem: an empirical investigation', *The Economic Journal,* 3: 416–428.

Hardach, K. (1976) *Wirtschaftsgeschichte Deutschlands im 20. Jahrhundert,* Göttingen: Vandenhoeck & Ruprecht.

Heimpold, G. (2010) 'Zwischen Deindustrialisierung und Reindustrialisierung. Die ostdeutsche Industrie – ein Stabilitätsfaktor regionaler Wirtschaftsentwicklung?' *Informationen zur Raumentwicklung,* 10–11: 727–743.

Herfert, G. and Lentz, S. (2010) 'New spatial patterns of population development as a factor in restructuring Eastern Germany', in Lentz, S. (ed.) *Restructuring Eastern Germany,* German Annual of Spatial Research and Policy, Berlin and Heidelberg: Springer, 91–109.

Herrigel, G. (1996) *Industrial Constructions. The Sources of German Industrial Power,* Cambridge: Cambridge University Press.

Hüfner, K. (2002) 'The challenge of unification and the reform of higher education in Germany', *Higher Education in Europe,* 1–2: 101–109.

Krull, W. (1991) 'What happened to East German research? Reflections on the Wissenschaftsrat's attempt to evaluate and restructure non-university research institutions is Eastern Germany', *World Affairs,* 1: 14–23.

Lentz, S. (ed.) (2010) *Restructuring Eastern Germany,* German Annual of Spatial Research and Policy, Berlin and Heidelberg: Springer.

Mohs, G. and Grimm, F., Heinzmann, J. and Thuermer, R. et al. (1984) 'The regional differentiation of the German Democratic Republic', *GeoJournal,* 1: 7–22.

Nemes Nagy J. (1979) 'Területi fejlődési tendenciák az NDK iparában' [Regional development tendencies in the industry of GDR], *Földrajzi Értesítő,* 3–4: 409–413.

Ostwald, W. (ed.) (1989) *Raumordnungsreport '90: Daten und Fakten zur Lage in den ostdeutschen Ländern,* Berlin: Verlag Die Wirtschaft Berlin.

Overy, R.J. (1995) *The Nazi Economic Recovery, 1932–1938,* New York: Cambridge University Press.

Page, W. (2002) *Germany's Mezziogiorno Revisited. Institutions, Fiscal Transfers and Regional Convergence,* Edinburgh: University of Edinburgh.

Ragnitz, J. (2005) 'Germany: fifteen years after unification', *CESifo Forum,* 4: 3–6.

Ragnitz, J. (2009) 'Prospects for regional development and entrepreneurship in East Germany', in *Strengthening Entrepreneurship and Economic Development in East Germany: Lessons from Local Approaches,* Paris: OECD, 13–27.

Sinn, H.-W. and Westermann, F. (2000) *Two Mezzogiornos,* Working Document Series. 378. Munich: CESifo.

Stack, H.M. (1997) 'The "colonialization" of East Germany? A comparative analysis of German privatization', *Duke Law Journal,* 5: 1211–1253.

Trigilia, C. (1994) *Sviluppo senza autonomia – effetti perversi delle politiche nel Mezzogiorno,* Milan: Il Mulino.

Urwin, D.W. (1982) 'Germany: from geographical expression to regional accommodation', in Rokkan, S. and Urwin, D.W. (eds) *The Politics of Territorial Identity: Studies in European Regionalism,* London: Sage, 165–249.

Villari, R. (1979) *Mezzogiorno dal feudalismo al capitalismo,* Naples: SEN.

6 Regional transformation and fragmentation in Russia

Spatial aspects of the power structure and economic development of the Soviet Union

Core regions in the Russian and Soviet empires

There was a breakthrough in the development of Russia the years of the late nineteenth and early twentieth centuries. A dynamic transformation took place in the Russian economy, although the prospects of achieving West European development levels seemed unrealistic. The moderate, (even, in some cases, more striking) signs of modernisation disguise the basic fact that Russia still remained a traditional society even at the beginning of the twentieth century and following a significant period of modernisation which involved radical change. The more modern they wished to make the country, the more underdeveloped became, and the adoption of Western patterns served the conservation of Eastern structures (Dixon 1999). One cause of the current underdevelopment of Russia is that market-determined development failed to bring the country closer to the West. Also in Russia, the modern state aimed from the outset at influencing development and counterbalancing market weaknesses. Support for this argument can be found in the writings of Alexander Gerschenkron who stated that, in Europe, competitive industrialisation simply increased the pressure on backward countries: on one hand it created ideologies of modernisation and industrialisation (including various versions of state Marxism) and on the other hand it also forced states and governments to support the development of national economies with their own resources (Gerschenkron 1962, 1970).

One of the visible signs of the underdevelopment of the country was the extremely high level of spatial differentiation. If we examine the economy, infrastructure, settlement network or the educational level of the population, the differences between European and Asian areas were huge. In the last decade of the nineteenth century the most developed industrial areas of the empire were the provinces of Moscow, Warsaw, Vladimir and St Petersburg. In these locations, industrial employment per thousand inhabitants was between 32 and 82 persons, while in the least developed areas it was between 1 and 7. According to data from 1892, 1.09 million people (1.2 per cent of the total population of 89.15 million in European Russia) worked in manufacturing and mining.

In the first decade of the twentieth century, industrial production data of the major regions showed 10–12 fold differences. At the beginning of the twentieth century, the production value of the manufacturing industry averaged 31 roubles for Russia as a whole, but 87 roubles for the Northwest regions and Baltic areas, 78 roubles for the Central Russian industrial area and a mere eight roubles for Asiatic Russia. In 1940, the spatial disparities in industry were even more significant. The per capita industrial production of the individual republics of then Soviet Union was 923 roubles in the Russian Federation and 71 roubles in Tajikistan. The differences in the industrial production indicators between the most and least developed areas increased from 11- to 13-fold during this 30-year period (Westlund *et al.* 2000). The favourable position of the Russian territories is clearly outlined by investment data: Russia was the clear beneficiary of Soviet investment policy for over 50years. This is evident from the changes in production volumes. However, in this latter case, the performance of the Baltic republics merits attention (Table 6.1).

The new economic policy (the NEP), which followed the war-time economy at the beginning of the 1920s, is the only period of regional policy in the Soviet Union when there was an extremely high demand for a reduction of spatial disparities. In the mid-1920s, the mobilisation of local resources became a fundamental task in the cause of economic reconstruction, but a lack of resources meant that the central government was incapable of implementing it, and for this reason the

Table 6.1 Ranking of Soviet republics – in terms of investment and production per capita, 1928–1978

Republic	Investment			Production value					
	1928–1932	1946–1951	1956–1960	1970	1982	1940	1956	1967	1978
Russia	1	3	2	4	1	1	4	3	3
Ukraine	3	5	4	9	11	3	6	5	6
Byelorussia	9	10	13	8	7	7	15	6	5
Uzbckistan	10	14	14	11	13	6	13	13	14
Kazakhstan	6	8	1	2	3	8	5	9	7
Georgia	5	4	12	13	8	5	12	11	10
Azerbaijan	2	2	6	14	12	2	7	12	11
Lithuania	–	12	6	6	5	–	8	4	4
Moldova	12	15	15	10	9	11	9	8	9
Kyrgyzstan	11	2	10	12	14	10	11	10	13
Tajikistan	5	12	10	15	15	12	14	14	15
Armenia	8	9	0	7	11	4	10	15	8
Turkmenistan	8	7	8	5	6	9	3	7	12
Latvia	–	6	6	3	2	–	2	2	1
Estonia	–	1	3	1	4	–	1	1	2

Source: Westlund *et al.* (2000).

economic organising authority of regional state institutions became important. The clear political ambitions of the proletariat and of the united peasantry brought an entirely new factor to the reorganisation of regional economies. Provinces with economically weak and underdeveloped industry were incapable of creating the necessary links between industry and agriculture and the problem of supplying the population with basic industrial products was insoluble (Shtoulberg *et al.* 2000). The scientific results of researchers into Russian economic geography concluded that to integrate the peripheral areas colonised by Tsarist Russia into one unitary state needed very special means.

The first general *industrial reform* of the Soviet Union was introduced in the so-called GOELRO Plan (State Electrification of Russia) which involved the electrification of the country. The public administrative conditions for implementing this monumental plan which included constructing power-stations and developing industry to utilise the energy produced, and the smaller regional units were unable to work out overall economic development programmes. Parallel to the plans for electrification, the work of transforming the public administration of the country was in progress. The government used proposals relating to the geographical regions of Russia early in the modernisation of public administration and the establishment of regional bodies of central state authorities (Tarkhov 2005). The first version of the GOELRO Plan suggested a total of nine regions to organise the implementation of the plan, but finally, after much debate, 21 economic regions designated by the Russian central planning committee were approved to devise energy and general economic development programmes and to oversee their implementation (Figure 6.1). Twelve of these regions were situated in the European part of the country and nine in the Asian part. However, local political elites effectively forced the creation of new economic regions, the first five-year-plan being devised for 24 of these regions and the second for 32. The political power of these regions lay in the fact that the local offices of the Russian national economy determined development plans for the whole region jointly with the local authorities within the regions and worked hard to gain more central resources.

During the NEP, fundamental changes were introduced into the administrative system of the country. The elimination of bodies dating from the old Tsarist administration had begun, but many elements of the old administration had coexisted with the new forms for 15 years or so. The Stalin constitution enacted in 1936 produced radical changes (Table 6.2).

The main area of activity in the first industrialisation concept of Soviet Russia was the already industrialised European part of the country (west of the Urals). More than half of the industrial investment was undertaken in the old industrial areas, bordering on the Volga and adjacent to the Urals and in the Kuznetsk Basin. The new industrial plants which were located close to raw material sources (not for spatial development purposes, but for defensive reasons) contributed to an eastward shift of the industrial heartland of the country, and in the 1930s these areas became the main focus of industrialisation. For example, in 1936 36 per cent of new investment was made in these areas, and in 1937 the output of the old industrial areas was 68 per cent higher than in 1925. Between 1930 and 1950, the growth in

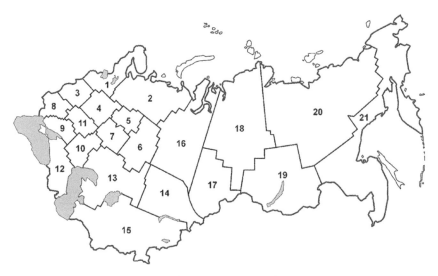

Figure 6.1 The economic regions of the planning committee, 1921

Legend: 1 – Northwestern; 2 – Northeastern; 3 – Western; 4 – Central (Industrial); 5 – Viatka–
Vetluga; 6 – Ural; 7 – Central Volga, 8 – Southwestern; 9 – Southern Highlands
(Industrial); 10 – Lower Volga; 11 – Central Black Earth (Chernoziom); 12 – Caucasian;
13 – Western Kyrgyz; 14 – Eastern Kyrgyz; 15 – Central Asian; 16 – Western Siberian;
17 – Kuzneck–Altaic; 18 – Yenisei; 19 – Lena–Angara; 20 – Yakut Länder; 21 – Far
Eastern.

Source: Khorev, 1981. p. 114.

the machinery manufacturing areas of Moscow, Gorky and Kuibishev was many
times higher than the production of the textile industrial area of Ivanovo. The
industrial output of Omsk, Novosibirsk and the Kuznetsk Basin was much higher
than the value of production in Tyumen, today's leading industrial area. Before
World War II the, collective industrial output of Moscow (the metropolitan area)
and the Moscow oblast was significantly higher than that of Siberia. The industrialisation of the Central Asian peripheries, on the basis of statistical surveys, seemed
to be an extremely large-scale operation: the increase in industrial output of
Kazakhstan, Armenia and Georgia was 12-fold, of Kyrgyzstan 14-fold and of
Tajikistan 26-fold between 1928 and 1937. At the same time, 300,000people
worked in the 3,500 newly established industrial plants, although employment per
plant averaged less than 100.

In the second half of the 1930s, quasi-democratic regional policy disappeared
from the Soviet Union. The regional economic councils were disbanded and the
federal republics, established under the 1936 Constitution, determined regional
policy. The economic management role of the republics was, in practice, very
modest and far less than that of the former economic regions. The economic responsibilities of the republics were limited to the implementation of their part of
any national plan: at most they had a degree of independence in arranging the modernisation of the peripheral ethnic areas.

Table 6.2 Regional units, 1922–1937

Name	1922	1929	1937
Federal republics	3	6	11
Autonomous republics	9	15	22
Autonomous regions	10	16	9
Border regions (krais), regions (oblasts)	–	8	47
Districts (including, ethnic)	–	176	35
Administrative districts	–	2,426	5,567
Governorates	84	16	–
Uiezd (administrative districts)	759	298	–
Volost (rural districts)	15,072	1,595	–

Source: The author's own construction based on Tarkhov (2005: appendices).

The dynamic development of new industrial areas started during World War II. From the Western parts of the country 2,600 industrial plants were relocated in the east. Of these, 58 per cent were moved to the Urals and the Volga area and 16 per cent to Western Siberia (Treivish 2002). In 1941, most Moscow companies were relocated to the east and to Siberia. As a result, the production of the European industrial areas was halved. According to data relating to value, the significance of Siberia was even less, but there was an essential growth in terms of numbers employed (Table 6.3). After World War II, the development of Western areas accelerated. Seven thousand five hundred factories which had been destroyed had to be rebuilt, while, in the Eastern areas, the oil, gas and other raw material-producing industries based on the geological research into natural resources dating from the 1930s began at the end of the 19s. The Eastern regions (Kazakhstan, Siberia and the Far East) strengthened their position in terms of raw material production(Table 6.4).

At the beginning of the last century the key areas in the development of manu-facturing or processing industries and in the modernisation of living conditions, both in Russia and in the Soviet Union, were the *historical city networks*. Until the Bolshevik Revolution, city development in Russia had progressed in much the

Table 6.3 The significance of Russia's three industrial regions based on employee numbers and production value, 1900–2000, per cent

District	Number of employed					Production value				
	1900	1925	1950	1975	2000	1900	1925	1950	1975	2000
Old industrial areas[1]	64	61	42	40	33	50	65	68	42	30
New European industrial areas	30	33	39	41	47	33	31	27	38	40
Eastern regions	6	6	19	19	20	17	4	5	20	30

Key: [1]St Petersburg and surroundings, Central industrial region and the Central Urals.
Source: Treivish (2002).

Table 6.4 Significance of the Eastern regions in specific product areas, per cent

Product area	1940	1960	1965
Electricity	9.2	21.6	29.4
Natural gas	0.5	2.4	78.8
Coal	28.7	35.9	58.8
Iron ore	1.7	11.1	16.3
Timber	23.4	26.2	37.3
Cellulose	–	9.3	29.6
Artificial fertilisers	6.9	15.9	13.7
Cement	13.5	21.4	26.0

Source: Shtoulberg *et al.* (2000: 43).

same way as in the rest of Europe. Occasionally, the normal flow of development was modified by administrative reorganisation and both favourable and unfavourable changes occurred. In Tsarist Russia, administrative functions as one means of encouraging city development (a factor of under-development) combined with economic factors, although with a significant time-lag. At the end of the nineteenth century, the urban population amounted to 15 per cent of the total. The first census in 1897 listed 461 towns or cities in the European part of the country and 51 in the Asian part. The urban population exceeded 20,000 in 15 per cent of the towns. Of the 76 larger cities, two (Moscow and St Petersburg) had populations of over 200,000, five (Astrakhan, Kazan, Saratov, Rostov-on-Don) between 100,000 and 200,000, while 17 had from 50,000 to 100,000 and 52 from 20,000 to 50,000. In 1926, the number of towns with a population of more than 100,000 increased to 22 (Table 6.5).

As part of the reform programme at the end of the nineteenth century, the Russian Interior Ministry elaborated a 20-year urban development strategy for the European part of the country. In practice, however, very little of this ambitious plan was realised: Murmansk, Tuapse and certain other settlements were given municipal rights. Urban settlements and other proletarian strong-points were seen as political allies of Soviet power and 90 settlements were given town status between 1917 and 1926. During the period of the first five-year-plan (1921–1925), most of these towns were developed in the Urals-Kuznetsk industrial area, and Novokuznetsk, Prokopevsk and Belovo were also elevated to town rank at that time. The rapid industrialisation resulted in a wave of plans for new towns, and by 1939, 100 new settlements were designated as towns, and within the Russian Federation itself the number of towns increased to 520 (Lappo 2005).

The logic of industrial development also left its mark on urban development during and after World War II. Characteristic of this period was the increase in terms of quantity of the Trans- Urals city network. Eighty per cent (that is, 182 towns) of today's 230 towns of Siberia and the Far East were raised to town status post-1917. In pre-revolutionary Siberia, there were 51 urban settlements 12 urban settlements during World War II. In the 45 years following the war, 107 settlements

Table 6.5 Population changes in today's large cities, 1897–2005, per thousand inhabitants

City	1897	1926	1989	2005
Chelyabinsk	25	59	1,030	1,095
Khabarovsk	16	44	598	579
Irkutsk	52	98	622	583
Yaroslavl	71	114	629	605
Yekaterinburg	43	136	1,363	1,304
Kazan	130	179	1,085	1,110
Krasnodar	66	163	619	715
Krasnoyarsk	27	72	912	917
Magnitogorsk	–	210[1936]	439	417
Moscow	1,039	3,641	8,677	10,407
Murmansk	13	73	472	325
Naberezsnije Celine	–	9[1939]	505	508
Novosibirsk	70[1915]	120	1,309	1,406
Nizhny Novgorod	90	186	1,435	1,289
Omsk	38	162	1,149	1,143
Perm	45	168	1,092	989
Rostov-on-Don	120	177	1,008	1,058
Samara	92	271	1,257	1,133
St Petersburg	1,265	1,616	4,435	4,600
Togliatti	5	–	629	705
Ufa	49	97	1,080	1,058
Vladivostok	29	108	631	587
Volgograd	56	148	995	999
Voronezh	81	120	882	849

Source: For 1897 and 1926: www.populstat.info/Europe/russiat.htm [6 April, 2008], for 1989 and
2005: Chislennost naseleniia RSFSR. 2001.

were designated as towns and 12 new towns were even projected in the 1990s (Leksin 2006).

The illusion of local and regional autonomy during the 1920s

The first decrees of the 1917 Revolution dealt with the transformation of power relationships. The first administrative orders of Soviet power, which concerned the Supreme Economic Council, labour supervision, the organisation of local authorities and the designation of new boundaries for regional authorities, aimed at implementing the administrative regional scheme and integrated economic zoning.

Conflict between different regional organisational strategies was rooted in the appraisal of autonomy and federalism from different points of view. The decision on 'The Federal Institutions of the Russian Republic', accepted in January 1918 at the Third All-Russia Congress of Soviets, was drafted in a spirit of democratic centralism, that is, it laid down quite clearly that federation could only be organised in such areas in which peculiar lifestyle or ethnic composition differs from their surroundings. Attacks were directed at the 'republics' which claimed semi-independent statehood, elected their own government and commissars and issued local banknotes. Regional autonomy was organised in different territories of the country. Considering its ideological grounds, the Siberian independence movement, the so-called 'oblastnichestvo' was the most respected organisation. The movement was founded by Siberian university students studying in St Petersburg in the 1860s and who, returning to Siberia, carried on the fight against Russian colonists and demanded the total autonomy of the region and a federal transformation of Russia. From 1918, the central authority continuously strove to eliminate the Siberian autonomist organisations (Bykova 2001).

As a result, and due to measures adopted by the 'republics' of the Urals, Kursk, Tver and Kaluga which conflicted with decisions of the central government, further organisation of new, larger regional administrative bodies (the so-called regional unions) was removed from the agenda. These regional confederations were one variation of the state's new regional organisational arrangements.

The conflict between different factions became most intense in the period when the first Soviet constitution was being prepared. The wing of the Bolshevik Party led by Lenin expected the constitution to provide for the effective harmonious co-operation of local and central bodies, while the regional federalists did not abandon their original ideas. In addition, there were other concepts which tried to develop a federal system of professional alliances. Lenin emphasised the dialectic connection of centralised state power and local autonomy and at the time of the publication of the decrees creating fundamental institutional systems of economic administration he committed himself in these terms:

> Every attempt to establish stereotyped forms and to impose uniformity from above, as intellectuals are so inclined to do, must be combated. Stereotyped forms and uniformity imposed from above, have nothing in common with democratic and socialist centralism. The unity of essentials, of the substence, is not disturbed but ensured by *variety* in details, in specific local features, in methods of *approach*, in *methods* of exercising control, in *ways* of exterminating and rendering harmless the parasites ... The more variety there will be, the better and richer will be our general experience, the more certain and rapid will be the success ...
>
> (Lenin Collected Works 1964: Vol. 26, 413, 415)

In time, the political fight between the followers and opponents of the Lenin wing turned to the field of economic policy. The first trade union debate, held in January 1918, showed signs of this, with different views concerning the duties of trade unions and the regulation of industry and labour supervision clashing. In their theses, published after the Treaty of Brest-Litovsk, the 'leftist communists', Bukharin, Preobrazhenski and others, expressed their opinion that: 'The form of public administration is bureaucratic centralisation and this has to develop in the direction of a regime of commissars, the stripping of autonomy from local Soviets and the effective abandonment of the bottom-up type of "common state"' (quoted by Szamuely 1979: 99–100). The authors highlighted their own economic management ideas in these terms:

> The management of companies should be passed to mixed bodies made up of workers and technocrats and these should be supervised and managed by national economy Soviets. The whole of economic life should be subordinated to the organising influence of these Soviets …

> (Szamuely 1979: 101)

To offer some insight into the deeper motives of the conflict, let us review, in the broadest possible terms, what happened in the field of economic organisation in Soviet Russia up to the Spring of 1918. The first steps to introduce a socialist state institutional system, the publication of orders concerning workers' control and the Supreme Economic Council, were taken in 1917. Both institutions, in the same way as privatisation in the economic sector, had an overall local organisation system. While the dominant feature of the Supreme Economic Council and its local bodies (the economic departments of the Soviets or, in the absence of these, the local bodies of the Supreme Economic Council) was a hierarchical management system, the All-Russia Workers' Control Council (a product of the influence of the Mensheviks) was incapable of effective operation. Since most industrial firms were privately owned, supervising the production of the private industrial sector was the basic activity of the Supreme Economic Council at the very beginning of its operation, and it was entitled to intervene only in cases involving a narrow range of state companies.

Later on, its local-regional bodies, as they grew stronger with the progress of nationalisation, were able to organise and regulate both the public and private economy in their area and to do this with relative harmony between local and state interests. In their operation, this dual subordination ensured the implementation of principles of democratic centralism. These were socially open organisations since the membership of these councils comprised the body elected by the councils of factory committees, representatives of the Soviets and company professionals. In this way, the regional economic councils organised, regulated and planned all economic sectors within their area of competence. Their decision-making power was, in practice, unlimited in the whole sector of production, distribution and consumption.

However, as matters developed, the cautious nationalisation efforts of the local economic institutions of central state power were made unworkable by the spontaneous actions of local workers' control councils and, due to this, the rapid nationalisation which had started in the country could not be followed by regularisation aimed at stabilising management relations. Soon the problems of socialist management were in the foreground of the political, and also the economic, conflict. Decentralisation, growing from nationalisation movements, did not slow down; rather it boosted economic decline and anarchy of production. In this way, the problem of combining the two management methods (individual responsibility and labour- controlled production) rose very sharply.

The conflict was a success for the Leninist faction. The decision concerning the management of nationalised enterprises was made from the top and promoted the harmonisation of local and central interests, implemented individual responsibility for management and ensured broad initiative from the working classes and centralism (the central discipline of management). Factory management boards (and directorates-general of 'mixed enterprises' operating industrial plants physically far removed from each other in terms of distance) were subordinated to bodies of regional national economy councils and regional management of nationalised enterprises (to the central directory in the case of enterprises managed directly by the Supreme Economic Council). Regional management (comprising candidates elected by the People's Soviet of representatives of factory management boards and the coalition of regional trade unions) were bolstered in their office by the regional national economy Soviet, and the mechanics of creating management bodies also stabilised the position of the individual management concept.

Within a short period of time, the management mechanism of the universal, rudimentary economic operational *war communism* seized control of the direct horizontal links between the basic units of production and the development of a strict vertical organisation management hierarchy, while the 'glavk' (chief committee) system eliminated, temporally inactivated, or, rather, stripped all power from every element of local-regional economy management which had formed and was gradually showing signs of operational maturity (Malle 1985). Article 61 of the first Constitution of the Russian Soviet Federal Socialist Republic (RSFSR) was drafted as follows:

> Regional, provincial county and rural organs of the Soviet power and also the Soviets of Deputies have to perform the following duties: a) Carry out all orders of the respective higher organs of the Soviet power; b) Take all steps for raising the cultural and economic standard of the given territory; c) Decide all questions of local importance within their respective territories; d) Co-ordinate all Soviet activity in their respective territories.
>
> (1918 Constitution (Fundamental Law) of the RSFSR)

It suggested the strengthening of centralisation in that the organisational system of the central authority was defined thematically and, perhaps, by the fact that in the basic law there was no mention of an organisational system of production management.

The operation of industrial centres, which were poor in terms of experience, professional individuals and methods and which coped with the performance of rudimentary plan indices with difficulty, was hindered by the high numbers of units managed (one industrial directorate looked after, on the average, some 60 firms which were widely separated in spatial terms). Therefore, what was started was the organisation of planning deconstruction and monitoring of the so-called unions or trusts at the meso-level. In the early 1920s, 179 trusts (comprising 1,449 firms) were in operation (Venediktov 1957). The two-tiered form of company management deriving from trusts organised on a sectoral base, clearly strengthened central influence. However, the creation of these American-style 'trusts' (groups of nominally independent companies which are centrally directed) to enforce regional discipline, suggests acknowledging the need to take steps due to a lack of horizontal connections.

There can be no doubt that there was a part to play by local economy management bodies in relaxing corporate verticalism. At the very beginning of the revolution, the managing bodies of regional economies were national economy councils operating in dual subordination. This type of body was not eliminated during the era of glavkism, but their former authority was withdrawn, and so they became the executive bodies, managing local small-scale industry for the Supreme Economic Council to the end of 1919. The effective organisers of the economy were the local branch organisations ('apparatus') of the industrial chief committees. These local council organisations increasingly started to point out the operational mistakes of economically isolated vertical unions ,not merely because of their economic bases being restricted to the extreme, but also because it became quite clear that maintaining production was impossible with the centralist methods due to fluctuations in production factors, chaotic transportation conditions, and so on.

Relatively soon, it also became clear that local economy management bodies, with their lack of proven methods and of trained professional staff, could only operate within a narrow range, primarily in the direct and operative management of production, based on decentralised decision-making authorisation. Since the Supreme Economic Council was incapable of effective management of the companies directly subordinate to it, regional industrial offices were created and many provinces came within their jurisdiction. On the one hand, these new executive bodies of the Supreme Economic Council directly managed the companies under their control, while, on the other hand, they harmonised the activity of all the economic units of a certain area. Their task was to manage the work of provincial (regional) national economy councils and the economic departments of the Soviets.

The changes in the field of economic management were uniformly adopted by the Eighth All-Russia Congress of Soviets in December 1920. The Congress passed important resolutions for each level of management. It suggested that the main task of the Supreme Soviet of the National Economy would be the overall planned management of industry and it also proposed the expansion of functions and authority of local national economy councils. The resolutions on local economy management bodies transformed the industrial directorates and chief committees of the Supreme Economic Council into the managing, regulatory and supervisory bodies of provincial national economy Soviets. The most important position adopted by the Congress might have been the resolution which suggested the creation of provincial and district co-ordination bodies, economic conferences (Russian: ekonomicheskoe soveschanie, abbr. EKOSO) to promote the implementation of a unified national economy plan.

At the very beginning of 1921, district and provincial economic councils met and regional co-ordination bodies were created in areas where existing organisational units were able to cope with the new functions. The Council of Labour and Defence created a specific committee to arrange the regulations of regional economic conferences. The Council of Labour and Defence passed the committee's proposal and a document was published entitled 'Provisional decrees concerning regional economic bodies'.

This resolution indicated the responsibilities of congresses – that is, that they needed to observe the implementation of economy-related decisions of supreme bodies, draw up the economic development plans for their region, coordinate the work of provincial economic congresses in their area of competence, control the execution of production programmes of the unified National Economy Plan and, last but not least, by means of their activity, encourage and improve the development of local innovation and initiative. The regional economic congresses operated as bodies of the Council of Labour and Defence and their president was appointed by the Council.

The Bolshevik leadership tried to restore the functions, defined in the original plan, of local economic bodies through the new economic policy. At the same time, the regional economy congresses, covering many provinces, embodied regionally organised centralism and it was necessary to be cautious of these becoming an obstacle to local initiatives and local economic policy. Therefore, the XI All-Russia Congress of the Russian Communist Party (Bolsheviks) considered it necessary to emphasise that:

> While we thought it appropriate both from economic and technical aspects that state companies with a similar profile or dealing with each other should come together under a unified management on a provincial, regional or nation-wide scale, at the same time we need to fight against the revival of the rejected system of 'glavkism'. Based on the resolution of the 9th Congress of Soviets, the companies placed in the hands of local Soviets together with their unions, remain under the management of provincial executive committees and they can only be handed over to national or regional unions by agreement or in the absence of such, by a decision of the Presidency of [the] All-Russia Central Executive Committee.
>
> (Congresses of the Communist Party of the Soviet Union (1972: 701.)

In August 1922, after debate by various bodies, the All-Russia Central Executive Committee and the Council of Labour and Defence passed a joint resolution concerning extending the authority of regional and provincial economic congresses. The economic and planning influence of Soviets was considerably strengthened by this resolution, which transferred the redistribution of state financial means between authorities to the jurisdiction of regional economic councils and defined specific responsibilities, ensuring greater independence for the creation and distribution of independent financial funds.

Democratic centralism in the operation of economic conferences was ensured by this dual subordination since they were required to report on their activity both to the competent executive committees of Soviets and to the Council of Labour and

Defence. However, the contradictions in the explanation of the relationship of centralisation and decentralisation left their mark on the new economic management system, not to mention the problems originating from disagreements over the creation of power-structural social relations.

At that time, dual subordination was not used mechanically. Lenin indicated, that

> Dual subordination is needed, where it is necessary, to allow for a really inevitable difference. Agriculture in Kaluga Gubernia differs from that in Kazan Gubernia. The same thing can be said about industry, and it can also be said about administration, or management as a whole. Failure to make allowances for local differences in all these matters would mean slipping into bureaucratic centralism, and so forth. It would mean preventing the local authorities from giving proper consideration to specific local feature, which is the basis of all rational administration.
>
> (Lenin Collected Works 1964: Vol. 33, 366.)

The institution of economic conferences, in terms of its organisational disciplines and its operational and characteristic features, was either already able, or soon to become able, to harmonise central and local objectives, to coordinate the vertical and horizontal socio-economical processes, to harmonise sectoral and regional interests and, last but not least, by enhanced financial and funding independence, to become an important link in the economic management of the planned economy. A well-functioning, co-ordinating institutional system of sectoral and regional planning and regulation was established without eliminating or radically transforming a satisfactorily functioning economic organisation system of socialism, and without having made any concessions at the expense of the functions of central government, so strengthening the totally planned nature of the economy. The economic Soviets could accomplish their direct economic management tasks effectively only with the involvement of the broad masses, and so it is no accident that they were kept in evidence as the essential sphere of action of economic democracy. The reports of the economic conferences accumulated much useful information about the spatial operation of the economy. These documents are a rich source material for today's researchers.

After the foundation of the Union of Soviet Socialist Republics in 1922, a republic-wide economic council was organised in the Russian Federation for the management of economic councils and, for a while, the co-ordination bodies of the other federal republics were the Councils of Labour and Defence, after which EKOSO-s were also organised in the republic. These organisational measures already managed to show some sort of centralisation tendencies which were proved by the partial reorganisation in 1923. At this time, only the district-level economic conferences were dismantled, but in the second half of 1924, elimination of most of the regional and provincial economic councils began. The two most effective, and furthest from central government with a specific power structure, the Siberian Revolutionary Committee and the Far East Revolutionary Committee (the institutions of oblastnichestvo) were only dissolved in 1925 and 1926 (Abdulatipov *et al.* 1992). What are the factors originating from the development of the Soviet economy of the 1920s and concomitant with the formation of power-political relations which strengthened the positions of the sectoral-central management of the economy, and, in no short time, disrupted the success of sectoral and regional aspects of the earlier balance of forces in the management of economic operations?

First, there is no doubt that the sphere of activity of central management in the economy was broadened by the economic policy programmes which ensured the proportionality of the spatial location of the country's forces of production. The Soviet Union selected its economic development strategy in such a way that, on the one hand, it would be possible to reduce the economic gap between it and the developed countries and, on the other hand, the rapid development of the areas actually trailing behind would start after the economic, political and social emancipation of nations and ethnic groups had been guaranteed. In this way, economic policy must, in the interest of the whole country, ensure effective spatial development and equalisation of difference in development levels of the regions.

Second, the degree of freedom of action of regional management of the economy was increasingly restricted by the tendencies towards centralisation of corporate management which developed in the company organisation system. An essential element of the new economic policy was the creation of opportunities for self-financing and independence. However, it soon became clear that most state firms were unable to cope with their production organisation functions (in the mixed economic relations situation which derived from fierce competition and with an under-trained specialist team), it was desirable to concentrate company management functions and force companies into uniting with others (forming trusts as mentioned earlier) and organising them in a vertical or horizontal way. At first, most of these 'trusts' were under the direct management of the Supreme Economic Council, but later they were transferred to the newly-formed economic Conferences of federal republics, although 72 defence and export-oriented companies producing important goods, or strategically important industrial and transportation trusts remained under the direct control of the Supreme Economic Council of the Soviet Union. The local industrial trusts operated under dual subordination (the republic's, provincial and regional economic conferences). I need hardly say that the management of the trusts demanded differentiation from central bodies. This reorganisation was typical of the Supreme Economic Council and, within the scope of it Central State Industry Directorate (consisting of sectoral directorates) was organised at federal level. The establishment of the centrally initiated and strongly centralised system of trade and product distribution for the industrial syndicates resulted in a further tightening of economic objectives and processes, managed by regional bodies. Both industry directorates and syndicates quickly built up their regional organisations, although these, because of their de-concentrated nature, were almost exclusively enforcing sectoral interests and the central will and were completely isolated from regional bodies. We can conclude that the establishment of the concentrated and centralised company structure is an obvious obstacle to the success of management relations which result clearly from the regional division of labour.

Third, parallel to this narrowing of the area of competence (and accelerating the process) of spatial economy management bodies, a hierarchical institutional system of national economic planning was set up., the regional economic conferences formed planning boards in order to compile and implement the national economy plan. The activity of these was, basically, the arrangement of the annual and long-term economic development plans of their region, but, beyond that, they carried out considerable fact-finding and conceptual work, such as the division of certain areas into districts. The regional planning committees gradually took over the fundamental planning functions of regional economic councils and these latter became local industrial departments, joining up with the communal departments of the Executive Committees of the Soviets. The significant changes in sectoral management which were confirmed by Supreme Soviet legislation up to 1932 clearly showed the sole leading principle of the economy.

Attempts at space-centric economic management at the end of the 1950's, and the failures of regional policy

As a consequence of the temporary loss of ground of the established Stalinist political regime, it became clear by the end of the 1950s that the multi-stage sectoral management systems of the planned economy had created a whole chain of adverse events. The majority of the negative influences arose from the over-centralised character of the decision-making process. No insignificant part in this process can be attributed to the fact that the structure of centralised management was so differentiated that the multi-coloured sectoral management made the effective development of inter-sectoral co-ordination, of inter-corporate co-operation almost impossible, and the product-oriented system of sectoral organisation became the bedfellow of sectoral chauvinism and autarchy. The excesses of sectoral management are, for instance, illustrated by the fact that, in the mid- 1950s, the number of industry-related ministries was around 10 (even in those republics with low economic potential) and the number of industry directorates subordinate to these was approximately several dozen. An additional source of difficulty was that, due to the large number of co-ordination duties appearing at regional level, co-operation between the local and regional management and control bodies (not only councils acting in tight dual subordination circumstances should be included in this, but regional parties also), was almost uncontrollable. The politico-economic practices of the era neither demanded horizontal co-operation nor considered it a fundamental principle of economic organisation.

The negative influences of hierarchic sectoral management exerted on regional development revealed themselves in a most complex manner in the Soviet Union. By the mid-1950s, the extensive industrialisation which significantly changed the regional structure of productive power was already complete. Economic necessity (according to which, if an increasing proportion of is spent on improving living standards and on the improvement of the retail infrastructure, increased economic performance can only be achieved with the increased utilisation of existing fixed assets together with a slowing down in the growth of new facilities) became evident for the first time. At the same time, the economic results drew attention to the fact that complicated sectoral management is quite unable to influence in any rational or direct way the fundamental units of the economy.

At the plenary session of the Communist Party in July 1955 the failings of the economy were voiced by a number of participants. They stated that the development of economically practical forms of production organisation, industrial co-operation and specialisation was stunted by the inflexible, sectoral industrial management so burdened with parallelism. The scope of measures, which were taken very rapidly after the plenary meeting, is shown by the fact that, in that same year, several Russian Federation ministries were dissolved and in the companies operating at republic and local and regional level the number of staff increased from 33 per cent in 1950 to 47 per cent (Bishaev and Fiodorovich 1961).

The need for radical changes in economic management was also voiced at the plenary session of the Central Committee of the Communist Party in February 1957. The resolution adopted in respect of the modernisation of manufacturing and construction industry organisations committed itself, among the various alternatives of multi-stage industrial management, to management on a sectoral basis. The plenum considered the principal starting-point of reorganisation to be the approach of management to production, the expansion of the spheres of authority of the federal and autonomous republics, the enhancement of the economic organisational role of local and regional bodies of the council, party and trade unions, and the increased involvement of the masses in economic management.

To provide a new basis for the regional management system was the direct consequence, and, in fact, to some extent a precondition for concepts to be realised. In the reformed regional scheme *economic regions* played a key role. Their establishment and designation were the fundamental motives for the establishment of the practical units of economic and administrative regionalisation. Economists and economic geographers of the era saw this as a guarantee of the effective operation of the new administrative regional units (Alampiev 1959, 1963; Kolosovskiy 1958, 1961). They tried to support their advantage over the former administrative units with several arguments. In the first place they asserted that the new administrative regions are economic complexes and, although much smaller than the former economic regions, their specialised character becomes more clearly distinct. The higher standard of specialisation provides more advantageous conditions for the establishment of simpler management forms and the opportunity to develop regional chauvinism and autarchy is smaller in the less structured units. Further arguments for the economic regions were the economic processes and the more reasonable concerted character of the operating basis of regional governmental organisations and those of the Party. The coincidence of the politico-governmental sphere of power and the economic sphere could significantly expand the sphere of authority of regional planning and regional management in general, and increase the depth of their potential for influence, so also enhancing local initiative.

A much profound change to the regional organisation system lurked behind the formal changes to the spatial basis of the economic management system. (Earlier, the new economic regions followed the boundaries of former regional administrative units.

At first, it was planned to establish 92 regions (oblasts), although their actual number turned out to be 105, and soon afterwards reduced to 47.) The economic councils established in the administrative regions became the organisational repositories of comprehensive administrative reform. These were bodies subordinate to the Council of Ministers. The Act of 1957 outlining their jurisdiction highlighted especially the fact that these economic councils are administrative bodies and can be controlled by the Council of Ministers of the Soviet Union only through the republic's councils of ministers. Thus, the control of the economic councils did not follow the traditional principle of dual subordination. Their relations to the regional councils was featured by the fact, that on the one hand they had to report on the activities of the companies operating under their jurisdiction to the executive committee of the council, and on the other hand, in complex economic development matters they were obliged to maintain close co-ordination with the councils. (Thus, in terms of organisational principles the economic councils significantly differed from the similar institutions of the 1920s. That is, the majority of the then existing regional economic bodies operated in dual subordination: as the independent organisational unit of the Soviet region, they were also under the control of the Supreme Economic Council.)

The law regarded the economic councils as regional management and special administrative bodies. Their structure closely followed sectoral principles. Through these sectoral bodies (directorates general, directorates) the economic council directly controlled the companies attached to it. The controlling authority of sectoral directorates covered the corporate operation in full. They were responsible for the material-technical supply of production, for the development of interregional co-operation and of co-operative relations within their district; they virtually controlled smallest details of industrial planning and organisation. Their task was to approve the corporate organisational and operating rules and regulations and to appoint the leaders of the productive industrial units. It was not accidental, therefore, that those criticising this organisational structure regarded it as the key inadequacy of the organisational system, that the 'Company – economic council' two-stage chain of control remained, in practice, three-stage.

The other organisational direction of the division of labour established in regional economy management was represented by Soviets (councils). While industrial organisations and organisations of the construction industry were controlled by the economic councils, local Soviets were responsible for agriculture, and for the non-productive sphere. Through the gradual decentralisation of administrative jurisdictions, independence of these councils in economic management was strengthened at the beginning of the reforms. However, at the beginning of the 1960s, a process began under which local industrial companies were withdrawn from local Soviet jurisdiction and finally transferred to economic organisations. Based on their management relations to the economic sphere, the government and power organisations (unified up to this point) were divided into two types: industrial (urban) and agricultural (rural) Soviets, and the political establishment was also reorganised based on production functions. In the agricultural areas, kolkhoz and sovkhoz (Soviet-style collective farms and state farms respectively) production directorates were established to undertake public administrative and party duties instead of district party committees.

The number of economic councils was reduced to 47 in 1962, and the three-stage planning system (economic region, administrative region and district) was replaced by a four-stage system. Sixteen economic macro-regions comprised the upper level; an increased number of regions of the economic councils made up the second, 137 autonomous republics, administrative regions (krais and oblasts) made up the third, while 2,724 districts formed the fourth level.

Summarising the results of this era of Soviet economic management, we can confirm that regional factors definitely outweighed sectoral management, and through this the higher decision-making levels were deprived of the possibility of uniform management, concept creation and execution. It is obvious that, in this way, a number of aspects of sectoral optima, represented by the specialised sectors and covering the entire country could not prevail. The mobility of budgetary investment instruments among the individual areas significantly decreased. As for industrial development, regional interests came into prominence: two-thirds of industrial investment was initiated and financed by the economic councils, and there was no uniform industrial development concept in operation, not even a sectoral one.

The economic councils aimed at the large-scale improvement of industry in their respective regions. Specialisation was overshadowed and economic relations between individual regions weakened. Even though the elimination of the hugely over-centralised management of industrial companies, of corporate isolation within a single economic district (due to subordination to the supreme authority) proved successful, the power of the local bodies formally increased. Nevertheless, reorgan-isations could not bring visibly better results in production, since it was only an organisational restructuring of management which took place: the administrative regulation methods of production remained dominant in corporate management (Zaleski 1967).

Management difficulties which could be linked to the organisational structure had not lessened; in fact, they had even increased to some degree through conflicts and disputes concerning the *delimitation of the regional units of public adminis-tration, economic management and planning*. Representatives of the disciplines dealing with the spatial aspects of socio-economic processes proved several times convincingly that spatial basic units – in contrast to the principles of reform – are not economic regions (Khrushchov 1966; Probst 1965; Shkolnikov 1965). The first version of the economic management regional system was unfavourable for long-term planning, while the second version was unsuitable to reconcile the complicated management relations which had developed in the region. The less stable regional organisational system also provided reasons for the strong differentiation of the economic productive capacity of regional units and of the standard of production. All of these hindered regional equalisation; it did in fact further increase the differences. This process was even supported by the fact that the regional orientation of economic management had scarcely any effect on regional planning; the degree of complexity of regional plans even decreased. The planning activity of the economic councils, however obvious the analogy seemed, could not be identified with regional planning. The planning activity of the local-regional bodies of the council covered only the relatively narrow local economy. Regional plans were, in effect, made only on the federal republic level (Pavlenko1984; Pchelintsev 1966, 1983). Despite the beneficial effects of the elimination of sectoral isolation which earlier hindered development, the uncalculated adverse effects (which conflicted with the basic concept of economic management) reduced the effectiveness of the economic operation, and this contributed to the long-term decline in the rate of economic growth in the Soviet Union.

We can identify several unique features of the regional economic structure of the Soviet era even though the prevailing state ideology and policy did not recognise the failure of the planned economic decision-making system in shaping the spatial structure. The main features of the regional organisations of the Soviet empire were:

1   The strong concentration of population and economy (especially industry and services) in the European part of the country. On the other hand, the focal point of the extraction industry was in the areas extending east and south of the Urals. In the mid-1980s, an annual 1 billion tons of raw material flowed from the Eastern regions to the Western industrial areas, involving up to 3,000 kilometre of haulage. Industrial development programmes of Siberia and the Far East were exclusively limited to the production of raw materials, and workers were not encouraged to leave the area. These solutions were both extremely expensive and unsuccessful.
2   The implementation of extreme, specialised regional development pro- grammes in the spirit of 'gigantomania' in the interest of demonstrating the superiority of sectoral ministries. In many regions and cities, development was based on a single sector of the extractive industry. For example, in the area of Ivanovo, the majority of output was provided by the textile industry, and in the Udmurt Republic, and in several Siberian cities and towns, by the defence industry. The spatial concentration was facilitated also by corporate organisa- tional means. In the different sectors of innovation-sensitive processing industry, huge monopolies had been established and by 1990 roughly 1,000 large companies controlled the Soviet manufacturing industry.
3   The autonomous operating conditions of settlements were restricted and the social sphere was heavily influenced by large companies. For example, the urban management of Magnitogorsk was exclusively undertaken by the steel- works and that of Togliatti by the automobile factory. Several other examples could be enumerated.
4.   The member republics of a formally federal, but essentially unitary, state possessed only restricted economy development powers.

The regional portrait of the new Russia

After the dissolution of the Soviet Union in 1991, with the switch to the market economy and with the disintegration of common economic space, the regional differences became much stronger. The effects of economic liberalisation were different in the individual areas of the country. The deep and protracted political crisis made its effect felt in every region of the country. Government investment (the main source of regional development funds) had been reduced to a minimum and the close economic bonds between constituent republics had been broken (Artobolevsky 1993). Industrial production decreased most significantly in the European Central, Southern, and Far East federal districts, while the decline of industry in the Siberian and North Russian areas, rich in natural resources, is minor, although still significant. The winners from these changes were exclusively the European centres of Russia. The development of Moscow and St Petersburg shows post-industrial features and a considerable proportion of the new market organisations (financial institutions, business service providers and export companies) are located in these two cities. Among the regions of the country, those who found themselves in the most acute situations were those whose economy was dominated by giant corporate concentrations, and narrow specialisation (Table 6.6).

After the dissolution of the Soviet Union, considerable regional reorganisation was introduced into the Russian Federation, and during the past 15 years or so the fundamental directions of changes influencing the country's economic and spatial structure were:

- A new state political position evolved after the collapse of the Soviet Union (the former internal peripheries becoming external peripheries).
- The elimination of the planned economy and the development of new market relations.
- The opening of the Russian economy to external markets.
- A new type of regionalisation in Russia, with the transformation of the economy producing several cross-administrative-border organisations – for instance in the energy sector and in transport.
- The evolution of a new stage of urbanisation, in which urban lifestyle and infrastructure are shaped, no longer directly according to industrial and technological requirements, but according to modern, environmentally friendly factors which better serve improvements to the quality of life and living conditions.

Table 6.6 Proportions of the population living in regions with differing development levels, Russia, 1993

Type of region	Population ('000s)	(%)
Backward	34,745	23.4
Depressed	35,073	23.7
Stagnating (temporarily)	30,527	20.6
Developed	47,900	32.3
Total	148,245	100.0

Source: The author's calculations based on Bandman *et al.* (1996: 211–243); Bilov and Smirniagin (1996: 181–183).

The switch to the market economy most of all affected the various industrial sectors. By the mid-1990s, industrial production was reduced to one-half of its earlier level, although the decline of production varied in the individual regions. The value of industrial production decreased by 50 per cent in the North Caucasus, by 63 per cent in the Kaliningrad region and by some 50 per cent in the Trans-Urals regions. When examining smaller spatial units (oblasts or provinces), a highly dramatic decrease can be observed. Industrial growth was characteristic of only 17 spatial units. The main driving force of regional differentiation was the transformation of the sectoral structure of industry. The decline was largest in the textile industry, precision engineering and in the chemical and timber industries. These, and the regions with economies based on some routine or undistinguished local industry, first, in the peripheral areas inhabited by ethnic minorities, demonstrate the worst features of depression. For example, in the multi-national autonomous republics unemployment rates are as high as 30 per cent, while the rate of unemployment in raw material-producing areas is only 4–5 per cent. When these two types of region are compared, the income of the population shows a 10 to 15-fold difference. In one-third of the county's regions, half of the population lives below the minimum subsistence level. The wages of the economic sectors also show significant differences: the average wages of those working in the fuel industry are three times higher than the national average and double those in light industry.

The regions which were established during the Tsarist regime and under the logic of the created regions (oblasts) encountered serious problems when faced with the free market. A considerable proportion of Russian public administrative units were unable to meet the competitive conditions set by market requirements. First of all, it was those regions which hit difficulties whose operation had earlier been determined by geopolitical factors (the production sites of defence-industry complexes were closed military districts), or whose growth had been influenced by a single, giant company. According to experts' estimates, as the direct consequence of inadequate regional management, the annual loss of GDP amounted to between 2 and 3 per cent (Novikov 1998).

Due to the lack of organisation, the market optimisation forces influencing the economy and the spontaneous migration of the population exerted significant pressure on the infrastructural networks in the emerging regions. At the same time, huge amounts of infrastructure-related plants lay unused in the ports, and in the large energy hubs. One tenth of Russian power-stations has not been producing for years and several hundred kilometres of pipelines through which, earlier, considerable export activity was realised, remained unused. The infrastructure networks of the two emblematic Russian metropolises, Moscow and St Petersburg, could no longer meet the requirements of economic development.

The inherited economic base has also contributed to the fact that Russia today may be regarded as an expressly raw material extracting country, and the raw material extracting regions can be considered as truly competitive on the world market. These regions rank first on the country's investment list and the largest amounts of capital and qualified labour force flow into them. The major proportion of infrastructural development over the last 10 years has been allocated to the road network of these areas; roads were constructed to link mines and quarries with seaports and border-crossings. However, the underdevelopment of a modern urban infrastructure represents a considerable obstacle to future innovative development in these areas.

Nevertheless, the new regional hierarchy does not help strengthen cohesion. The outdated public administrative structure of the country and the rigid regional boundaries hinder the spatial expansion of beneficial economic and social processes. Leading regions are unable to exert pressure on other regions, and the losses due to regional segregation are very significant. For example, due to the lack of co-operation, different regions of Northwestern Russia are developing their ports and road-networks individually.

One of the signs of weak cohesion is the large differences among regional units. Based on gross regional product (GDP) per capita, the difference between the poorest and the richest oblasts (provinces) in Russia was 44 fold (double that of the income difference between the world's poorest and richest countries). Among the (then) 89 regions, the GDP per capita exceeded the national average in only 16 oblasts (Figure 6.2). Although over the whole country (which was divided into seven macro-regions (the so-called 'federal districts', managed by a Presidential plenipotentiary envoy), the performance of four of these macro-regions exceeded the national average and large variations can be seen among their individual units. The GDP per capita of the Urals federal district, comprising four oblasts, is 208 per cent of the national average. The figure the Tyumen oblast, the Russian region with the best performance in this federal district, is 564 per cent in contrast to the other units of the region (whose average is 40–80 per cent). In the least developed Southern Federal District (which comprises eight regions with national minorities and five oblasts with a Russian population), the average GDP per capita amounts to 49 per cent of the national average.

After turn of the millennium, regional differences widened still further. In 1994, the GDP per capita of the 10 most developed Russian federal regions was 2.50 times that of the national average, while in 2002 it was 3.3 times. In 2004, out of the 89 regions, 10 produced more than half of the country's GDP (Table 6.7).

The majority of regional units show weak competitiveness in the global markets, and the lack of success of Soviet regional development is shown by the fact that not even a single modern, regional productive cluster has been established: monoculture is characteristic of one-quarter of the Russian regions. Productive relations do not manifest themselves in networks, but large vertically organised companies manage economic co-operation. Sixty per cent of the output of the timber industry in the (long industrialised) Tver region, which has a relatively diversified economic structure is produced by four large companies, and 44 per cent of the production of the engineering industry is produced by three large companies. Mono-functional cities are located in the Central, Urals and Siberian federal districts in the greatest numbers. They account for 61 per cent of urban settlements and, as the population of four-fifths of these settlements exceeds 50,000, their share of the city network is considerable. One-point-five million

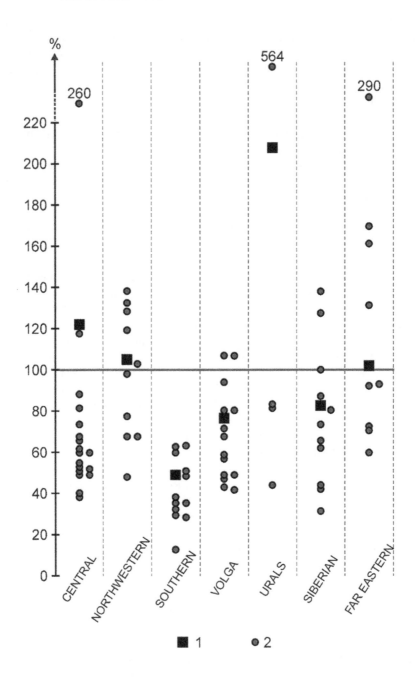

Figure 6.2 GDP per capita in the Russian federal districts, 2004, Russia = 100
Key: 1 – Federal district; 2 – Region (oblast).
Source: The author's compilation based on the data of Osnovnye pokazateli sistemy nacional'nyh
          schotov.

Table 6.7 The 10 most important Russian federal regions in national GDP terms, 1994–2004

1994		2004	
Subject	*(%)*	*Subject*	*(%)*
Moscow (City)	10.2	Moscow (City)	19.0
Tyumen	6.3	Tyumen	13.0
Sverdlovsk	3.8	Moscow	3.8
Moscow	3.6	St Petersburg	3.6
St Petersburg	3.2	Tatarstan	2.8
Samara	3.2	Sverdlovsk	2.6
Krasnoyarsk	3.0	Samara	2.5
Nizhniy Novgorod	2.8	Krasnoyarsk	2.3
Bashkiria	2.7	Krasnodar	2.2
Chelyabinsk	2.7	Bashkiria	2.1
Total	41.5	Total	53.9

Source: Konceptsiia strategii social'no-ekonomicheskogo razvitiia regionov Rossiiskoi Federacii, p. 5.

inhabitants live in the mono-functional cities of the Sverdlovsk region(42 per cent of the region's urban population). The situation is more unfavourable in the Volgograd, Tyumen and Archangelsk areas, since, in these, more than half of the urban population live in cities which are maintained by a single industrial sector. According to this indicator, Siberia's position is no better either, since 41.0 per cent of the urban population there is concentrated in such cities. (Table 6.8). First and foremost this city-network feature explains why the majority of Russian investment and infrastructural projects flows into the extraction industries and into large companies, since, in these terms, sectors which are competitive on the international markets carry insignificant weight.

Regional social problems

Sharp demographic and social inequalities are characteristic of Russia's current spatial structure. In the first place, the unequal spatial distribution of the population may be considered as the greatest. The Central-Western and Southwestern regions can be deemed the demographic gravity zones of the country, totalling one-quarter of the country's area, but three-quarters of its population. All of this is reflected in the extreme differences of the indicators of population density (Figure 6.3).

As a consequence of forced industrialisation, a large proportion of Russian settlements are unable to increase their population in any regular manner. The agglomerations of the large cities show long-term stagnation in respect of demography and migration. Among the 13 largest Russian cities with populations of more than 1 million, only the populations of Moscow, Rostov-on-Don and of Volgograd have continuously increased. For example, Perm, which earlier had 1 million

Table 6.8 Regions with a large number of mono-functional cities, 2004

Region, republic	Number of cities	Number of mono-functional cities	Proportion of population living in mono-functional cities (%)
Chukotka	3	3	100
Khakassia	5	4	80
Karelia	13	10	77
Ivanovo	16	12	73
Sverdlovsk	47	33	70
Kemerovo	20	14	70
Nizhniy Novgorod	23	17	68

Source: Konceptsija strategii social'no-ekonomicheskogo razvitiia regionov Rossiiskoi Federacii, p. 9.

inhabitants, no longer features in this category. The population of Russian cities decreased between 1991 and 2002 by more than 4.5 million (3.9 per cent). On the basis of industry-based urbanisation, new types of population-reproducing phenomena became general, with both the birth-rate and the mortality-rate decreasing. Over most of the country, the natural increase steadily dropped, and, while in 1990 this could be seen only in the ageing Central and Northwestern regions, by 2003 it was characteristic of 73 spatial units (oblasts) of the country. The only exceptions to this phenomenon are the Eastern and Southern peripheries where high birth rates are still common today. The country has several regions where, during the last 15 years, settlement populations decreased by one-third, and it is the first time in the country's history that the village has lost its self-reproductive capacity.

If we assume the indefinite continuation of current natural increase rates, Russia's population loss by 2050 may reach 1.8 per cent per annum, while the proportion of the senior citizen population may grow from the 20 per cent of 2002 to 34 per cent. In the meantime, the ageing population remaining in work will also decrease. By 2010, the number of those on the labour market is expected to be 3.6 million lower, and this number will decrease by a further 7 million by 2015. The dramatic decrease of the country's population and the migration tendencies also involve risks in geopolitical terms. In Siberia and the Far East a demographic vacuum may develop, and this may be an opportunity for mass immigration from the surrounding countries, a development which would be clearly inconsistent with the economic and political interests of Russia.

Beyond the one-sided nature of the migration processes, the adverse situation evolving due to a significant decrease in the number of immigrants and to a steady increase in the number of emigrants, the low rate of mobility of the population also hinders regional development. There are several regions in the country where development is handicapped by serious shortages of labour, and, according to predictions, from 2006, these areas may show an increase in their shortage of labour over a five-year period from 0.25 per cent to 1.20 per cent. However, to maintain

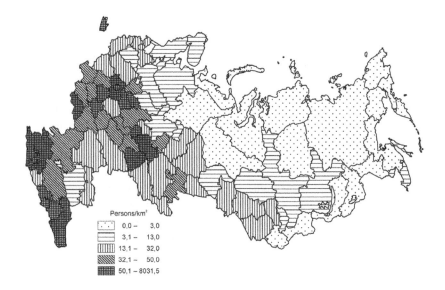

Persons/km²

[ ] 0,0 – 3,0
[ ] 3,1 – 13,0
[ ] 13,1 – 32,0
[ ] 32,1 – 50,0
[ ] 50,1 – 8031,5

Figure 6.3 Population density indicators of the Russian federal regions, 2002, persons/km²

a 7 per cent growth rate of GDP would also require the same growth rate in the working age population. These problems could be remedied with an increase in population mobility, but mobility is currently impeded by several factors:

• The bureaucratic infrastructure for registering labour and residence has not yet been set up. People do not find homes in the places where jobs are to be found and cannot find jobs where they live.
• Financial resources for public utility services needed to retain their population are lacking in the regions.
• High travel costs deter commuting by workers.

The commuting habits of the inhabitants of Russia today differ little from the features of early industrialisation. The poor level of mobility can be explained by the level of education of much of the workforce. The education system has not yet adjusted to market conditions. Institutions of vocational training were established under the old Soviet system, and significant changes have not yet been implemented. Even in those areas which are still growing strongly, the labour market shows a one-sided picture: in respect of technical activities there is a significant lack of a skilled workforce, while, in many branches of the humanities, considerable over-education is evident. Effective working relationships between education and the economy have not been established.

As a consequence of spontaneous spatial development, Russian society shows a very diverse picture. According to sociology surveys, 3 per cent of the population can be regarded as wealthy (even as millionaires), 20 per cent belong to the middle-class, 70 per cent can be included in temporary groups, whose members may sometimes climb a rung of the social ladder, but often slip back. Among the latter, 30 per cent can be considered definitively poor and 10 per cent live in extreme poverty. The social division of Russian society hinders social reform, exerts an adverse effect on the growth of the internal market, and the current consumption level is an obstacle to more rapid economic growth. Due to the low income levels of the population as a whole, it is impossible to introduce modern forms of financing. One cannot rely on any contribution to development from the population and the workings of civil organisations are slow and protracted (Consultations with the Poor ... Russia; Sharpe 2007).

After the change of regime, radical changes took place in the relationships of ethnic groups living in the country. Earlier, relations with ethnic minorities had a favourable influence on the cultural development of the multi-national empire. In fact, the Russian proportion of the population of the old Soviet Union was 55 per cent, while the Russian population of today's Russian Federation is 82 per cent (Table 6.9). Regional educational and cultural institutions of the different ethnic groups were closed down. The evolving ethnic enclaves and a lack of institutions needed for ethnic communities to exist has led to ethnic seclusion over the regions of the country. The mobility rate of ethnic minorities is also somewhat low. Social problems in the ethnic regions tend to accumulate. Economic growth is low and the unemployment rate is high. Social stagnation incites conflict and in many cases central government needs to deploy the military to maintain order in these regions.

The Russian settlement structure

The clear beneficiaries of forced industrialisation and political ideology were, for many decades, the cities. The urbanisation level of the country can be regarded as outstanding even in international terms with 73 per cent of the population living in *cities*. The urban population reached its peak in 1990 when the population of Russian cities reached 108.9 million. A steady reduction, however, produced a decline to 104.7 million by 2005. It is quite understandable that, in the more thinly inhabited areas, city networks are also rare (Bradshaw and Palacin 2004).

In Russia at the beginning of the twenty-first century, there were 1,097 cities registered as such. This means that the number of cities had doubled and that the urban population had increased seven times over 100 years. In 2001, the population of 15 per cent of these cities (specifically, 163) exceeded 100,000. There were 11 cities with more than 1million inhabitants, 23 with 500,000 to 1 million and 57 with 200–500,000 inhabitants. Most of the remaining 900 or so small- and medium-sized cities are located in European areas.

Elements of the Russian city network established in the Soviet era – more than half of them – appeared very weak during the period of regime change. The ability of companies to set up in towns and cities collapsed. Companies previously producing almost exclusively for the internal market took part in running cities, and with considerable funds. As a result of the change to a market economy, thousands

Table 6.9 Proportion of ethnic minorities in the Russian population, 2002

Ethnic group	People ('000s)	(%)	Percentage of 1989
Russian	115,869	79.8	96.7
Tatar	5,558	3.8	100.7
Ukrainian	2,944	2.0	67.5
Bashkir	1,674	1.2	124.3
Chuvash	1,637	1.1	92.3
Chechen	1,361	0.9	151.3
Armenian	1,130	0.8	212.3
Mordvinian	845	0.6	78.7
Belarus	816	0.6	67.5
Avar	757	0.5	139.2
Kazakh	655	0.4	103.0
Udmurt	637	0.4	89.1
Azerbaijan	622	0.4	185.0
Mari	605	0.4	94.0
German	597	0.4	70.9
Kabard	520	0.3	134.7
Ossetic	505	0.3	128.0
Dagestan	510	0.3	144.4
Buriat	445	0.3	106.7
Yakut	444	0.3	116.8
Kumi	423	0.3	152.4
Ingush	412	0.3	191.5
Lesg	412	0.3	160.0
Total	145,164	100.0	98.7

Source: Konceptsija strategii social'no-ekonomicheskogo razvitiia regionov Rossiiszkoi Federacii, p. 21.

of companies were closed, and military orders also dropped significantly. (Military establishments had a prominent position in every fifth city in Russia.)

However, the two groups of the Soviet-type city network, the present and former capitals (Moscow and St Petersburg) and the *administrative centres of the regions* (regional capitals) were the absolute winners in the change process. There are significant differences between these two federal cities. The 21 per cent of the Russian GDP is produced in Moscow, while St Petersburg which has half of the population of Moscow, produces less than 4.0 per cent of GDP. Moscow is a typical post-industrial metropolis. Eighty-four per cent of its GDP comes from the services (in St Petersburg, 63 per cent GDP originates from services) (Zubarevich 2006).

The regional centres are, in general, the largest cities of their federal division or region and their share of the population of their territory is large. The city of No-vosibirsk consists of 53 per cent of the population of its region (oblast), Tomsk 47 per cent and Kaliningrad 45 per cent of their oblasts and Izhevsk 40 per cent (of the Udmurt Republic). Forty to 70 per cent of a region's GDP is produced in the centres of the public administration units; almost every economic indicator exceeds the regions' averages by 10–30 per cent. Likewise, these regional capitals spend the major part of the budget of their region: Yekaterinburg 50 per cent, Perm 60 per cent and Chelyabinsk 75 per cent. Inhabitants of the regional capitals spend, on the average, 42 per cent more on market services and consumer goods, and build significantly more apartments. In the city of Yaroslavl, for instance, each inhabitant purchased 65 per cent more in the way of services and consumer goods in 2004 than those living in the Yaroslavl oblast (i.e., the federal subject) (Leksin 2006). Ninety per cent of undergraduates study and 80 per cent of scientific researchers work in these cities. These centres are the clear beneficiaries of the post-Soviet transformation: 95 per cent of privatised state assets are to be found in these cities, and the expansion of the banking system and international relations also helped to enrich the interest groups living here. The middle classes of these regional centres and 'Oil Cities' comprising *c.* 2.50 million people enjoy 90 per cent of the annual income (50 billion dollars) of this social stratum.

Russia is the archetypal example of the fact that *contradictions may arise between the degree of urbanisation and the extent of urbanisation.* The Soviet Public Administration Law set the administrative requirements for the promotion of a town to quantitative requirements relating, primarily to the size of population, although the circular infrastructure and institutions of urban lifestyle were almost totally absent from the Russian small- and medium-sized towns. Following the change of regime, a transformation of Russian cities began. Changes are traceable both in the number of cities and in the urban population. The number of urban settlements actually decreased in Russia, and the reason for this unusual phenomenon is that, during the temporary period of crisis, many agricultural towns applied to be downgraded to village or settlement level to enable its inhabitants to pay lower public utility charges and to be able to take up allowances related to agricultural production. Due to the collapse of large city economies, large cities (those with over 500,000 inhabitants) had lost 2.6 million inhabitants by the mid-90s, while the population of cities with fewer than 100,000 inhabitants increased by 1.6 million. A majority of cities in this latter category are located in the Southern, poorly urbanised, regions and in the territories of ethnic minorities, but it is a general rule that the growth of cities in the emerging regions has increased steadily, while in depressed areas the crises primarily occurred in cities.

A reorganisation of *the industrial performance* of Russia's larger cities also took place. Table 6.10 shows significant changes in the order of the 15 Russian cities with the largest economic capacity. Moscow and St Petersburg have maintained their positions during the past 25 years, while the home of the textile industry, Ivanovo (the Russian Manchester, together with the important engineering centres of Yekaterinburg and Rostov rank lower, and Nizhniy Novgorod slipped back from third or fourth place to eleventh. Chelyabinsk, Ufa and Samara (all with a diversified economic structure) were able to retain their positions. The spectacular advance made by Togliatti, a city with an innovative industrial structure (automotive and petrochemical industries) should be an example for Russian city development. The cities included in this ranking in 1970 produced 28 per cent, and in 1996 20 per cent of Russia's industrial output.

The dominance of some regional centres of public administration which, earlier, had had leading positions in the Russian network of large cities, came to an end, and new competitors appeared in the regions. The development of the regional city-competition is at the same time proof that the existing image of Russia as a strongly centralised Russia may slowly change.

The rural population of 39 million people (23 per cent of the country's population) lives in 155,000 settlements, but the size of these rural settlements is very small with an average population of 249. The population of 95 per cent of all villages is below 1,000. However, the proportion of the population living in these small villages was, in 2002, only 52 per cent of the rural population.

The spatial arrangement of the village network is also uneven. There are large differences in the density and size of rural settlements. A settlement network with small villages is typical of the Northwestern and Central federal districts and for those along the Volga; in these large regions the population of less than 50 per cent of the villages is over 100 people (Zolin 2006.). According to the census returns for 2002, the population of only 0.1 per cent of villages exceeds 5,000. Three-quarters of the villages categorised as large or very large (631 villages) are situated in the Southern and Siberian federal districts and along the Volga. The population living in large villages amounts to 16 per cent of the total village population. This is highest in the Southern Federal District at 23 per cent (Vserossiyskaya perepis' naseleniya 2002 goda).

Deficiencies in regional development policy

The slow process of institutionalisation of regional policy

Following the change of regime, almost all the elements of Soviet-type regional development collapsed. The largest loser in the economic disintegration was the Russian Federation which had earlier clearly profited from artificial integration. Disintegration also strongly influenced the regional position of the Russian economy and can be characterised by:

- Increase of transport costs, devaluation of product structures, decline of consumption, and, as a consequence of the possibilities for establishing newly directed economic relations, the interregional exchange of commodities significantly changed. The degree of contraction in interregional product turnover exceeds that of the decrease in production.
- Regional budgets collapsed and the steady resources gap and increasing debt stock stepped up the tension between central government and the regions.
- Maximising increases in income resulted in unrestrained exploitation; the economic separatism of regions became general.
- Owing to increasing transportation costs, the interregional flow of labour dropped to a minimum level.

Table 6.10 Cities providing the largest industrial output, 1970–1996

City	Position in ranking order		Share of Russian industrial output (%)	
	1996	*1970*	*1996*	*1970*
Moscow	1	1	5.80	8.50
St Petersburg	2	2	2.50	5.00
Togliatti	3	64	1.90	0.30
Chelyabinsk	4	3	1.50	1.50
Omsk	5	7	1.30	1.10
Novokuznetzk	6	9	1.20	1.00
Lipeck	7	30	1.20	0.50
Samara	8	6	1.10	1.20
Ufa	9	10	1.10	1.00
Cherepovetz	10	26	1.10	0.60
Nizhniy Novgorod	11	4	1.00	1.50
Surgut	12	–	0.90	–
Norilsk	13	32	0.90	0.50
Krasnoyarsk	14	8	0.90	1.10
Magnitogorsk	15	18	0.80	0.90
Perm	17	12	0.70	1.00
Yaroslavl	18	11	0.70	1.00
Kazan	23	15	0.60	1.00
Yekaterinburg	24	–	0.60	–
Novosibirsk	26	16	0.60	0.90
Rostov-on-Don	45	17	0.30	0.90
Cheboksary	51	14	0.20	0.90
Ivanovo	52	17	0.20	1.00

Source: Treivish *et al.* (1999: 278).

After the downfall of communism, divergent processes crept into the economic and political fields as well into the Russian state which was declared unitary. Among political factors, the central government and the division of power between the regions played a significant role. In principle, the new Russian Constitution regulated power relations and eliminated most of the regulations which discriminated against the regions. However, the economic crisis of 1998 made it clear that economic collapse could not be prevented solely by political means, and integration organised on a market basis must be supported by means of economic policy. From that point onwards, we may speak of the re-evaluation of regional economic policy. The concept of regional policy first appeared in Russian governmental documents in 1992. In that year, Boris Yeltsin addressed a regional political Presidential message to the State Duma (the Russian Parliament). Regional political committees had been established in the Lower and Upper Houses, and the political parties had also included the problems of regional development in their manifestoes. In 1996, President Yeltsin issued a decree concerning 'The main directions of regional policy in the Russian Federation'. The presidential document considered the goals, means and institutions of regional policy. Its key elements were:

- The economic, social, legal and organisational principles of the federation must be elaborated.
- Starting from the constitutional regulation, the basic requirements of social security must be defined independent of the type of development potential which an individual regions may have.
- The principle of equal opportunity must be established in all regions of the country.
- Regional environmental programmes must be prepared.
- Serious attention must be paid to the development of strategic regions.
- The climatic and natural endowments of regions must be fully exploited.
- Guarantees must be in place for the operation of local government.

This series of duties did not differ much from the regional political goals of the Soviet regime, but it can still be considered a major success as the prelude to modern regional policy in Russia. The document gave rise to wide-ranging debate and the dialogue initiating the improvement of Russian public administration also originated primarily within political and professional circles.

In order to finance regional political duties the, State Duma established a fund to subsidise federal regional units, the source of which was 15 per cent of the net revenues form customs and import duties. The primary aim of the fund was to subsidise regions struggling with acute problems, but almost every region obtained assistance. Of the 89 regions (oblasts), no fewer than 81 benefited from these funds, the majority of which were spent on solving budgetary problems.

This attempt to establish stability for operating regional development institutions failed. In the central institution of Russian economic policy, the Presidential Executive Office, a regional policy unit had not been established, and initially the Ministry of Economy was in charge of regional policy. Basically, however, its duties did not extend beyond preparing the government's annual report. In the mid-1990s, a new central organisation (the Ministry of National Problems and Federal Relations) was charged with responsibility for regional policy, and in 2000 an independent Ministry of Regional Policy was set up. In the first phase of Russian regional policy – according to the unanimous opinion of experts – there were only formal results to be reported. However, the concept of policy has taken root and its institution has appeared on the scene in the area of central public administration, although, to date, factual results can be seen only in the elaboration of some regional programmes (Artobolevsky 2000).

The stabilisation of the state budget and accelerating economic growth have enabled the government, from the end of the 1990s, to spend more on reducing regional differences. However, the experiences of the past five years or so have made it clear that the government's regional measures are not effective, and the measures applied have exhausted all of its (initially promising) potential. In the application of regional policy, the Russian government faced new challenges. While earlier, during the era of primary industrialisation, it aimed to reduce regional differences by establishing industries which required a large workforce and which concentrated on producing standardised mass products, the new policy, although with the same targets, had to employ strategies to open new markets and enlarge the domestic market. The 'levelling' subsidies granted from the budget to backward regions in respect of their adaptation to market conditions clearly reduced the effectiveness of the national economy, since, even though the purpose was redistribution, these subsidies took considerable resources away from the leading regions. The mechanism also put the developed regions into a difficult position, in that they were not able to adapt to international market competition. 'Levelling' as a regional policy objective became an obstacle to stimulating the regional expansion of innovation, and also to meeting the requirements of competitiveness. Leading regions could only utilise their development motivation in a very limited way, and in the subsidised regions the feeling of dependence harmed public morale.

The proposed package of regional policy measures was also poor, and a major proportion of those applied consisted of governmental transfers and objective programmes. Modern regional policy measures appeared only slowly in state policy, and to a limited degree. The reform of public administration and the reorganisation of the budget made their effect felt only at macro-level. The meso-level remained unchanged since conditions for regional development had not been established.

No comprehensive analysis in respect of the regional situation had been elaborated and different forms of development had not been drawn up. No information was available on regional features. Owing to such deficiencies, it was simply impossible to apply differentiated regional policy. The planning system of the units of regional public administration is underdeveloped, with settlement and regional planning not in harmony. The concept of interregional co-operation is almost unknown in Russia and there are no valid principles and rules for utilising budgetary resources. The country does not have a regional development strategy, and so the government's concepts and decisions cannot include any concrete and regionally differentiated concepts regarding the suppression of poverty, the increase of GDP, the modernisation of industrial regions in decline and a homogeneous country. Measures influencing the development of individual regions falling exclusively within the new regional organisation of the country do not appear in legislation and budgetary planning. The national settlement network development concept, adopted in 1994, is not taken into account either by local authorities or by business.

Outdated territorial administrative structure

The regional public administration of the country is outdated. Today Russia is divided into 83 regional public administrative units, including 21 republics, seven border territories (krais), 46 provinces (oblasts), one autonomous region, six autonomous districts and two federal cities. In 1917, Russia consisted of 56 regions (gubernia). By 1950, this had changed to 84 regional administrative units. During the last half-century, the number at meso-level (disregarding new and abolished units) remained unchanged. The sizes of the regional administrative units show considerable differences. The 22 larger oblasts, those with more than 2 million inhabitants, comprise 25 per cent of the number of administrative units, while 56 per cent of the country's population live there. The administrative borders hamper new forms of development and they fail to meet the requirements for economies of scale. The legal regulation of regions does not comply with international standards, and the country has hardly ratified a single document on European regional co-operation. A review of 'regions' is under way in the spirit of the reform of Russian public administration, and, to date, a few have been merged, with further mergers expected. Each region (federal subject) has its own government, ministries and budget, and, if necessary, subsidies can be granted from the central budget.

In 2000 seven *federal districts* were established by Presidential Decree. In 2010, new North Caucasian Federal District was split from Southern Federal District. Each of these 'super regions' embraces a number of existing regional administrative units, and, according to the presidential concept, the new seats of the districts became the regional centres of the subordinated regions (Figure 6.4, Table 6.11). The duties of the Plenipotentiary Representative of the President of the Russian Federation appointed as the leaders of the districts involve ensuring that the regional leaders of the district observe Federal laws and budgetary policies, elaborating new social and economic programmes and gathering statistical data for the central administration.

Figure 6.4 Federal districts of Russia from 2010

Table 6.11 Main data of federal districts, 2010

Description	Area, thousand km²	Population, millions	Administrative centre	Population of district centre, thousands	Urbanisation level (%)	Employed in industry (%)
Central	653	38.7	Moscow	14, 382	81.7	21.2
Southern	417	13.9	Rostov	1,089	62.4	17.4
North-western	1,678	13.7	St Petersburg	5,028	81.9	23.3
Far Eastern	6,216	6.3	Khabarovsk	577	76.0	20.2
Siberian	5,115	19.3	Novosibirsk	1,524	70.4	22.4
Urals	1,788	12.2	Yekaterinburg	1,425	80.2	25.6
Volga	1,038	31.6	Nizhniy Novgorod	1,250	70.8	25.6
North Caucasia	172	9.5	Pyatigorsk	143	48.8	15.0

Source: www.gks.ru [15 November, 2013].

President Putin hoped that the districts would boost the regions' political and economic relations with Moscow, and that the effectiveness of public administration would improve. Instead of holding governorship elections in the Russian regions, the regional leaders were appointed by the central administration in 2004 (although the decision had first of all to be approved by the local parliaments); it was a measure aiming at centralisation. Both the Russian opposition and foreign political circles strongly criticised the curtailment of regional autonomy and the democratic changes of the 1990s in such a manner (Lynn and Kuzes 2002, 2003; Petrov 2002).

According to the logic of centralisation, decentralisation only promoted the break-up of the federation and supported the measures taken in favour of regional separatism – something which, in the case of Chechnya, arose in its worst possible form. According to leading Russian opinion, the self-interest of corrupt local elites replaced those alleged fundamental principles of autonomy which, in the Soviet era, had led to the establishment of the federal state of Russia. The governing political forces were filled with increasing frustration at the deterioration of regional problems and inequalities and their own incapacity to retain the key elements of the federation under their control. The Kremlin, therefore, became convinced that it is fundamentally necessary to restore Moscow's firm power over Russia's regions in order to preserve national homogeneity and to protect the public against the dual dangers of separatism and terrorism. The Russian president made clear that his objective is to have the governors report to the president, to make them serve the Russian state and not the local mafias. The officially formulated goal of the centralising reforms is to eliminate thoroughly the wide-ranging and lavish corruption and manipulation which, by influencing local elections and politics, committed regional leaders to local interest groups rather than to Moscow, and, finally, to make local leaders personally responsible for the completion of developments implemented in their respective regions (Leksin 2005).

Administrative reforms have their internal logic, and it seems that these changes, by explicitly and deliberately eliminating local participation in decision-making through election, will inevitably reduce Moscow's ability to govern the country effectively in the future. The changes raise the question as to whether Russia will continue to be considered as a Federal state when power is divided between the centre and the regions. It seems likely that it will not. In addition, the administrative reforms will very likely enhance the political tensions in such republics as Tatarstan, where the dangers involved in the independence movements at the beginning of the 1990s could be averted by transferring certain areas of economic and political sovereignty from Moscow to Kazan. Basically, the reaction against considering Russia as a multi-ethnic/multi-territory state has begun. Ethnic territories, such as Tatarstan and the republics of the North Caucasus are downgraded to 'regions'. The autonomy of Tatarstan, which was outlined in a far-ranging treaty concluded with Moscow in February 2004, has been considerably curtailed since Putin came into power in 2000. Moscow no longer concludes similar power-sharing treaties with other regions, and it has also begun to restrict the validity of those treaties already in existence. The Russian Ministry of Nationalities (which was more or less removed from the ministerial system was reorganised in March 2004 as the Ministry of Regional Policy). In the course of the debate in Moscow on the appointment of regional governors, new suggestions were made with respect to limiting the authority of regional parliaments, to the direct appointment of mayors, and even to the total elimination of autonomous republics and regions, effectively demanding the return, albeit in an altered form, of the Tsarist provincial system (Shvetsov 2006).

The concept of a 'bottom-up' approach to federal organisation, most visibly supported by Tatarstan and its president, *Mintimer Sajmijev*, and which urged an even division of political power between the centre and regions, was rejected by Moscow, leaving no doubt that the Federal order, if it is to be retained at all, will be created on a 'top-down' basis. It will not be based on mutual agreement between the centre and the regions, but on what Moscow considers to be right to authorise the regions with (Vardomskiy 2006).

Fundamentals of the new regional development strategy

The Ministry of Regional Development completed the country's regional develop-ment strategy in 2005 (Kontsepciya strategii social'no-ekonomicheskogo razvitiya ...). The eight-chapter document gives a general survey of the regional differences of the country, and it outlines the requirements of regional policy. The document defines the basic principles of modern regional policy in the following terms:

1 *Multi-pole development policy.* Measures aiming to diminish regional differ-ences must be developed according to the features of the individual regions. Development resources must be concentrated and directed to poles which are able to initiate and maintain innovation processes. As the modernisation of the country has just begun, innovative measures should be directed towards growth centres. In order to realise this policy, pilot regions should be delineated (Table 6.8).

2   *Complexity.* In the interest of implementing the principle of equal opportunities set out in the constitution, and of realising national cohesion goals, budgetary assets should be redistributed to those regions which had been overlooked in the realisation of current programmes. Backward regions falling outside of the range of prioritised growth poles should not be ignored. Development concepts must also be prepared for backward regions. The duty of central federal bodies is to determine the regional development sources in a differentiated manner which takes into account all of the options which best serve reform.

3   *Complementary effectiveness, synergy.* Regional policy goals must be determined in close harmony with other reforms in progress in the country. In allocating regional development funds, the co-operation of the regions must be considered and individual forms of subsidy need to be reconciled.

4   *Differentiation of regional policy.* Russia's move towards global integration affects the individual regions of the country in different ways. There are considerable differences in development potential and in the situation of individual regions. Diversified and differentiated measures will be necessary in the different types of region (Table 6.12).

5   *Subsidiarity.* Local organisations must be given a great degree of independence in the social and economic development of regions. The most comprehensive means of this is the decentralisation of power.

The regional concept indicates that the modernisation of the country and an increase in GDP can be achieved by improving the activity of the regions. It defines the goals of central (federal) level regional policy as follows:

- To improve the living conditions of the population living in the territory of Russia.
- To establish conditions for stable, high-quality economic development.
- To strengthen the competitiveness of Russia and of its regions on the international market.

The draft lays down the goals for regional policy as:

1   *Establishing the competitiveness of Russia and its regions.* By considering aspects of the market economy it shall enable the achievement of economic growth resources through the concerted development of the economy and settlement network. Comprehensive infrastructural development programmes shall be initiated. Internationally competitive production clusters shall be organised in the innovation-intensive sectors.

2   *Encouragement of new regionalisation processes, reconsideration of regional resources.* Regional cohesion and the development of a unified economic area shall be established by respecting regional and local independence. Obstacles to the free movement of labour, goods and services are to be eliminated and regional markets have to be opened. Small- and medium-sized enterprises have to be supported.

Table 6.12 Problems and development tasks in the individual regions

Regional configurations	Development problems of the regions	Tasks to be undertaken
Raw material extraction regions	Infrastructural backwardness. Environmental and settlement development. Conflicts of interests.	Human resource development. Labour force settlement. Environmental programmes. Effective settlement policy.
Border regions Endangered zones	Extensive emigration of population. Narrowing of social infrastructure. Defective communication networks. Weak cultural interaction. Conflicts arising from identity. Problems threatening public order.	Organisation of cross-border co-operation. Establishment of transport, cultural and logistics centres. Extension of labour resources. Stabilisation of population numbers. Infrastructural improvement.
Regions affected by ethnic problems Regions threatening state order and the integrity of the country	Events threatening the safety and life of the population, state order and national integrity.	Strengthening of social security institutions. Revision of legal regulations. Strengthening of border guards and improvement of public security.
Technology transfer regions	Lack of workforce. Lack of industrial areas. Weak infrastructure. Poor business services.	Importing of developed technology. Encouragement of strategic investors. Human resources development.
Innovative regions	Lack of regional components of national innovation system. Weak institutions of market organisation. Lack of qualified labour force.	Elaboration of regional innovation strategies. Improvement of communication. Education of labour force. Organisation of technology transfer centres.
Cities of international importance	In Russia, the number of international cities being able to successfully participate in the global competition is limited. The city network is outdated; the cooperation between cities is weak.	Settlement of international corporate centres. Acceleration of infrastructural development. Establishment of high-quality urban environment. Establishment of administrative and service provider institutions of Federal importance.
Old industrial regions	Living conditions of inferior standards. Outdated technical facilities. Weak market relations. Lack of qualifications.	Organisation of industrial parks. Reindustrialisation. Rehabilitation of former industrial settlements. Diversification of the economy.
Newly industrialised regions	High rate of unemployment. Weak infrastructural fundamentals of city development. Many social conflicts. Low development level.	Programmes serving the migration or adaptation of the population. Employment enhancement measures. Extended budgetary resources. Infrastructural development.

Source: Konceptsiia strategii social'no-ekonomicheskogo razvitiia regionov Rossiiskoi Federacii, pp. 27–28.

3 *Development of human resources, enhancement of the spatial and sectoral mobility of the population.* Improvement of the country's population reproduction indicators, financial encouragement for young people to establish families must be established. Through the improvement of the educational

system, the skilled labour stock of the regions and the stability of the population must be increased. Migration programmes must be elaborated in order to harmonise the demographic and employment processes of the individual regions, in order to promote the adaptation of migrants to Russian society. The ethno-cultural behaviour of the population must be improved.

4   *Improvement of the ecological condition of the regions.* Economic development programmes must be subjected to environmental analysis. The ecological systems of the regions must be improved by energy- and raw material-saving technologies.

5   *Improvement of the quality of public administration, budgetary reforms in the regional units representing the regions.* Encouragement of public administrative organisations to use new management methods (strategic planning, efficiency- enhancing measures, different forms of co-operation, public–private partnership).

The draft document defines five priorities for regional development. First, it highlights the need for the fastest possible change from the policy of basic gap-reduction to that of polarised development. Different levels (international, regional, district) of growth centres of the country must be determined for concentrated development policy.

Regional units which:

1) are characterised by high commodity and demographic turnover rates;
2) have scientific and higher educational institutions of international and national importance;
3) produce innovations of national importance;
4) have growth rates above the national average;
5) have high-quality intellectual capital and a skilled labour resources;
6) have strategic partnerships already established, or be relatively easily established between the participants in public administration, the civil sphere and the economy; and
7) have the capacity to stimulate the development of neighbouring regions within a decade may be considered as 'incentivising' regions.

The document mentions the regional elements of the national innovation system as the *second* priority. With respect to this, it mentions several possibilities: the integration of closed regions (old military complexes) into regional economies, huge support for the seven Russian Science Cities in order to establish technological transfer centres, the designation of regional research universities (support for basic research and research transfer) and the organisation of special economic zones in the prosperous regions.

The *third* priority of the concept is industrial modernisation and the organisation of competitive industrial clusters. The employment of new industry organising possibilities, serving the development of a network-like economy, will face the traditionally vertically organised Russian industry with serious difficulties. Support for the new economy will necessitate a great deal of government assistance.

The *fourth* priority includes employment policy and population mobility activity and it enumerates countless means and institutions of modern European practice. The *fifth* priority refers to administrative and budgetary matters. The administrative modernisation programmes on the agenda include the reorganisation of inter-departmental co-operation and the establishment of monitoring systems. The reform of the budgetary sphere represents the biggest challenge. The overall financing system of local governments must be reorganised.

One measure serving the realisation of the strategic concept was the establishment of an inter-departmental committee within the framework of the Ministry of Regional Policy which will primarily undertake 'soft' reconciliation tasks, prepare itself to revise the implementation of the concept and will operate the monitoring network. The concept proposed to set up a federal regional development agency which would undertake concrete organisational and consulting tasks with respect to the implementation of regional and inter-sectoral programmes and would also manage resource co-ordination. The other institution to be set up is a National Regional and City Planning Institute, which, in the form of a holding company, would be an important player in regional planning.

References

Abdulatipov, R.G., Boltenkova, R.F. and Yarov, Ju.F. (1992) *Federalizm v istorii Rossii,* Mosco: Respublika.

Alampiev, P.M. (1959) *Ekonomicheskoe raionirovanie SSSR,* Tom 1. Moscow: Gospolitizdat.

Alampiev, P.M. (1963) *Ekonomicheskoe raionirovanie SSSR,* Tom 2. Moscow: Ekonomizdat.

Artobolevsky, S.S. (1993) 'Regional'naia politika Rossii: obzor sovremennogo sostoianiia', *Region,* 3: 21–37.

Artobolevsky, S.S. (2000) 'Recent trends in Russian regional policy and use of then EU countries experience', in Horváth, G. (ed.) *Regions and Cities in the Global World,* Pécs: Centre for Regional Studies, HAS, 192–201.

Bishaev, M.A. and Fiodorovich, M.M. (1961) *Organizaciia upravleniia promyslennym proizvodstvom,* Moscow: Gosudarstvennoe izdatel'stvo planovo-ekonomicheskoi literatury.

Bradshaw, M.J. and Palacin, J.A. (2004) *An Atlas of the Economic Performance of Russia's Regions,* Birmingham: University of Birmingham.

Bykova, S.S. (ed.) (2001) *Sibirskoe oblastnichestvo. Bibliografecheskii spravochnik,* Tomsk: Vodolei.

Congresses of the Communist Party of the Soviet Union, Moscow: Politizdat, 1972.

Dixon, S. (1999) *The Modernisation of Russia, 1676–1825,* Cambridge: Cambridge University Press.

Gerschenkron, A. (1962) *Economic Backwardness in Historical Perspectives. A Book of Essays,* Cambridge, MA: Belknap Press of Harvard University.

Gerschenkron, A. (1970) *Europe in the Russian Mirror: Four Lectures on Economic History,* London: Cambridge University Press.

Khrushchov, A.T. (1966) 'Sootnoshenie poniatii "territorial'naia organizaciia" i razmesheniia promyshlennosti' *Vestnik MGU. Seriia geogaficheskaia,* 3: 99–102.

Kolosovskiy, N.N. (1958) *Osnovy ekonomicheskogo raionirovaniia,* Moscow: Gospolitizdat.

Kolosovskiy, N.N. (1961) 'The territorial-production combination (complex) in Soviet economic geography', *Journal of Regional Science,* 1: 1–25.

Lappo, G.M. (2005) 'Itogi rossiiskoi urbanizacii k kontsu XX veka', in Glezer, O.B. and Poljan, P.M. (eds) *Rossiia i ieio regiony v XX veke: territoriia – rasselenie – migracii,* Moscow: OGI, 187–214.

Leksin, V.N. (2005) 'Prostranstvo vlasti i mir cheloveka', *Mir Rossii,* 1: 3–61.

Leksin, V.N. (2006) '"Regional'nye stolicy" v ekonomike i social'noi zhizni Rossii', *Voprosy ekonomiki,* 7: 84–93.

Lenin Collected Works. Volume 26., 33. Moscow: Progress Publishers, 1964.

Lynn, D.N. and Kuzes, I.Y. (2002) 'Regional variations in the implementation of Russia's federal district reform', *Demokratizatsiya,* 1: 5–18.

Lynn, D.N. and Kuzes, I.Y. (2003) 'Political and economic co-ordination in Russia's federal district reform: a study of four regions', *Europa-Asia Studies,* 4: 507–520.

Malle, S. (1985) *The Economic Organization of War Communism, 1918–1921,* Cambridge: University Press.

Novikov, A. (1998) *Risk Factors Associated with Russian Regions and Municipalities,* Moscow: Institute for Urban Economics.

Pavlenko, V.F. (1984) *Planirovanie territorial'nogo razvitiia,* Moskva: Ekonomika.

Pchelintsev, O.S. (1966) *Ekonomichesskoje obosnovanie razmeshcheniia proizvodstva,* Moscow: Nauka.

Pchelintsev, O.S. (1983) 'Intensifikatsiia i regional'noe upravlenie', *Regional'nye sistemy,* 3: 8–14.

Petrov, N. (2002) 'Seven faces of Putin's Russia: federal districts as the new level of state – territorial composition', *Security Dialog,* 1: 73–91.

Probst, A.E. (1965) *Effektivnost territotial'noi organizacii proizvodstva (metodologicheskie ocherki),* Moscow: Mysl'.

Sharpe, M.E. (2007) 'Russian society in different dimensions: based on materials from a Conference in memory of L. A. Gordon', *Russian Politics and Law,* 1: 31–50.

Shkolnikov, M.G. (1965) 'O territorial'noi organizacii promyshlennogo proizvodstva', in *Voprosy razmesheniia proizvodstva v SSSR,* Moscow: SOPS, 5–68.

Shtoulberg, B., Adamesku, A., Khistanov, V. and Albegov, M. (2000) 'Soviet regional policy', in Westlund, H., Granberg, A. and Snickars, F. (eds) *Regional Development in Russia. Past Policies and Future Perspectives,* Cheltenham: Edward Elgar Publishing, 37–83.

Shvetsov, A. (2006) 'V ozhidanii liberal'noi modernizacii gosudarstvennoi regional'noi politiki', *Kazanskii federalizm,* 3: 37–55.

Szamuely, L. (1979) *Az első szocialista gazdasági mechanizmusok. Elvek és elméletek* [The first socialist economic mechanisms. Principles and theories], Budapest: Közgazdasági és Jogi Könyvkiadó.

Tarkhov, S.A. (2005) 'Dinamika administrativno-territorial'nogo deleniia Rossii v XX veke', in Glezer, O.B. and Poljan, P.M. (eds) *Rossiia i ieio regioni v XX veke: territoriia – rasselenie – migracii,* Moscow: OGI, 33–75.

Treivish, A. (2002) 'Promyslennoszt' v Rossii za 100 let', in Danilova-Daniljana, V.I. and Stepanova, S.A. (eds) *Rossiya v okruzhaiushchem mire: 2002. Analitichesky iezhegodnik,* Moscow: Izdatel'stvo Mezhdunarodnogo nezavisimogo ekologopolitologicheskogo universiteta, 1–12.

Vardomskiy, L. (2006) 'Politika tsentra – instrumenty i rezul'taty', *Kazanskii federalizm,* 3: 89–96.

Venediktov, A.V. (1957) *Pravovoe polozhenie sovnarhoza i podvedomstvennyh iemu proizvodstvom,* Tallin: Valgus.

Westlund, H., Granberg, A. and Snickars, F. (eds) (2000) *Regional Development in Russia. Past Policies and Future Prospects,* Cheltenham: Edward Elgar.

Zaleski, E. (1967) *Planning Reforms in the Soviet Union, 1962–1966. An Analysis of Recent Trends in Economic Organization and Management,* Chapel Hill, NC: University of North Carolina Press.

Zolin, P. (2006) 'Sistema sel i poselenii', *Ekonomist,* 2: 76–84.

Zubarevich, N.V. (2006) 'Goroda kak centry razvitiia sovremennoi Rossii', in *Gorodskoi al'manah,* Vyp. 2. Moscow: Fond Institut ekonomiki goroda.

7 Regionalism in a unitary state

Decline of competitiveness of the
Hungarian regional development policy

Historical antecedents

In Europe, the state and national development of the nineteenth century shaped the regional structure of different countries in different ways. In the multi-centred states (Italy, Germany, Spain) the industrial upswing and the creation of a transport infrastructure involved a number of urban areas which underwent an almost identical development cycle, and the main driving forces of the economy, culture and politics rooted themselves in different places. In the monocentric countries (France, Austria, Hungary, most East-Central European countries and, partially, in the UK) the performance of the peripheries away from the dominant capitals was weak and the railway network was developed in a radial structure mainly to serve the state centre where cultural and political functions were also concentrated. The most important industrial stakeholder circles were generally interested in the development of integrated national markets, their economic interests on several occasions forcing regional elites to concede over issues of protectionist taxes versus the strengthening of regional autonomy.

In the Austro-Hungarian Monarchy, developing along the normal lines of the multi-polar economic area, similar economic interests prevailed. Owing to the dominance of the Hungarian agrarian economy, relatively little attention was paid within the Empire to the development of industry. Outside the capital, the largest industrial centre was Bratislava (Pozsony), whose manufacturing operations employed 6,000 people – followed by Timişoara (Temesvár), Arad, Braşov (Brassó), Miskolc, Debrecen and Pécs, whose industrial labour forces each amounted to approximately 4,000–5,000 (Beluszky 2001, 2002).

The modernisation programmes in Hungary in the Dual Monarchy era (railway and water-works construction and state-financed public works) introduced serious changes in the regional structure of the country, being overwhelmingly a force for concentration. Although governments in those days did not work out any spatial development policy by today's standards, they had to respond to the demands for modernisation being formulated in the underdeveloped regions of the country: various levels of action in the peripheral areas were supported by the National Economic Association (OMGE), while the first governmental development programme was started in the NE Carpathians at the end of the 1890s as a result of decisions arrived at by the Székely Congress. A governmental 'gap-bridging' strategy for the institutional system of Székelyföld (the land of the Székely people), one of the most backward areas of the country, was formulated. Although the nation's stormy history prevented the proposals from being executed, the Congress minutes are still interesting today and are useful methodological reading for specialists in regional development. At the end of nineteenth century, the National Statistical Office designated statistical regions of the country and started to collect statistical data (Figure 7.1).

After World War I, ongoing regional processes in historical Hungary were disrupted following the Trianon Treaty. The areas of economic development were fragmented, national borders intruded, natural gravity zones and hinterlands cut off and connections linking production factors severed. The economic structure of the new country showed an extreme degree of imbalance. The dynamic industrial development of previous decades mainly favoured Budapest, 50per cent of industrial employment, and 90 per cent in machine industry being concentrated there. Outside the capital, only Győr had a notable machine production capacity. The territorial structure of direct tax revenue, accurately reflecting the general performance capacity of the economy, draws a clear unipolar picture of the country: the contribution of Budapest to this item of state income amounted to 59 per cent (Table 7.1). On this basis, consequently, all the basic characteristics of today's regional structure had appeared at the beginning of the twentieth century: the highly developed city of Budapest, the relatively well developed region of North Transdanubia and the remaining (underdeveloped) two-thirds of the country.

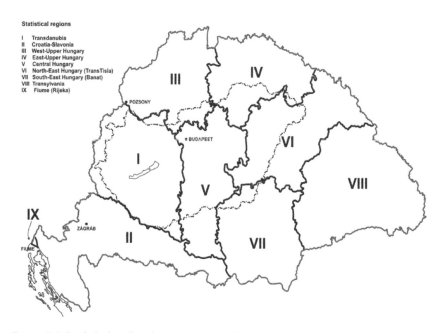

Statistical regions

I   Transdanubia
II Croatia-Slavonia
III West-Upper Hungary
IV East-Upper Hungary
V   Central Hungary
VI North-East Hungary (TransTisia)
VII South-East Hungary (Banat)
VIII Transylvania
IX Fiume (Rijeka)

Figure 7.1 Statistical regions in Hungary in 1900

Between the two World Wars these regional structural differences remained. Furthermore, the modernisation of the machine industry structure once again strengthened only the position of the capital, with 60 per cent of industrial employees being concentrated there in 1930. The centres of the dynamically developing industry lay, almost without exception. in the capital. R&D facilities were almost exclusively established here, and, in 1938, 54 of the 13,000 university students studied in Budapest institutions.

The development of the weak regional structure of new Hungary became the centre of debate in the second half of the 1920s. It was mainly academic experts in jurisprudence and public administration who debated the issues of the balance between centralising and de-centralising solutions, participants in other spheres of the economy and social management rarely expressing any opinions (Hencz 1973). The viewpoint of Kuno Klebelsberg, the Minister of Education at that time on the subject of development of intellectual centres outside Budapest could be considered a rare exception. As a criticism of state policy in the twentieth century, we can see what he wrote in the *Pesti Napló* on 15th of September, 1927:

> In Budapest the 'Lágymányos Pool' is the last open area and so either there will be a university-city there or, on the basis of foreign examples, we should consider the possibilities that the hubs of our scientific life should be relocated to Szeged and Debrecen… Is it only Budapest which can take a share of all state institutions and construction free of charge? This system cannot be sustained any longer, bearing in mind the principle of equitable distribution.
>
> (Klebelsberg 1928: 75)

Table 7.1 The regional structure of direct tax revenues[1] in Hungary, 1913

Region	Total of direct taxes, per thousand crowns (Korona)	Distribution, (%)	Population inhabitants (in thousands)	Distribution (%)	Allocation quotient[2]
Budapest	188,525	58.6	930	14.4	4.07
North Transdanubia	37,066	11.5	1,175	18.2	0.63
South Transdanubia	22,822	7.1	1,222	19.0	0.37
North Hungary	17,375	5.4	993	15.4	0.33
Great Plain	55,876	17.4	3,128	33.0	0.53
Total	321,664	100.0	6,448	100.0	1.00

Note: [1]Direct taxes (land tax, housing tax, earnings, income and corporate taxes, mining, transportation, capital gains and annuity tax, and other direct taxes) comprised 32 per cent of state revenues. [2]The intensity of concentration is represented by the well-known regional economic indicator, the allocation quotient, which is the quotient of the population ratio of the given region and the ratio of the direct taxes in that particular region.

Source: The author's own calculation on the basis of Edvi Illés and Halász (1921: 74).

Despite the fact that decentralisation in the priorities of the economic and cultural development of big cities in national organisational plans between the two World Wars was advocated by several intellectual groups, professional organisations and even by elements of government, major changes in the regional structure of the Hungarian economy did not take place.

In the 1950s, signs of regional development were hardly detectable at all, apart from the fact that developed industry was not exclusively limited to the capital, and the ratio of industrial workers there had decreased to 44 per cent. New industrial regions emerged, mainly in the Hungarian Uplands area, with Miskolc as its centre. Industrial centres were established in the areas of Nógrád, Pécs-Komló, Tatabánya, and Várpalota. Thus, Hungary's North-East to South-West directional industrial axis was formed.

The extremely centralised state and economic system could not accept that underdeveloped regions or settlements were attempting to go ahead on their own initiative. The council system, introduced in 1950, dismantled the otherwise under-developed local government system of the settlements and decreed that the sole task of these councils should be to carry out orders from the centre.

The reform of the economic administration in 1968 opened up a new era for regional development too. To a certain extent, decentralised economic decisions supported geographically dispersed development, and an increasingly larger part of the settlement network became affected by the modern economy. In 1971, a new regional development policy was set by means of two decisions of the Council of Ministers. For the first time in the history of spatial development, a socio-political aim was set: the alignment of the living conditions of the population in the different regions of the country.

However, spatial and settlement development reform followed the change of the economic administration after an interval of some years, but this delay in terms of the content was considerable. Meanwhile, opposition to the reform was preparing a strong counter-offensive and re-centralisation started. For example, the regulation of the financial arrangements system of local authorities removed the real economic basis from local government as had been originally planned. In the 1970s, central interference increased still further – a negative response to increasing economic difficulties.

Economic regulations introduced by the reforms had their effect only somewhat indirectly, and direct regulation proved effective only to a limited extent. Such regulations were the creation of the central spatial development funds, which amounted to some 2,5 billion forints during the fourth five-year plan (of which 800 million forints were spent for the transfer of industry from the capital, 400 million for the industrial restructuring of the mining areas, while the rest served the industrialisation of underdeveloped regions (Enyedi 1983).

The fact that industrial companies established many manufacturing units into rural towns and the larger villages as a continuation of the large-scale development to increase the size of the labour force, had a very important influence on development. From the end of the 1960s to the middle of the 1970s, a very strong regional distribution of industrial production took place, and, since that time, very little has changed in the regional spread of industry. As a result of the great importance of corporate decisions, the geographical location of new industrial units came to reflect their interests. Forty per cent of rural industrial units had their headquarters in Budapest, and, in the case of the larger units in the machinery industry, more than 70 per cent were managed by companies in the capital. Therefore, the very wide geographical spread of industry produced only low numbers in urban centres. We can nevertheless mention several modern rural industrial establishments, although it frequently happened that plants established in underdeveloped areas were allocated simpler, less modern and unprofitable – often polluting – activities, while R&D, organisational and decision-making functions were concentrated in corporate headquarters. Regional effects appeared as a form of re-creation of underdevelopment, in which underdevelopment was indicated not by a lack of industry, as earlier, but by its old-fashioned structure and technology.

The 40 years of centrally-planned economy produced an ambiguous situation in the development of the Hungarian regional structure. Delayed industrialisation, several elements of which resembled the industrialisation of the West European peripheries, contributed to a slowdown in the growth of regional imbalances, but it also blocked the spatial dissemination of regional driving forces. The reason for this was unquestionably political in origin. We cannot speak of decentralisation in real terms, since the regional establishment of industry was not linked to power-sharing. The narrow concept of decreasing regional disparities concentrating on the superficial indicators of underdevelopment attached to infrastructure favoured the survival of the redistribution system.

After transformation, and in spite of the fact that important changes took place in all areas of activity with a bearing on regional development, the driving forces of real decentralisation have still not asserted themselves. In the 1990s the Regional Development Act set up institutions and provided a few tools, but new differentiation processes appeared in the regional structure of the country, now moved by market forces. This was despite the fact that the concentration level of post-industrial regional driving forces was as high as had been experienced in earlier development periods.

A one-pole country

In terms of territorial disparities, Hungary shares characteristics with other EU countries. As in Italy and Germany, the disparities in Hungary between large geographical areas are significant where an East–West divide was clear after the transition. However, unlike Italy and Germany, disparities are also evident at smaller territorial levels. Central Hungary, Central Transdanubia and West Transdanubia are the best performing territories which are developing more quickly than the national average. South Transdanubia and, even more so, North Hungary and the Northern and Southern Great Plain, however, are burdened with problems and fall short of the average in almost all respects. The Southern Great Plain represents the median in some respects, showing signs of revival and growth potential (Table 7.2).

Table 7.2 GDP per capita by region in Hungary, 2004

Region	GDP per capita as percentage of national average	GDP per capita as percentage of EU27, PPS
Central Hungary	163	106
of which: Budapest	213	139
Central Transdanubia	94	62
West Transdanubia	99	65
South Transdanubia	69	45
North Hungary	66	43
Northern Great Plain	64	41
Southern Great Plain	68	44
Hungary Total	100	65

Source: National Accounts, Hungary, 2004–2005.

The economic changes of the transition period have led to greater territorial disparities. Highly specialised regions with little flexibility in rigidly-organised heavy industry, mining or agriculture were strongly affected while those with a more flexible structural base recovered from the depression more rapidly and produce higher-than-average growth and employment rates. The winning regions managed to reorganise their industry so as to upgrade products and processes permanently and target competitive market niches. At the same time, their attractiveness was reinforced by the new economic policy put in place during the transition based on tax allowances to joint ventures, foreign investment and new business. The most prosperous territories include those with a high share of manufacturing – especially machinery – and a large export potential resulting from high FDI. Foreign capital has been concentrated in the economic centres, protecting the renewal of the economic structure, still favouring Budapest and its surrounding areas (OECD 2001).

Disparities in income levels, unemployment, and poverty are high in Hungary. The exclusion of unskilled workers from the labour market and the impoverishment of many households have created social problems. Variegated industrial mix, the concentration of FDI, and highly uneven R&D capacities, all contribute to this lack of cohesion and tend to reinforce existing territorial dichotomies: East–West, centre–periphery, and urban–rural.

Budapest and its surrounding area have always dominated Hungary, but never so significantly as today. One in five Hungarians lives in Budapest, which comprises the country's smallest and most densely populated territory with the most dense economic activities and social facilities. Its share of GDP in 2004 amounted to 34.6 per cent of all Hungarian output. Although its share of industrial employees significantly decreased during the period (to less than 20 per cent), its share of business employees reached almost 40 per cent. In addition, industries with the highest levels of R&D and innovation are still based in Budapest. Its dominance in the service sector and high-technology industry, and its outstanding infrastructure and telecommunication facilities are some of the reasons for the heavy weight of the capital in Hungary's spatial structure (Horváth 2005). Even in terms of social facilities such as health services and education, Budapest is much better endowed than its population would suggest.

Despite the fact that, from the end of the 1920s until today, all the various documents have contained the idea that major cities had their importance in the creation of their own regions, and short-termist political elites have continually obstructed the possibility of any critical mass being created (apart from their own county seat) which could have become the force behind the decentralisation of power (Konrád and Szelényi 2000). Even today we can quote several examples of decisions being generated in county seats motivated solely by the political wisdom of the day. Some three-quarters of a century later, Klebelsberg's dilemma was resolved (not by accident) by university campuses lined up around the Lágymányos (Muddy Pool), while, in the provincial intellectual centres, institutions of higher education are forced to integrate (formally) to obtain small grants. In the current regional structure of Hungarian higher education and research, it is a pointless exercise to discuss the future of knowledge-based regional development, the size and the weight of the larger university centres being unsuited to solving new tasks (Table 7.3). Only one-quarter of university students are to be found in the four university centres immediately following those in Budapest, while, in other European countries with a similar population level to Hungary's, the proportion is one-half or one-third (Figure 7.2).

Hungary is regaining its former position within Europe as it undergoes a profound transformation. These changes, however, are not being felt equally in all regions. Regional economic, social and infrastructural disparities are continuously growing both among counties and regions. Performances diverged and disparities increased when the period of growth was established. Fuelled by substantial waves of FDI, Western Hungary, as well as the capital and its surrounding area, were the

Table 7.3 The distribution of students in higher education among the regional centres, 1938–2008

University centre	Student numbers			Distribution (%)		
	1938	1985	2008	1938	1985	2008
Budapest	7,178	44,900	159,501	54.3	45.2	43.4
Debrecen	1,103	7,291	23,055	8.3	7.3	6.3
Miskolc	312	3,953	13,143	2.4	4.0	3.6
Pécs	1,342	6,480	23,150	10.1	6.5	6.3
Szeged	1,151	8,999	27,000	8.7	9.1	7.4
Others	2,142	27,721	121,095	16.2	27.9	33.0
Total	13,228	99,344	366,947	100.0	100.0	100.0

Source: The author's own calculations on the basis of the Hungarian statistical yearbooks.

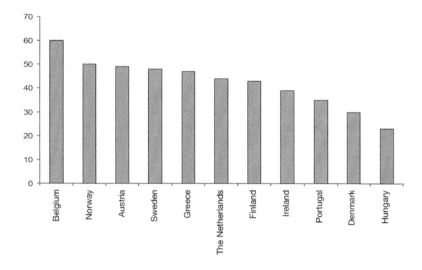

Figure 7.2 The four largest university centres outside the capital – their share of numbers
of students in higher education, 2008, per cent

Source: The Author's design on the basis of national statistical yearbooks.

fastest to restructure and to take advantage of cumulative effects, whereas counties
in the Northeast still suffer from the difficult restructuring of heavy industries and
mono-sectoral activity. The the Great Plain and the Southeast are experiencing a
decline in agriculture. While North-Eastern regions were among the most developed during the communist period, growth has now shifted to the West. This
East-West divide, the trend towards metropolitanisation encouraging suburbanisation around Budapest, a rural exodus and the accompanying process of
urbanisation are increasing territorial fragmentation. These trends are widening
income disparities between the countryside and the main cities (Horváth 2005).

The changes in performance can, first of all, be explained by the level of industrial
production, employees, investment and export capacities. In the period 2001–2003,
the value of investment in manufacturing industry in Pest county was €1.3 billion,
€0.4 billion in Győr-Moson-Sopron county, €0.1 billion in Somogy, and €0.2 billion
in Szabolcs. Similar discrepancies can also be noted in industrial exports. Three-
quarters of the industrial production of Győr-Moson-Sopron and two-thirds of that
of Fejér county reaches foreign markets, while only one-quarter does so from
Baranya and Tolna counties.. The export of the Audi Hungária Company in Győr is
15 times higher than that of the total industry in Baranya county (formerly a highly
industrialised county dominated by mining and light industry).

The emigration of young professional intellectuals from the regional centres is
a further warning sign. Well-qualified university graduates cannot find jobs
requiring high qualifications, which is a threat to fulfilling the concepts of the
development of the knowledge-based economy. It is a common complaint that the

universities produce too many graduates, but we should also consider whether the economy has been intellectualised to the required level. Developing business services, R&D and international functions, which currently show up weakly in the regions, might result in thousands of highly qualified jobs, and these could clearly serve the development of the economy.

Modifying these trends is recognised as being the key to the modernisation of Hungary, since they are a major reason for the weakening competitiveness of the country. A country where there is an extremely high concentration of modern regional development driving forces is not capable of establishing an active and competitive cohesion policy.

The Hungarian regions occupy positions in various groups of the European ranking list. The Central Hungarian region can be found at the end of the middle third of this ranking list, together with Corsica (France), Sardinia (Italy), the Highlands and Islands region of Scotland, Castile and León (Spain) and Namur (Belgium). The second most developed Hungarian region, Western Transdanubia, stands at the head of the bottom third of the ranking list. This group of regions is exclusively from the Cohesion countries and includes the North, Central and Alentejo regions of Portugal and the Peloponnese and Thrace (Greece). The position of the Central Transdanubian region is similar and to some Greek and Portuguese regions and with other, more developed, East European regions. The remaining Hungarian regions, alongside other, exclusively East European, regions are ranked in the middle of the bottom third.

If we regard Budapest as a separate territorial unit, then, with its €33,000 per capita (PPS) GDP, 145 per cent of the EU27 average, it would feature in the group of the 30 most developed regions.

Building up of the institutions of regional development policy

The formal renewal of regional policy

Since 1990, a series of reforms decentralising state administration, re-establishing the autonomy of local government and delegating to them broad responsibilities in delivering local public services were introduced. The reforms of the early 1990s, and in particular the reform of local government, were characterised by the strengthening of the role of the locality (municipalities, local communities) at the expense of the counties. The emphasis of this first wave of reform was on demo-cracy and independence from the central state, while efficiency and rationality, important concerns in Western European states (Stewart and Stoker 1995), were somewhat neglected. Fragmentation, low levels of efficiency and the near-doubling of local authorities were the main outcome of this first wave of reform.

The establishment of the regions was supposed to create a forum for interest intermediation and policy formulation more close to the central state. However, the limited role of both local public actors and pressure groups, such as chambers of commerce, NGOs, and so on, in the regional development councils after the 1999 amendment of the Act and the key role of sectorally-minded central state officials in the regional development councils has substantially decreased their role as an alternative locus of interest articulation at the meso-level of government. Therefore, the identification of the main actors in terms of interest representation is found primarily at county level (Figure 7.3).

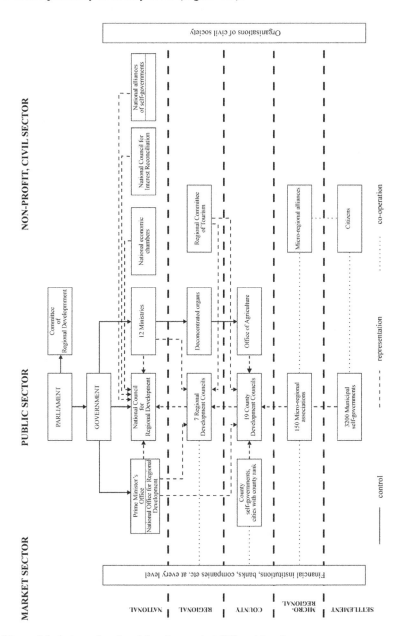

Figure 7.3 Actors of regional development at different levels
Source: Pálné Kovács et al. (2004).

The importance of the first Regional Development Act is illustrated by the fact that it has made possible decentralised development and the incorporation of the concepts of social justice and impartiality into politico-economic decisions. To fulfil these basic constitutional requirements, the Act established institutions and made decisions regarding financial tools. There might be a possibility for different regions to assemble their ideas and to supplement the resources of local stakeholders with central subsidy.

Hungarian policy was the first in East-Central Europe to elaborate comprehensive regulation for the regional modernisation of the country. However, the Regional Development Act and the Parliamentary Decree on the Concept of Regional Development – due to incomplete reforms in other spheres of social administration – could not in themselves bring about the necessary change of direction. Although the reports on Hungary made by the European Commission since 1998 continuously warned of the gaps in EU compatibility of regional policy, it was always subject to the narrow political interests of the Hungarian government of the day.

In most accession countries, regional development acts were introduced and both central and local institutions of regional policy were established, while in Hungary the Act was amended unfavourably and central government's administration organisation for regional development was changed several times (a similar amendment was introduced only in Romania). All of this could give the impression that, in Hungary, the concepts of regional development are used only under pressure from the EU and that only formal requirements are targeted for fulfilment.

This impression, however, was, step-by-step, turned into reality. In the second half of the 1990s, the enthusiasm of the numerous professional groups active in regional matters had worked out a large number of regional strategies, concepts and programmes, but, by the early 2000s, they had run out of steam, and belief in the viability of decentralisation had been destroyed by central government's passivity and further attempts to centralise.

Disappointment peaked with the National Development Plan, which, contrary to original expectations, contained only one regional operative programme for the 2004–2006 period. In the Czech Republic and Poland almost 40 per cent of the subsidy available for development was directly at the disposal of the regions, while in Hungary this proportion was 18 per cent. Following the subsequent abandonment of the earlier regional concepts, pro-regionalists, losing hope, became interested in traditional mechanisms, reviving lobbyist bargaining, something which they had earlier wished to forget. Hungarian regional policy, instead of becoming Europeanised, fell instead into the trap of provincialism.

Resources are fragmented, and the strategies and programmes of the regions and the counties are not considered significant. The relatively small, although continuously expanding, regional development resources are contested for by micro-regional stakeholder groups, and, as a result of occasional alliances and concessions, effectively based on existentialist motives, a minimum amount of development resources is spread thinly over different areas of the county. Meanwhile, many continue to gaze piously and in hope towards the heavens, and so, perhaps, it is small wonder that they cannot see the neighbouring county, town or university, amongst which there is no ongoing debate about the fulfilment of common aims, since their leaders are busy lobbying in Budapest, sometimes squabbling with each other for peanuts.

The legal regulation of regional development

With the Act on Regional Development and Physical Planning of 1996 and its amendment in 1999, the Hungarian government introduced a system of regional development whose most distinctive feature was the creation of a new regional level. The macro-regions are supposed to implement regional policy and assume or co-ordinate responsibilities which lie beyond the scope of the local level. The European Union has had a strong impact on shaping the new level since it considers an adequate territorial structure imperative for implementing its various pre-accession and Structural Funds. The new regional actor is generally viewed as a central government partner for regional policy implementation; some consider it a core for a full government level between central and municipal levels. However, since regional development institutions run parallel to the existing framework, the new system has created some confusion. The distribution of responsibilities between new regional development bodies and existing government institutions is unclear, and disputes on project implementation are quite common. Institution building is a core issue for decentralising the Hungarian State (Pálné *et al.* 2004).

The present state of development planning in Hungary is characterised by the comparatively strong role of local government, by an, as yet unclear, role of the new regions, and by a, rather traditional and partly contradictory, handling of responsibilities at national level. As described earlier, new regions were created in Hungary during the second half of the 1990s. First, the government introduced the statistical designation of the seven macro-regions and encouraged the establishment of voluntary Regional Development Councils (RDCs). However, since counties were free to choose their partners to unite into regions, the statistical regional system and the development regional system did not match. Furthermore, many counties belong to more than one region. Several RDCs were established, although most have not been operational for some considerable time, due mainly to a lack of any firm commitment to the creation of a regional level and strong resistance from the counties.

The introduction of the regional level has not clarified power-sharing in the Hungarian territorial government and regional development system. One of the crucial issues of Hungary's current regional development approach concerns, on the one hand, the still undefined future role of today's counties, and, on the other, that of the newly created regions – as well as the role of the central state. While there is probably no reason to question the opportunity to maintain and strengthen local government at county level, whether the size of the country justifies dividing development planning and programming into county and regional levels is questionable. Aspects of efficiency and the European Union requirement to dispose of operational development programmes at NUTS 2 level might lead to the conclusion that a single level should be responsible for preparing and implementing development plans and programmes.

At local level, the practical ability to prepare and decide upon feasible development programmes based on priorities determined in corresponding regional development plans depends to a large extent on the existing financial system. The fact that counties and regions do not have sufficient financial resources to take their own decisions independently of complementary funding decisions at national level seriously handicaps any effective decentralisation (Horváth 2001).

In sum, the introduction of regions seems to be a reaction to the current weakness of the county level rather than a response to a specific need for a new political level. Although most policies can probably be performed or implemented at county level also, the geopolitical context and the need to ensure EU policy compatibility should obviously be taken into account. It is important, however, that the introduction of regions does not lead to confusion on the delimitation of power between the two proximate levels. If both are to be maintained, the dual system of counties and regions needs to be clearly assigned both tasks and policy responsibilities.

Co-operation in regional development decisions

The rationale of the Act on Regional Development is based on the concept of partnership. However, it also takes into consideration the basic thesis that regional development is not the result of separate actions or decisions, but the product of a large number of market participants playing a common game. The operation of the market economy partly depends upon individual decisions, but collective (governmental or other group) choices also have an important role. The emergence of a specialised economic science studying collective choice also indicates that serious difficulties appear when we wish to make common choices on the basis of individual values (Pearce 1986).

Collective activity is the basis of the development of partner connections. Partnership is essentially a formal or informal agreement among the actors in regional development to achieve a specific economic objective. This objective is, in many cases, rather general and formal, but there are also examples of exact conditions of co-operation being recorded in a contract. Consequently, in these cases, co-operation will extend beyond compiling the common objectives to taking common steps. However, the participants in a partnership frequently do not have equal rights and chances of participation in respect of their financial resources. We can, therefore, differentiate between average and leading participants.

The number of those organisations which exist in the sphere of the above group of stakeholders is quite high. Co-operation among them can take various forms, depending on local and regional conditions. In categorising the possible partnerships, a number of markedly characteristic types can be differentiated (Bennett and Krebs 1991). No matter what form of co-operation is in question, it should satisfy two basic types of requirement at one and the same time: it should be connected to a development activity and actively contribute to sustaining the co-operation. To become an important participant, any partner should know precisely the aims of development, their regional effects, the expected consequences and the steps to be taken.

Partnerships among the participants in the vertical levels of the economic processes are normally regulated by Act of Parliament, but the fostering of horizontal relationships can be provided only partially with the help of legal tools. Much more important than this is the fact that the critical mass involved in the outcome and processes of the development should agree on their mutually supported, collective aims (Marin 1990).

The regional development practice in Western Europe also had difficulties with the organisation of partnerships, almost a decade being needed to experience the characteristics of the operation and to suggest successful forms to those regions desiring co-operative regional development. Currently we already have access to sufficient West European analysis to be able to determine the general and specific features of partnership or to draw conclusions for Hungarian regional development (Bennett and Krebs 1994; Leonardi and Nanetti 1990).

The first characteristic feature is that the type, the leading actors and the partic- ipants in the partnerships show noticeable differences in different types of region. In less developed regions, the local authorities and the mayor are the key figures in development, while, in the rural areas, the number of participating actors is much higher. The most diversified partnerships are to be seen in the industrially deteri- orating regions, and here the number of actors is the highest. The leading positions within the programmes are, in most cases, in the hands of regional and local government, but the development agencies and chambers of commerce also play an important role.

The second characteristic feature, especially important in Hungary, is that universities and research institutions currently participate in development programmes as often as the financial and the private enterprise sectors, proving that development is innovative in character. We cannot overlook the fact that, in one-half of the programmes, the regional authority plays the leading role, although this potential key player is currently inadequate in Hungary. We should, therefore, accept that building up partnerships under domestic circumstances will have to face a considerable number of difficulties.

The third characteristic is the multi-coloured nature of the co-operation activities. The partnership is not exclusively financial but rather a co-operation covering a wide range of regional development actors.

The fourth characteristic feature is linked to the cascade connection between the elements of the co-operation network. Although participants are closely linked together in co-operation, depending on the activities and on the type of region, dominant partnerships can be seen. The most frequent forms of co-operation involve groups of local authorities, regional government, and other local actors.

Consequently, the key to success in decentralised regional economic develop- ment is control over local development projects and the new domestic regional development system must also face this problem. The circle of activities which have an influence on regional development is widening, and the development factors most appropriate for a given area need to be selected from the wide range of programmes available, and partners need to be found to carry out and finance them.

The new regional development system in Hungary also increased the number of the development tasks, widening both the circle of participants and the channels of finance. Consequently, the structure of the institutional system, and the rules of operation and power need to be examined from the standpoint of whether they represent sufficient organisational power. In our opinion, the internal operational system and powers of most regional development actors are still incapable of organising efficient partnerships. Local authorities are perhaps best prepared for participation in regional development programmes, although the office structure of larger cities and the committee structure of their assemblies still do not fit the differentiated tasks emerging in these settlements. County councils can only be very modest players, while the chambers, absorbed in building up their own organisations, can in no way be regarded as a dynamising force. The county development councils, therefore, will not be in an easy situation, since the partners involved will be mainly interested in obtaining subsidies rather than in combining their own resources (Pálné *et al.* 2004).

Although the new Act on Regional Development provided a theoretical opportunity for introducing West European-style regional development practice into Hungary, the fetishism surrounding settlement independence, infrastructural underdevelopment and, last but not least, the development practice followed in recent years in Eastern Hungary together foreshadow that county councils would prioritise the removal of infrastructural weaknesses.

Traditional infrastructural development, however, is incapable of creating jobs, of bringing about a reasonable increase in export capacity and of digging out the roots of underdevelopment: market institutions, product and technology development, the financial infrastructure of rural enterprises and financial organisations capable of combining scattered resources are needed in each region of Hungary. Suitable responses to these key issues of modernisation and competitive readiness can be given only within the framework of a comprehensive decentralisation policy.

The new paradigm and the institution of the region

The region is a territorial unit serving the sustainable growth of the economy and the modernisation of the spatial structure, having independent financial resources, following an autonomous development policy and equipped with the rights of self-government. On the basis of this definition (whose components have naturally changed in different ways in the various periods of European development) regions so far do not exist in Hungary, except as naturally defined by certain geographers (Tóth 2004). Form without content in itself is incapable of influencing the regional structure of the country in a favourable direction, decentralising the new regional driving forces and creating the terms of multi-polar development. The region defined as the framework of regional research is incapable of organising the regional driving forces of the twenty-first century without powers, institutions and tools.

Hungary needs regions since European regional development proves unequivocally that the region as the sub-national administration level, based on concepts of self-government, with its economic capacities and structural potential is:

- the optimal spatial framework for the assertion of regional policy targeting economic development;
- the appropriate area for the operation of post-industrial, regional organisational forces and the development of their reciprocal connections;
- the important setting for the enforcement of regional and social interests;
- the most appropriate size of spatial unit to construct modern infrastructure and the professional, organisational, planning and executive institutions of regional policy; and
- the defining element of the decision-making process of the EU's Regional and Cohesion Policy.

The decentralised state structure system can be established organically as a result of complex, legal regulation. The concepts providing its pre-requisites should be established in the constitution (or, lacking consensus, in a decentralisation law), laying down the reciprocal share of powers between state and region, contributing to the mitigation of spatial differences and creating equal opportunities for accessing public services, fostering economic decentralisation and delegating rights and resources to local authorities and the regions.

In the transition period, the strengthening of the spatial development regions cannot be postponed. In the years following accession, Hungary's ability to utilise Structural Funds will be the decisive reference for the regional political decisions of the EU. Post-2007, regions must be maximally prepared to be able to manage directly the regional operative programmes. To achieve this, their legitimacy should be strengthened in the spirit of partnership, their professional level in terms of efficiency and transparency and their resources in terms of additionality, complexity and concentration.

The need for regionalisation in today's Hungary emerged neither from the public administration point of view nor EU membership. At stake is the growth of the Hungarian economy, the modernisation of the country, a decrease in regional differences and the future positions to be occupied in the European division of labour. Regionalism might be the new power for initiating modernisation in Hungary at the beginning of the twenty-first century. Moreover, the current regional institutional system of spatial development is unable to fulfil even its original aims. The regional agencies basically have the task of collecting projects; and so they serve to execute the central will and not to realise regional ideas. In the performance of the regional agencies, there are considerable differences between innovative and traditional, execution-oriented agencies.

As the results of empirical research show, the decentralised model evokes the strongest opposition precisely within the circle of government ministries. The results also indicate that most of those involved in the creation of regions support reform in theory, but they are not convinced that the current regional borders and centres have been well defined, and their regional ties are limited to a narrower circle. However, on the basis of opinions expressed by the actors, it seems that it would be impossible to create more acceptable regional borders than the current ones. It is extremely important not to distract attention from the basic issues, that is, the functions which regions should have and what rights the central state administration should delegate. Even the ministries now seem to be shocked that they themselves might face change. But why should central state administration assess applications for a couple of million forints? Why is working out the vital sectoral operative programmes not the most important task for central state administration? Why are there no well-elaborated, long-term development concepts?

Not only operative, but also important strategic planning tasks can be delegated to the regions. Moreover, because in the new programming period, the method suggested by the central offices cannot be used. The tried and tested methods from one corner of the country cannot be used in another corner. Each region should work in its own way. The successful EU member states are those where the country is developing along various regional orbits.

Throughout the development of Hungarian regionalism, the interests of economic and societal actors are apparent in addition to political reasoning. In the period of the planned economy, establishing an optimal market size played a role, albeit to a limited extent. Large corporations weighed regional factors while organising their subsidiaries. However, the spatial proximity of such units did not result in their efficient co-operation, and the interior economic cohesion of various regions could not strengthen. Elements of vertical control remained dominant in economic administration.

The possibilities of involving spatial considerations in the economy increased due to changes outside the state borders in the mid-1980s. At the end of the 1970s, a period of organising cross-border co-operation agreements was started in the member states of the EEC. The Alps-Adriatic Working Community, spurred by initiatives from Italy, became a notable Central European venue of institutionalised interregional co-operation. The founding Italian, German and Austrian regions wished to make use of the possibilities in co-operating with East European economies, and administrative units of Hungary became the first in Eastern Europe to become members of the Working Community. Participation in its working groups widened the international experiences of Hungarian county officials. At the beginning of transformation, these representatives hoped that democratic government would also result in the decentralisation of external political and economic powers. This concept also motivated the thinking of economic actors operating in the western territories of the country. Unfortunately, changes in the Hungarian political system were not supportive of the aims of institutionalised para-diplomacy. While Hungary currently plays an active role in organising cross-border co-operations (18 were registered as of 2010), their effects on economic development are barely visible (Baranyi 2003).

There has also been no meaningful progress in regionalising public administration. Although parties have made declarations about regionalism and the decentralisation of state organisation in election programmes, their promises were quickly forgotten in a governing position due to their political interests. Notable changes occurred in 2006, when the socialist-liberal government brought before Parliament a planned law on creating administrative regions. The opposition, however, refused its support, and so, since the measure would have required a two-thirds majority, it failed to be enacted (Pálné Kovács 2009, 2011).

Political argument against regional public administration claims unfavourable changes in the accessibility of services. Opponents of regionalism stress that the new administrative level would be more distant from citizens, and that, in consequence, access to quality services would become harder. Fears of weakening local democracy also play a serious part. Opponents expect constraints on local independence and worsening financial means for municipalities. Occasionally, arguments against regions also demonstrate a degree of Euro-scepticism, while populist groups think of the need for establishing regions merely as an obligatory formal requirement set by the European Commission. Naturally, these simplified and merely politically motivated views are erroneous, as establishing regional public administration also requires the strengthening of local services, the latter contributing to the rising living standards of inhabitants, not to mention the fact that transforming the (by now obsolete) unitary state into a decentralised one involves transferring powers from the central governments to the regions.

In 2010, due to the huge two-thirds majority of the conservative government, the process of regionalisation and slow decentralisation stopped, and a new model of the centralised state started to develop, including county and district-level government offices (Buzogány and Korkut 2013; Pogátsa 2013). All the institutional results of the regionalisation have been cast away, and the subsidiarity has disappeared from political vocabulary.

Possible future images of the regional tier

One of the most frequent elements in professional and political argument supporting a comprehensive reform of Hungarian public administration is matching the structural framework of regional development functions with EU requirements. It is evident that the region could be the optimal size for regional development, not only because of the involvement of NUTS 2 regions in relation to Structural Funds, but also because, in Hungary, counties are quite incapable of achieving success in the economic competition of the European regions.

Consequently, the strengthening of the regions in relation to spatial development is necessary, even where there might be doubts regarding the viability of total regional reform in the near future. Undoubtedly, the most successful organisational model for managing economic and spatial development would be a directly elected, self-governing authority where the region is a complex unit with multi-layered functions and institutions.

On this basis, the key issue of public administration reform is how development management functions appear at regional level. In addition to the sphere of authority and resource allocation, it is most important to give serious thought to organisational, operational and executive questions – that is to say, to the management of regional development, which, in many respects, lays different demands on public administration.

Regardless of which organisational model is the most appropriate, we can state, in general, that, in laying the foundations of regional competitiveness, the pre-eminent factors are:

- strategic alliances;
- public and private partnerships;
- inter-sectoral coordination;
- entrepreneurial activity by the public sector;
- inclusion of local actors in solving current economic and social problems;
- support and strengthening of synergies, system integration; and
- the capacity to renew the organisation.

To catalyse these functions, to integrate the various resources and actors and to foster and build up networks – these are the tasks of regional government. This involves a more active assumption of responsibility than would be necessary with a liberal market model, but one which is significantly less centrally directed and less hierarchical than the welfare model. In the current economic development period, regional authorities need to say not what must be done, but, rather, how and with whom.

By way of summary, we can state that decentralisation, the spread of non-governmental inter-sectoral forms, networking and complexity are the key terms which characterise the management of regional policy in general. The main objective is not to create a new layer of local government, but to achieve what is necessary. In those cases where regional-local authorities are operating, it would be appropriate for them to be delegated planning rights. At the same time, it is questionable whether the body, no matter how democratically elected, would satisfy partnership requirements. It should, therefore, be guaranteed that the concept of partnership be asserted in the planning process, at the very least in a consultative capacity. The planning arrangement mechanism can even be regulated by regional authorities, although it would be safer to introduce some form of compulsory regulation for this purpose, for example through the establishment of parallel evaluative bodies.

There is a solution available from within the circle of member states of the EU, in which the central law details those bodies which must be included in the planning process, although the decision as to the forms and details of the process remain within the power of planning bodies. Consequently, the current regional development councils, with only minor changes to their composition and sphere of authority, could remain solid institutions of the Hungarian regional institutional system.

Regional authorities can take over the resource distribution role currently played by development councils at regional and county level. Regarding resources, regional authorities will decide in terms of size and targets, depending on whether there will be county-level distribution and whether county-regional development councils will survive. In addition to size, other highly important issues are the responsibility for resource allocation and the operation of the different subsidising systems, the procedural order and mechanisms local authorities will use to carry out these responsibilities.

Presumably, even in respect of the distribution of national resources, it is not practical to carry out direct institutional management of project systems. Should the body be given a role in operating normative, state-subsiding systems, the rules and aims of distribution and application should appear in institutional decisions, and then the body should also be endowed with controlling rights.

Obviously, this body could make decisions regarding project applications which it had initiated itself, including the self-financing part. In consequence, authority over domestic resources does not mean only the power to distribute those resources, but also to finance self-initiated projects. From this point of view, it would be highly important that the regional authority itself should be the initiating partner of the economic and private sectors and the local authorities of the settlements.

The issues relating to planning and finance include the mechanism to be used for the harmonisation of central, regional and other resources and for EU and private sources to be collected for the projects aiming for EU support. It has become clear that introducing planning contracts on the basis of the French example, already applied by Poland in its regional development policy, would be expedient. Regions might have a role of key importance in the signing of the planning contracts, since only directly elected, regional authorities can be considered to be a legitimate partner and to carry sufficient weight to set against that of central government. The main question is the mechanism for the harmonisation of regional and central priorities, the linking of resources and the assertion of common priorities. In planning contracts, it is possible to agree on common development priorities, including the level and form of state intervention (by subsidy, loan or loan guarantee, etc.). This pattern is convenient, even in the respect that subsidy from the state can be also planned alongside the region's own resources.

The planning contracts would be a part of the state budget and would have the result that, unlike the operational budgets, they would cover periods longer than a year and could be modified with much greater difficulty. Details of the planning contracts could even be defined as a part of a separate law on planning. The setting-up of regional authorities would have the obvious advantage that the acceptance of both physical plans and development plans would fall within the sphere of authority of the same body. The body itself could decide what sort of agreement and procedural order should be followed in carrying out the dual planning exercise.

It is important to emphasise that there is a need for the establishment of regional authorities, and not simply because it is required by the EU. Independent of the EU's Structural Funds, the organisation of regional authorities can have, above all, the advantage of creating a regional actor equipped with overall rights and spheres of authority, in whose interest it is to manage and put to advantage the economy of the region, to create an environment favourable to and fostering the economy: regional marketing, international networking, human resource development, education and training.

The National Development Plan

Targets

The overall objective of the current planning period is to reduce the income gap relative to the EU average. The reduction of this gap to a large extent depends on how successfully Hungary can increase her income, and so actions should contribute to this overall objective (the New Hungary Development Plan 2007).

The *first objective* of the National Development Plan is to increase the competitiveness of the country and its regions, at both international and European Union levels. In general, the choice of this objective is justified by low productivity, the scarcity of capital, the low level of technology, a weak SME sector, the low use of agricultural potential and modem IT applications offered by new ICT technologies, by the weak use of products of the information society, poor R&D activity, the inadequate transport infrastructure and the under-utilised potential for tourism.

The strength of the economy depends on modernising productive capacities, on stimulating capital accumulation, taking over new technologies, improving the quality of products and building business infrastructure: all these make a positive contribution to the objective. The introduction of new technologies is required, not only for these purposes, but in order to reduce environmental risk, and reduce pollution. The NDP will support these areas by *promoting investment* and providing physical investment to improve the performance of the productive sector. This is particularly important in those regions where under-utilised labour can be found.

Competitiveness in Hungary is particularly dependent on the *SME sector.* The upgrading of their technology, improved management skills, improved opportunities in the capital market, a better business infrastructure, and developing SME's e-capacities to help communication with their environment and business partners will all lead to higher value-added and will strengthen considerably overall competitiveness. There is significant potential to develop better supply-chain links between SMEs and large firms and among SMEs also, so that they can integrate more effectively into international markets. The strengthening of women's participation in the SME sector should also be promoted via equal access to business support measures and entrepreneurial training. A more intense innovation, the new knowledge of the workers and the management all increase productivity. The strengthening of the development of new products, technologies in R&D centres, in both the corporate and the non-profit sector will help to attain the objective. These actions are especially important outside the capital, in areas where R&D activity is low, and where there is underused local potential to pursue research (e.g. universities). The dissemination of research results and bringing new ideas to the market will help to increase competitiveness, something which is currently weak in Hungary.

The potential of the *tourism* sector in Hungary is large. To strengthen overall competitiveness in the sector, investment is required. To improve the quality and quantity of accommodation, services and skills must be addressed by utilising the cultural and natural heritage of the country. These tend to generate higher spending per tourist and lead to an extended stay of visitors in the country. Appropriate attention must be paid to the preservation of the environment so that the country's natural resources are not harmed by this development.

In order to increase the benefits from *local and regional potential,* accessibility between and within regions is desirable for increased competitiveness. This requires new social and business links to be established which improve local competitiveness. Such partnerships improve local administration, facilitate the rehabilitation of brown-field sites and establish better networks between local universities and the business sector.

Improvements in the quality of the *environment* based on environment protection (sewage- and waste-management, improvements to water or air quality) and in nature preservation, increase the attraction of the country as a tourist destination. They also improve the capacity of the population to work and so increase competitiveness. A good community environment is also crucial in attracting investment. Steps which promote the more efficient use of energy in the productive sector also have a positive impact.

An efficient *transport system* connected to the European transport network is a major and direct contributor to economic competitiveness. It will facilitate the integration into the European market and allows the development of new activities in the domestic market. Hungary should benefit from its geographical position by attracting high-value services related to transport. However, due to its poor quality, the transport infrastructure risks have restricted development. Improvements to the infrastructure will improve the accessibility of the country and its regions for tourists. The construction of transport infrastructure will mitigate the effects upon the environment and seek to preserve its natural resources.

Increasing economic competitiveness requires a better use of *human resources.* Active labour market policies to encourage increased employment will also help to reduce unemployment. In Hungary the elimination of the mismatch between education and the labour market would allow the development of a more productive and active labour force. The improvement of education and training as part of life-long learning continuously increases the skills of those in work or still in education. Life-long learning, self-motivated learning and the acquisition of skills and knowledge will be promoted by lowering the cost of learning through the use and widening access to the Internet and web-based information and data sources. Increased competitiveness also requires better involvement of disadvantaged social groups. It is particularly difficult for women to return to the labour market, despite the fact that they are well-educated. A further under-utilised and large social group are the Roma, whose greater involvement in the enterprise sector would mean a better use of the country's human potential.

The second objective of the NDP is to increase employment and to develop human potential. The choice of this objective is justified by the low participation rate in the labour market, the high share of long-term unemployment, social exclusion (of the disadvantaged and the Roma), discrimination against women in the labour market, the low flexibility and ability of education and vocational training in meeting labour market needs and its weak infrastructure, and the weakness of services which promote employability.

Higher level human capital would help to bring Hungary into line with the rest of Europe by making it easier for individuals, businesses, civic and government institutions to co-operate across borders. Countries with highly skilled labour forces and better human capital have a better chance to catch up, and so it is crucial for Hungary to develop its human resources. In addition, the skill-biased technological change and growth patterns observed in the world economy suggest that those countries which channel a major part of their resources into developing human capital should significantly benefit from technological development.

Action over a wide range of areas can lead to a better use of human resources. Promoting and improving *active labour market policies,* preventing and tackling unemployment and the strengthening of labour market institutions together contribute to a higher level of employment. Actions which ease the social and employment discrimination against *disadvantaged groups* in society (such as the Roma) increase social cohesion. These social groups are concentrated in micro-regions which lag behind. Ensuring equal opportunities starting from the school system and support for social inclusion offer huge benefits for the future labour market performance. Direct measures to improve the current labour market position of the disadvantaged enhance their employability and lead to the improvement of their social status. The improvement of access to ICT services and data, information and knowledge in underdeveloped areas, where disadvantaged groups are concentrated, contribute to local community and overall cohesion. It would also facilitate their inclusion in the information society and help their social integration.

The need for a higher level of human capital makes it necessary for people to obtain the necessary knowledge required by the continuously changing economy. The rapid advance of knowledge and skills requires a permanent upgrading of the basic skills of the people. This learning means *life-long learning.* The basis of this should be laid down already in primary education with the attainment of skills and competencies indispensable for life-long learning. The concept of life-long learning will help people to retrain and to upgrade their knowledge, thus improving labour market participation by tackling skills obsolescence and improving employment prospects. In order to benefit more from this, the content and methodologies of teaching and training need to be adequately developed. Vocational education and training systems should also fit the needs and structure of the labour market.

In Hungary the state of *infrastructure of education* in some areas is poor and the quality of the building stock and of the equipment in many areas causes problems in meeting the needs of education. The remedy for this situation is investment in the infrastructure of education which contributes directly to the objective by improving the quality of education.

The poor *health* condition of some of the population seriously restricts employa-bility and results in high inactivity, leading to a shorter working-life. Communication between the service providers in health and the improvement of equipment in health are major bottlenecks identified in the area. Upgrading these areas will help to raise the quality of the labour force and also increase competitiveness in the productive sector.

The role of R &D in contributing to a better use of labour resources takes several forms. The low level of aggregate and corporate R&D activity and spending in Hungary restricts national competitiveness. An increase in R&D spending and the spin-off activities both help competitiveness and improve labour demand. A well functioning R&D system directly contributes to a higher quality workforce in the field and their greater employability. The improvement in spin-off activity serves to create new industries with a high-quality workforce, and this in turn leads to activities with high value added.

Actions relating to the *environment* improve employability by improving the health of the population. In a number of areas there exists a clear need to improve the environment and this in turn serves the aim of better employability by means of a better quality environment for the national labour force. This, of course, requires increased environmental awareness from the population and appropriate training.

A good transport infrastructure improves the accessibility of underdeveloped regions and areas, both from within the country and from outside and so improves work opportunities by increasing the competitiveness of the regions and areas that benefit from such development projects. It also helps people to find work by increasing the range of jobs which can be taken since these projects improve the conditions for commuting.

There are large *regional and local differences* in employment opportunities but many forms of action would help to mitigate these. However, local knowledge can best be used at local level, and so action at local level has high potential to contribute to a better use of human resources. Enhancing the social economy contributes to job creation and help to reintegrate the most disadvantaged. The improvement of employability and the flexibility of local SMEs are also feasible fields of action to achieve the objective. This is particularly so in the case of tourism, where the use of local potential has high rewards.

In *rural areas* the improvement of employment opportunities requires the diversification of local activities away from agriculture and the so there is a need for the training of people for new activities and the introduction of new sources of income. A better preservation of local cultural and natural heritage help the development of tourism as a dynamic industry providing new employment.

The *third objective* is to raise the quality of the environment, to provide for sustainable natural resource management, and to achieve a level of development which is more balanced regionally. The choice of this objective is justified in general by the need for the reduction of the environmental burden and by the large regional disparities in quality of life across the country.

Although, in general, the state of the *environment and nature conservation* is not bad relative to the EU, considerable improvement is required in a number of important respects. These areas for action are closely related to the community environment. Waste- and water-management, the improvement of water quality and the reduction of air pollution are issues which have a considerable effect on the welfare of communities. A further field for action which is of great concern to the community is the improvement of both flood control and water pollution.

For these environmental improvements a *better use of energy* is also required. Currently, one unit of GDP is produced using 50 per cent more energy than the EU average. If this were to continue, it would ignore totally the value of energy conservation and lead to an unsustainable use of resources. Likewise, the state of the environment must not be harmed by damage to *biodiversity*. A reduced level of biodiversity is undesirable from the point of view of preservation, and it would have serious consequences for tourism and related local activities. These actions all contribute to a better quality of environment.

Regional disparities in the quality of life embrace a number of factors. Differences in local and regional skills, accessibility and the potential for linking with other regions and communities varies, and so does the quality of public services, and the share of disadvantaged communities in local population. Action to mitigate disparities depends on improving the potential of local enterprise to absorb capital, to attract new kinds of investment and to create job opportunities which correspond to local labour-force patterns. Special attention should be paid in the regions to all sections of society to ensure equal opportunities for men and women. A better use of domestic potential requires local universities to co-operate with local enterprise more closely, since this helps to find new sources of competitiveness. This would be particularly effective in the poorer parts of the country. Other sources of local potential are the utilisation of brown-field sites and the improvement of the community environment so as to increase regional and local quality of life. The elimination of transport bottlenecks which threaten to hinder local and regional production activities is also needed for the better use of resources. At local level, the construction of bypasses and ring-roads to ease local traffic, improve the quality of life and increase the safety of the inhabitants are also seen as necessary to development.

In *rural areas* the potential for development is based not only on tourism, on the modernisation of agriculture, food processing, forestry and fishery. The diversification of activities into handicrafts and the production of essentially local products, that is, the preservation of local culture, all contribute to the introduction of new sources of prosperity. Support for the development of basic services in rural areas helps the development of new businesses and serves the needs of the local population.

Financing cohesion policy

In the first period of the membership, between 2004 and 2006, Hungary received greatly increased sums in development resources from the structural funds budget. Within the framework of the National Development Plan, developments and investments have been completed (or are still being implemented) in nearly 2,000 settlements across Hungary. Development resources amounting to €2.85 billion awarded to more than 18,000 successful applicants have contributed to the creation of something approaching 50,000 new jobs around the country (Table 7.4).

Hungarian actors, local authorities, entrepreneurs and NGOs, have mastered the ins and outs of the application process over the past three years. Naturally, the contracting authorities have also passed the test with flying colours: they were

Table 7.4 Allocations for Structural Funds operations, 2004–2006, million euros

Fund	2004	2005	2006	Total
Structural Funds	448	620	786	1,854
Cohesion Fund	340	280	374	994
Total	788	900	1,159	2,847

Source: National Development Plan, 2004–2006.

required to learn and apply the intricacies of the EU application procedure. Step-by-step, the system is being established: the government, fully aware of the teething troubles of the system, has taken into account the viewpoints of applicants when transforming and, where possible, simplifying administrative regulations.

The distribution of resources between sectoral and regional operational programmes is dependent on the role of the regional level. In 2004–2006, the share of funds allocated to regional development was only slightly over 17 per cent (Figure 7.4).

The experiences of the 2004–2006 period have been of particular importance since Hungary now stands at the beginning of the new EU budgetary period, when Hungarian applicants have access to even greater development resources from the Brussels budget.

The preparation of the first National Development Plan was a considerable challenge, and one from which Hungary gained a great variety of experience. No single and coherent database had previously been prepared. The strategy was neither in harmony with, nor connected to, the NDP's financial planning, and the allocation of resources among the programmes was made without exact, quantified

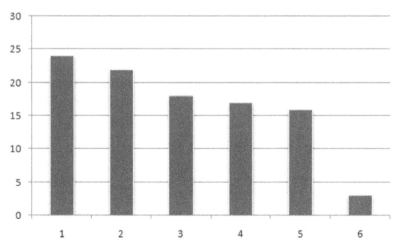

Figure 7.4 Share of expenditure of operational programmes, 2004–2006, per cent
Key: 1 Economic development. 2 Human resources. 3 Agriculture and rural development. 4 Environment and infrastructure. 5 Regional development. 6 Technical assistance.
Source: Designed by the author.

and accepted result indicators. In the planning process, driven by resource allocation, strategy was not created in a target-oriented way, but tool-oriented. As the Structural Funds use a basically regional approach, the responsibilities for the respective objectives or professional content were not settled among the ministries working in a sectoral approach. The task of organising programmes of this size was also a considerable challenge for state administration, since thinking in terms longer than the annual budget was totally lacking. The experiences of partnership demonstrated that poorly organised social debate and the mass involvement of partners with no experience in the regulation of Structural Funds could significantly slow down the planning process.

Between 2007 and 2013, Hungary will have the opportunity to implement one of the largest-scale development programmes in its history, supported by the European Union. Following the agreement reached by the Hungarian Government in December 2005, the country is to receive a total of €33bn in support over the seven-year period (taking into account agricultural subsidies). This includes nearly €25bn for development, regional and social gap-closing, as well as for agricultural and rural development. The EU Cohesion and Structural Fund subsidy amounts to €24.8bn for these seven years – which also means that Hungary ranks second among member-states in terms of the amount of development resources per capita. Cohesion fund support is supplemented by EU support for rural development in excess of €3bn.

As a result of Cohesion Fund and rural development support and of the domestic co-financing of development, resources will be provided (at current prices) during these next seven years which represent, in annual average terms, three times the funds available in the 2004–2006 period.

Hungary was entitled to receive €24.8bn in development funds, calculated at 2004 price levels, from the Cohesion Policy Funds of the EU between 2007 and 2013, which is supplemented by domestic co-financing and private capital (Tables 7.5 and 7.6). Also, an additional total of (approximately) €3.4 billion is available from the European Agricultural and Rural Development Fund and the European Fisheries Fund.

Of the seven Hungarian regions, six qualify under the terms of the Convergence Objectives and one, notably the Central region will qualify under those of the Phasing-in Regional Competitiveness and Employment Objective. The aspects considered when planning the distribution of funds were:

- relevant European Union regulations on the use of the Cohesion Fund and Structural Funds;

Table 7.5 The allocations for structural funds operations, 2007–2013

	Billion euros	*Percentage share*
ERDF	12.6	50.8
Cohesion Fund	8.6	34.7
ESF	3.6	14.5
Total	24.8	100.0

Source: The New Hungary Development Plan.

Table 7.6 The share of individual operational programmes, 2007–2013

	EU contribution, billion euros	Percentage share
Economic development	2.5	10.0
Transport	6.2	24.9
Social infrastructure	1.9	8.3
Environment and energy	4.2	16.8
Social renewal	3.4	13.7
Convergence regions	4.3	17.3
Competitiveness region	1.5	6.0
State reform and e-government	0.8	3.0
Total	24.8	100.0

Source: The New Hungary Development Plan.

- the relative weight of certain areas of intervention in attaining the main objectives set;
- developmental obligations in the protection of the environment and transport arising from Hungary's EU membership;
- the size and relative level of development of individual regions of the country;
- the assumed absorption capacity of individual areas of intervention.

References

Baranyi, B (2003) 'Before Schengen – ready for Schengen. Euroregional organisations and formations on the eastern borders of Hungary', *European Spatial Research and Policy,* 1: 85–94.

Beluszky, P. (2001) 'The Hungarian urban network: historical perspectives', in Turnock, D. (ed.) *East-Central Europe and the Former Soviet Union,* Environment and Society. London: Arnold, 51–70.

Beluszky, P. (2002) 'The transformation of the Hungarian urban network after 1990', in Horváth, G. (ed.) *Regional Challenges of the Transition in Bulgaria and Hungary,* Discussion Papers. Special. Pécs: Centre for Regional Studies, HAS, 27–48.

Bennett, R.J. and Krebs, G. (1991) *Local Economic Development: Public-Private Partnership Initiatives in Britain and Germany,* London: Belhaven Press.

Bennett, R.J. and Krebs, G. (1994) 'Local economic development partnerships: an analysis of policy networks in EC-LEDA local employment development strategies', *Regional Studies,* 2: 119–140.

Buzogány, Á. and Korkut, U. (2013) 'Administrative reform and regional development discourses in Hungary. Europeanisation going NUTS?' *Europa-Asia Studies,* 8: 1555–1577.

Enyedi, G. (1983) *Földrajz és társadalom* [Geography and society], Budapest: Magvető Könyvkiadó.

Hencz, A. (1973) *Területrendezési törekvések Magyarországon* [Territorial organisation efforts in Hungary], Budapest: Közgazdasági és Jogi Könyvkiadó.

Horváth, G. (2001) 'Consequences of the interrelationship between institutions of regional development and of integration in Hungarian regional policy', *European Mirror,* Special Issue: 119–154.

Horváth, G. (2005) 'Decentralization, regionalism and the modernization of the regional economy in Hungary: a European comparison', in Barta, G., Fekete, É., Kukorelli Szörényiné, I. and Timár, J. (eds) *Hungarian Spaces and Places: Patterns of Transition,* Pécs: Centre for Regional Studies, HAS, 50–63.

Klebelsberg, K. (1928) 'Budapest, Szeged és Debrecen, mint tudományos székvárosok' [Budapest, Szeged and Debrecen as scientific city centres], in Klebelsberg, K. *Neonacionalizmus* [Neonationalism], Budapest: Atheneum Irodalmi és Nyomdaipari Rt. 71–76.

Konrád, G. and Szelényi, I. (2000) *Urbanizáció és területi gazdálkodás* [Urbanisation and regional economy], Szeged: JGYF Kiadó.

Leonardi, R. and Nanetti, R. (1990) *The Regions and European Integration: The Case of Emilia-Romagna,* London: Pinter Publishers.

Marin, B. (ed.) (1990) *Generalized Political Exchange. Antagonostic Co-operation and Integrated Political Circuits,* Frankfurt: Campus Verlag.

'National Development Plan of the Republic of Hungary, 2003', Budapest: Prime Minister's Offices.

OECD Territorial Reviews: Hungary, Paris: OECD, 2001.

Pálné Kovács, I. (2009) 'Regionalization in Hungary: options and scenarios on the "road to Europe"', in Scott, W.J. (ed.) *De-Coding New Regionalism. Shifting Socio-Political Contexts in Central Europe and Latin America,* London: Routledge, 199–214.

Pálné Kovács, I. (2011) *Local Governance in Hungary – The Balance of the Last 20 Years,* Discussion Papers, 83, Pécs: Centre for Regional Studies HAS.

Pearce, D.W. (ed.) (1986) *Macmillan Dictionary of Modern Economics,* London: Macmillan Press.

Pogátsa, Z. (2013) 'The recentralization of economic development in Hungary' in Palermo, F. and Parolari, S. (eds) *Regional Dynamics in Central and Eastern Europe,* Leiden and Boston: Martinus Nijhoff.

Stewart, J. and Stoker, G. (eds) (1995) *Local Government in the 1990s,* London: Macmillan.

The New Hungary Development Plan. National Strategic Reference Framework of Hungary 2007–2013, Budapest: National Development Agency.

Tóth, J. (2004) 'Kell-e nekünk régió?' [Should we need a region?], in *Mindentudás Egyeteme 3*, Budapest: Kossuth Kiadó, 193–212.

Part III

Inter-regional co-operation in Central Europe

8 Working communities and Euroregions

In future years the space, structure and modernisation of Central European economic development will primarily be determined by co-operation with dynamically developing countries. In addition to developing the market economy, the key aspects of development strategy are reintegration into the international division of labour (at both macro- and micro-economic level) and the related overall social adjustment. Opportunities for economic growth are mainly linked to strengthening the nation's export capability and utilising the advantages of the international division of labour. Foreign economic relations should also be based on decentralised forms of participation in international regional integration and the evolution of appropriate structural and institutional systems.

Central Europe is a tender field of the inter-regional co-operation. Regional interrelationships have had both positive and negative historical background. On one side, the ties between the former members of the Austro-Hungarian Empire remained stronger than any other economic-commercial relationship in Europe, and on the other the new nation states formed after World War I hindered integrated development of former attraction zones alongside the new border (Berend and Ránki 1982; Good 1984). Some recent development processes are affected by this dichotomy.

Attempts before systemic change: Alps-Adriatic Working Community

Different parts of Central Europe have different attributes for formulating their responses, and it has been almost 30years since a few Hungarian counties started to play a part in Central European regional co-operation. This experience has provided numerous lessons, not only for formulating development concepts in the counties involved, but also for other programmes of co-operation (J. Horváth 1998).

Inter-regional relations played an important role in strengthening the competitive position of the large Central European region. However, provinces of the region chose another way to develop regional co-operation. Bilateral co-operation agreements were gradually replaced by multilateral international associations – which is how *Euroregio Basiliensis,* cited as a classic example in the literature, emerged in 1971. This comprised Upper Alsace (France), the Canton and City of Basel (Switzerland) and Baden (Southern Germany) The old Franco-German conflict was replaced by harmonious economic and cultural co-operation. The three regions are closely linked as a result of working together on infrastructural development (joint airports, express rail network, integrated communication facilities, joint training on special university courses, etc.) and on establishing modern industrial production sectors.

In 1972, the International Lake Constance Conference (six Austrian, Bavarian, and Swiss territorial administrative units) came into existence, and, at the same time, 10 Austrian, Swiss, Bavarian and Italian provinces organised the Alps Working Community. The Alps-Adriatic Working Community followed in 1978, and in 1984 the *Western Alps Working Community* (COTRAO) was set up by the Italian regions of Valle d'Aosta, Piedmont and Liguria, the French regions of Provence-Alpes-Côte d'Azur and Rhône-Alpes and the Swiss cantons of Vaud, Valais and Geneva. In 1990, the Working Community of Danubian Countries Provinces was established. The main initiators of these co-operation programmes are the Free State of Bavaria and the Lombardy Region. These two regions found (as a programme) their regional growth centre role in Central European co-operation. The essence of this co-operation lies in the modernisation of the economy, of corporate structure and of technology, in the development of R&D provided by the regional co-operation between the various administrative units.

The two Central European regional co-operating groups (the Alps, and Alps-Adriatic) overlap each other's territory to some extent. Bavaria, Ticino, Salzburg and Trentino-Alto Adige (South Tyrol) region are members of both organisations (Figures 8.1 and 8.2). The population of the two blocs was very similar, as is their economic structure. However the Alps–Adriatic Working Community covered a substantially larger territory (Table 8.1), and has marked interior differentiation (due to the provinces on the Eastern periphery).

In 1978, when Europe was still very divided and the seeds of the concept of a unified Common Market idea had just emerged, the representatives of two Northeast Italian regions (Friuli-Venezia Giulia and the Veneto) and four Central Austrian provinces (Carinthia, Styria, Upper Austria and Salzburg), together with Bavaria, Slovenia and Croatia met in Venice and decided to form an Action Association for harmonising different fields of regional development. Trentino-Alto Adige joined in 1981, Lombardy in 1985 and the Burgenland (Austria) in 1987. Between 1986 and 1989, five Hungarian territorial administration units, Győr-Moson-Sopron, Vas, Zala, Somogy and Baranya counties, also participated in this inter-regional organisation. With the admission of the Swiss canton of Ticino in 1990, the organisational foundation of the Community was complete.

The task of the community was formulated by the founding Joint Declaration (Venice, 20 November 1978) as a common informative, professional discussion and harmonisation concerning problems falling within the interests of the members. The areas emphasised were:

- trans-Alpine road links;
- port traffic;
- generation and transmission of energy;
- agriculture;

Figure 8.1 The Alps Working Community

- forestry;
- water management;
- tourism;
- environmental protection;
- nature conservation;
- landscape care;
- settlement development;
- cultural relations; and
- contacts between scientific facilities.

Figure 8.2 The Alps-Adriatic Working Community

The three decade-long operation of the Alps-Adriatic Working Community and the work of its expert committees allow us to draw conclusions. Summarising these experiences is important since they may offer guidance for further regional co-operation in Central Europe. The main conclusions are that:

1   The Working Community was built up gradually. In the first phase of its operation, those regions which had previously maintained intensive bilateral relations with each other became members; regions joining later depended heavily on their own relations with some of the existing member regions. An important organisational principle is that only regions with national borders can become members (a principle of all European regional organisations) and territories with no common borders with 'member-states' cannot join the Working Community, even under strong political pressure. A good example of this is Lower Austria, which has not been admitted to the Alps-Adriatic Working Community in spite of intensive political and economic propaganda.

Table 8.1 Member regions of the Alps-Adriatic Working Community, 1988

Member region	Surface area		Population	
	Thousand km²	Country (%)	Thousand km²	Country (%)
Bavaria	70,553	28.4	11,043	18.1
German Land	70,553	28.4	11,043	18.1
Lombardy	23,856	7.9	8,856	15.5
Trentino-Alto Adige	13,620	4,5	882	1.5
Friuli-Venezia Giulia	7,847	2.6	1,210	2.1
Veneto	18,364	6.1	4,375	7.6
Italian regions	63,687	21.1	15,353	26.7
Upper Austria	11,980	14.3	1,270	16.8
Burgenland	3,965	4.7	270	3.6
Styria	16,387	19.5	1,187	15.7
Salzburg	7,154	8.5	442	5.9
Carinthia	9,534	11.4	536	7.1
Austrian provinces	49,020	58.4	3.705	49.1
Croatia	56,538	100.0	4.672	100.0
Slovenia	20,251	100.0	1.937	100.0
Győr-Moson-Sopron	3,837	4.1	426	4.0
Vas	3,337	3.6	227	2.1
Zala	3,784	4.1	311	2.9
Somogy	6,036	6.5	349	3.3
Baranya	4,487	4.8	432	4.1
Hungarian counties	21,481	23.1	1,745	16.4
Total	281,530	–	38,455	–

Source: National yearbooks of statistics, 1988.

Finally, there must be some limit to the number of member regions. The experience of the Alps-Adriatic Working Community demonstrates that an organisation with more than 15 members is more difficult to operate (with a deeply structured network of committees and: working committees). A gradual enlargement of the Working Community (and the preliminary granting of observer status) is also justified by the fact that, in the initial phase, the differences of interest which inevitably emerge can be harmonised more easily with a smaller number of members, and co-ordination mechanisms can be introduced more easily.

2   The founding and core regions of the Alps-Adriatic Working Community developed regional co-operation at a time when their economies had actually set out along this development path. Developing international co-operation became an important element of the internal regional policy of the member

regions, and the regions also helped to increase the competitiveness of their business organisations with their own resources.

The standards of the European Community aiming at the integration of the internal market were also good incentives for developing co-operation. Uniform customs and tariff regulations and the development of the Western European linear infrastructure in this region also meant the strengthening of cross-border relations. It is a specific motive of the development of this Central European regional co-operation that its members are considered the most dynamically developing regions within their countries, and that they play an outstanding role in the bilateral foreign trade relations of the countries. (For example, the Alps-Adriatic regions of Italy supply 52 per cent of Italy's exports to Germany, 58 per cent to Austria, and 66 per cent to the former Yugoslavia.)

3   Inter-regional co-operation exceeded the limits of formal relations when the market players had established their own co-operation networks. The collaboration of various types of marketing organisation had been institutionalised, and they had developed their own modus operandi which no longer needed administrative coordination. The institutions of the Expo and Fair Cities, chambers of commerce, business, entrepreneurial and technological centres, the airports of the working community are all in continuous contact with each other today on their own in initiative. One of the problems of integration in the Eastern (Hungarian, Slovenian, and Croatian) regions is that these institutions are either under-developed or totally lacking, and, while the engines of co-operation are market organisations, this role is still played by various forms of administrative institution in the Eastern counties.

It is, therefore, our conclusion that public administration has a general political and co-ordinating role to play in regional co-operation, while a dense network of co-operation can be established by organisations or the direct collaboration of market actors.

4   A general task of regional administration is to represent and defend the interests of this co-operation in the face of central government. Organising the Alps-Adriatic Working Community was not free of conflict between central and regional interests. Owing to its specific constitutional system, the Bavaria has the greatest freedom of movement. On the contrary, the Italian regions and the Austrian *Länder* could only extend their right to international co-operation by means of long constitutional debate – which has not yet ended. In the former Yugoslavia, even the constituent republics had only limited autonomy in foreign trade affairs, and in Hungary this question was hardly ever raised.

Constitutional debate flared up, especially after 1980, when the Council of Europe in Madrid reached an enabling agreement which indicated the necessity of decentralised organisations for cross-border co-operation. This agreement prescribes the freedom of regions to choose, on the one hand, the forms of border co-operation, and, on the other, guarantees that the state is empowered to inspect and control the maintenance of state sovereignty. Although the agreement has not obliged any ratifying state to reform its internal legal system, it was an important measure to develop the institutional and legal means of regional co-operation, and so these autonomous endeavours of the regions should not be considered anti-constitutional. After the ratification of this agreement, further national laws were enacted: the 1987 decree of the Italian Constitutional Court extended the rules of the basic agreement to regions removed from international borders (and from the Italian side this has legitimised the Alps-Adriatic Working Community). In preparing Austrian constitutional reform, it was unanimously agreed that the *Länder* should be able to sign international agreements concerning issues which lie within their authority.

Independently of these legal outcomes and the clearly more extensive rights, power positions, and financial means of the regional meso-level when compared to Hungary's, Centre region conflicts of interests are constantly present. In the case of the Alps-Adriatic Working Community, the Italian, Austrian, Yugoslav and Hungarian states have tried to restrain, rather than encourage, the rate of development of this Central European integration, especially after the organisation of the Pentagonale (Central European) Initiative.

In order that the Hungarian economy should be able to integrate, on a regional basis, into Europe, a radical renewal of regional policy and administration is necessary. Power must be divided between central and local government, and their regional communities, in such a way that adaptation to modernisation centres should be influenced not only by central norms, but also by responding to market signals with autonomous local and regional decisions.

The reform of the regional and administrative structure of the country is a pre-condition for realising an innovative regional development strategy, and for establishing international regional competitiveness – one which cannot be neglected. The current Hungarian counties, because of their economic potential, market size and the extreme weakness of their market organising power, are neither suitable to fulfil the role of independent fields of action in the international division of labour, nor to be equal partners of West European regions. A partial solution to this could be the organisation of a meso-level of democratic representation (which could even be the county, although focused on international relations rather than on an association of counties).

The Carpathian Basin as an economic area

The political changes and economic reforms of the 1990s have produced ambiguous results in the development of natural regions, economic spaces and administrative units of the Carpathian Basin.[1] The gradual and problematic transition to a market economy has led to profound spatial differentiation in every country. The collapse of the former economic structure and the building of the new economy have affected the different areas in various ways. Territorial differences have started to grow, and the benefits of the regime change do not show a spatially even distribution either.

Among factors producing a beneficial effect on economic restructuring, an important role is played by the European integration relationships in countries recently joining the European Union. As a basic condition of accession, the new member-states were to be prepared for the implementation of an efficient regional policy, set objectives and use resources in the implementation of their economic policy aimed at the reduction of spatial differences, establish new institutions, and create the possibility of cross-border development of regional cohesion. A long-term result of EU membership may be the revival of centuries-old former integration relationships in the Carpathian Basin developed through centuries. Due to the geopolitical situation, and the varying degree of integration maturity, achieving the desirable outcome provides tasks for politicians, researchers and economic professionals alike for the decades to come.

The transformation of the economy has produced particularly negative effects in most Hungarian communities beyond the borders. Beneficiaries of the market economy have emerged in large cities and settlements with a particularly favourable geopolitical position. This former group includes several successful border settlements, which initially exploited the informal, and later on co-operation-based economy and labour market demand. The majority of ethnic Hungarians live in rural areas, while well-paid jobs in tertiary branches, financial services, and export-based enterprises have been created in cities. Following the collapse of large-scale industry, the under-qualified rural population formerly commuting to towns was deprived of a steady income.

Nationality factors have played a limited role in the spatial diffusion of development. State subsidy policy can of course influence the development of individual areas. State influence may have positive and restrictive aspects. In several Western European countries, special advantages were granted to encourage the economic closure of under-developed areas with an ethnic minority population, and additional resources were provided to support culture and education. In the meantime, ethnic areas in Eastern Europe have been neglected for a long period and negative discrimination still seems to haunt economic and regional development policies. It is a fact that modern regional development policy, including the structural and cohesion policies of the European Union, emphasises the spatially homogenous distribution of economic advantages. This implies an equal distribution of the positive effects of economic growth among all ethnic groups in the area.

Regions with uneven development

The territory of the Carpathian Basin, as measured by European standards, is characterised by general backwardness. Disregarding developed Slovenia, the indicators of performance per unit of the countries reach only a half or third of the EU average. Among the regions, only Bratislava and Budapest surpass the average GDP per capita of the European Union (Table 8.2). The reduction of state subsidies, the changes in the geographic orientation of foreign relationships, the disintegration of large companies, the crisis of heavy industry and agriculture resulting from the collapse of the planned economies have affected the core and peripheral regions in diverse ways. Even though the process of restructuring had a negative impact on traditional development poles, former metropolitan areas with a more complex economy and socio-economic functions are less severely affected by the transformation process than monocultural industrial regions and rural areas. The success of marketisation and the development of modern economies can be observed in Transylvanian large cities, Slovakian medium-sized cities, and in the core region and tourism centres of Croatia. The number of private enterprises and the share of FDI significantly surpass the national average in these areas. The tertiary sector is on the road to become the most dominant sector of the economy, due largely to the expanding business and financial services. The most dynamically growing regions are producers of major innovations and new products, and members of international economic co-operations as well.

Among the countries of the area, Romania's case illustrates the failure and ineffectiveness of the former state spatial development policy. The main conclusion regarding the present state of economic and social structures is that after the establishment independent Romania, economic policy based on various ideologies had only a modest impact on the country's traditional spatial structure, and while regional disparities decreased in quantity, the territorial pattern of developed and backward regions remained largely unchanged in the twentieth century despite the efforts of forced industrialisation demanding great sacrifices Bucharest and some large cities (Craiova, Piteşti and Constanţa) with their surrounding areas show structural characteristics which enable them to embark on the road to modernisation. Transylvania, which belonged to a different economic system 90 years ago, was more or less able to conserve its advantages inherent in its settlement structure (dense network of small towns) and qualified human resources. Out of the three administrative regions of Transylvania, two had GDP per capita rates above the national average. The Western region (Hunedoara, Arad, Timiş and Caraş-Severin counties) is the second most developed region after Bucharest, where GDP per capita exceeds by 14 per cent the national average, while the Central Region (Mureş, Harghita, Covasna, Braşov, Alba and Sibiu counties) comes third. Central Region income rates are 13 per cent higher than the national average. The northern areas of Transylvania and the North-west region comprised of Bihor, Satu Mare, Sălaj, Bistriţa-Năsăud, Maramureş and Cluj counties, ranks the sixth among the eight Romanian regions. Its economic performance is 90 per cent of the national average. According to the global development index, 4 out of the 16 Transylvanian counties can be called highly developed, 3 developed, and six medium developed, and there are only three under-developed counties in the three regions of Transylvania.

The same degree of spatial disparities characterises the rest of countries in the Carpathian Basin. Those areas where Hungarian minorities are dominant reveal large developmental disparities: there are relatively developed areas in a more favourable position than the national average (e.g. the areas of Žitný Ostrov near Bratislava or certain parts of Vojvodina) and there are several underdeveloped peripheral regions (e.g. the Eastern Slovakian counties, Zakarpattia oblast, and Croatian Slavonia). In the Slovakian counties of Trnava and Košice with large Hungarian populations, GDP per capita almost reaches the national average; in Banská Bystrica and Nitra, it reaches only 75 per cent. The income levels of the regions shown in Table 8.2 depict the disparities of demographic potential, labour force and income positions as compared to EU standards. Both data sets show NUTS 2 units (the EU's statistical development regions) in the countries. A sign of the economic vulnerability of the Carpathian economy is the persistence of traditional features in the employment structure. The Eastern regions are characterised by the predominance of the agrarian sector and the weak presence of the tertiary sector (Figure 8.3).

Regional situation report

The different political-economic environment of the regions of the Carpathian Basin led to the development of an economy functioning in the form of highly segmented, largely independent submarkets.

Market fragmentation in our days is further strengthened by the fact that different countries are at different phases in the Euro-Atlantic integration process, therefore the free movement of manpower may be inhibited by factors such as the variety of border crossings and the temporary legal restrictions on employment opportunities. With the advancement of the integration process, the system of relations of the different market segments will significantly improve; however, the problems in Zakarpattia (Transcarpathian) oblast and autonomous province of Vojvodina will likely persist in the long run, since Serbia and Ukraine unlikely to become members of the EU in the foreseeable future and in these cases restrictive external border policies will be maintained.

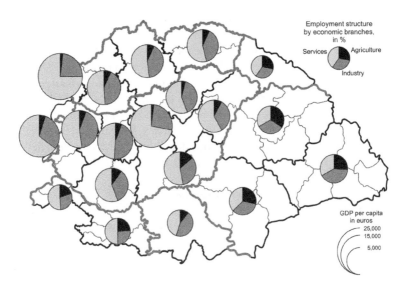

Figure 8.3 GDP per capita and structure of employment by economic sector in the regions of the Carpathian Basin, 2010

Source: Author's calculations based on national statistical yearbooks.

Table 8.2 Major data of the NUTS 2 regions of the Carpathian Basin, 2010

	Population thousands	Density of population, person/km²	Unemployment rate (%)	GDP per inhabitant in PPS, Euro	GDP per inhabitant as percent of the EU27 average	R&D expenditure of GDP (%)
Hungary						
Central Hungary	2,956	414	8.8	26,100	107	1.6
Central Transdanubia	1,098	100	9.3	13,900	57	0.7
Western Transdanubia	996	88	7.4	15,900	65	0.6
Southern Transdanubia	945	68	12.7	10,800	44	0.5
Northern Hungary	1,209	93	16,7	9,700	40	0.6
Northern Great Plain	1,492	86	14.5	10,100	41	1.1
Southern Great Plain	1,318	73	10.6	10,400	42	1.0
Slovakia						
Bratislava	622	295	5.8	43,100	176	1.1
Western Slovakia	1,866	124	10.7	16,700	68	0.4
Central Slovakia	1,351	83	15.9	14,600	59	0.4
Eastern Slovakia	1,585	100,	18.7	12,100	49	0.5
Romania						
North-west	2,720	81	5.9	10,200	42	0.3
Centre	2,524	103	9.0	10,900	45	0.2
West	1,919	61	6.4	12,900	53	0.2
Croatia						
Continental Croatia	2,956	92	13.6	14,500	59	1.0
Slovenia						
Eastern Slovenia	1,085	89	10.6	17,000	69	1.4
Ukraine						
Transcarpathia	1,253	98	7.0	5 000	22	0.1
Serbia						
Vojvodina	2,003	94	14.2	9 000	40	0.3

Source: http://epp.eurostat.ec.europa.eu, Statistical yearbook of AP of Vojvodina; Statistical yearbook of Ukraine.

Nonetheless, development differences may not only serve as a factor inhibiting co-operation; on the contrary, they may well improve its chances. The political-economic changes of the 1990s brought forth totally new conditions of operation with the opening of borders and the possibility of co-operation between border areas. Through their labour demand and export activity, economically more advanced areas were and will still be able to stimulate the labour market of neighbouring regions. This, of course, will not happen if the countries' peripheral and backward regions encounter each another, for there will be a total lack of the necessary development dynamism (the labour market indices of Southern Transdanubia and East Croatia provide a good example).

All the regions of the Carpathian Basin witnessed an improvement regarding their labour market before the global financial crisis, with rising employment and declining unemployment. Available data indicated that this phenomenon might become a permanent tendency if major shocks did not occur; however, the global economic recession has put this development into question. Since we are talking about sensitive labour markets in highly vulnerable economies, the inversion of the positive processes may occur with the speed of light, and the most up-to-date forecasts seem to hint at this possibility.

The prolongation of the recession poses a great threat to the further integration of the labour market, since several regions will be forced to enter into competition instead of co-operating, even within their national territories. Rising market tensions hardly create favourable conditions for employment in the neighbouring countries, not to mention the general lack of foreign language skills. Potentially accessible jobs on the other side of the border provide no benefit if the available professional knowledge cannot be utilised due to difficulties in communication. Already, there are examples of this unfortunate situation, since it was partially due to this reason that Southern Slovakian industrial parks and other prospering companies were unable to employ Hungarians (knowledge of Slovakian and/or English is a basic requirement).

The exchange of employees between regions of the Carpathian Basin can be further hindered by emerging political conflicts stemming from the common historical heritage, but the Western orientation among the circle of mobile employees is even more characteristic. In most cases, the neighbouring region is not the final migration destination, but serves only as a stepping-stone towards domestic labour markets with higher wages or more likely towards the more developed countries of the EU (this tendency is clearly visible in the case of foreign citizens employed in Hungary). The willingness to migrate does not decrease among employees of the Central European countries in question; however, after returning voluntarily or out of necessity to their home countries, there are fewer chances that Western workers reappear on the given submarket due to the economic recession.

The intensity and direction of workforce migration is not by any means constant, and radical changes might occur as a result of changing macro-economic conditions. The Hungarian-Romanian border illustrates this phenomenon, since in the 1990s, Hungary was the only recipient of occasional mass migration flows, while today, due to the dynamically growing Romanian economy and rising wages, employment on the other side of the border, a formerly unthinkable alternative, becomes a realistic possibility for Hungarian rural population living in enclosed under-developed areas (Baranyi 2003).

In Slovakia, the concentration of economic activities in the Bratislava Region does not equal that of Central Hungary. The region has a 25 per cent share in the country's GDP. Its leading position is affirmed by the level of wages exceeding the national average by one-third, and labour market relations characterised by excess labour demand. The region's economy is mainly based on industry, particularly in the Volkswagen-centred automotive industry, but also oil refining, organic and non-organic chemical industry production hallmarked by Slovnaft and Istrochem. In addition to Volkswagen and Slovnaft, other large-scale employers are Železničná Spoločnosť Cargo Slovakia (railway transport), Sociálna Poisťovňa Ústredia (social security), Orange, T-Mobile (telecommunication), DELL (IT) and Coca-Cola.

A wide range of large industrial plants and the proximity of the capital play a significant and positive role in the life of the West Slovakian Region. The predominant role of Nitra, the region's largest city, where regional central functions are concentrated, is further enhanced by the presence of the Volkswagen Elektrické Systémy, the largest subcontractor of the mother company in Bratislava. The second largest city in the region is Trnava, where the French PSA Peugeot Citroen set up the country's second largest car factory half a decade ago. In addition to the automotive sector, the electronic industry hallmarked by South Korean Samsung (Galanta) and Japanese Sony (Trnava and Nitra) are responsible for a large share of regional output. The most important petrochemical complex in the area, the Duslo chemical works in Šaľa, produces nitrogenous fertilisers and rubber industry products in addition to natural gas processing. Other significant employers are Danfoss Compressors in Nitra, Osram in Nove Zamky, Slovenské Energetické Strojárne in Levice, Euroobuv in Komarno and SEWS in Topol'čany.

Central Slovakia is a region showing no above–average characteristics. The largest share of industrial output is provided by the traditionally important mechanical engineering, chemical, pharmaceutical and paper industries. The country's largest printing firm was developed in Martin. The South Korean automotive company Kia set up its single European plant near Žilina. The tourism potential of the region is great, but the low quality of tourism services and the lack of marketing activity led to the under-exploitation of this asset. The southern part of the region (the area of Lučenec and Rimavská Sobota) has faced the most severe problems of unemployment in the country for almost a decade.

Eastern Slovakia is the most under-developed region in the country. Economic activity is mainly concentrated in Košice. The largest employers are US Steel in Košice, Východoslovenská Energetika, Tepláreň Košice (thermal power station), Yazaki Wiring Technologies, BSH Drivers and Pumps (Michalovce), Gemtex (Kežmarok), and Embraco and Panasonic AVC Networks (Spišská Nová Ves). The 300-hectare industrial park in Kechnec, one of the most successful industrial parks of the country is located in this region. Kechnec has a Hungarian population and 12 foreign companies with 2,000 employees are located there. An important factor of regional competitiveness is Košice airport registering 500 thousand passengers per year.

Transcarpathia is the region showing the weakest economic performance among those discussed here, with a GDP per capita below 25 per cent of the EU average. However, it is in a relatively good position compared to other Ukrainian regions. According to surveys about the investment attractiveness of Ukrainian regions (regarding the general level of economic development, state of market infrastructure, financial sector, state of human resources, operation of local enterprises and local governments) the most attractive destination after Kiev and Lviv is Transcarpathia. Another positive sign is that according to the complex regional development index, Transcarpathia was among the most dynamic regions of Ukraine in the last few years. Regarding the adequate functioning of the labour market, the situation is much less favourable; Transcarpathia performs well below the average in terms of entrepreneurial activity. The general performance of the economy is illustrated by the fact that 16 per cent of workers are employed in industry and producing over 50 per cent of GDP. The number of industrial employees fell by 60 per cent by the beginning of the twenty-first century. The areas of Mukacheve and Uzhhorod show signs of depression. The role of foreign direct investment is still modest at present. The most significant foreign investment in the region, the Škoda and Volkswagen car-assembly factory is located near the Hungarian border in Solomonovo.

The Romanian Northwest region has an agrarian type economy based on the number and proportion of agricultural workers (the agrarian sector is the major source of income for over 50 per cent of the population); however, light and heavy industrial branches also play an important role in the nationally significant regional industrial centres (Cluj-Napoca, Oradea, Baia Mare and Satu Mare). Due to its economic structure, the region's GDP per capita remains below the Romanian average, despite the fact that Cluj-Napoca and Oradea are the most dynamically developing cities of the country. These large cities offer a wide range of business services with elements that are otherwise only characteristic of Bucharest. Foreign Direct Investment amounting to €1.7 billion (4.6 per cent of the total FDI in Romania) represents a minor or major share in 13,000, and has created a large number of new jobs (this area also includes the entrepreneurial zone in Borş, situated directly on the Romanian-Hungarian border, a potential destination for Hungarian workers). This region may be considered the main destination of Hungarian investment activity in Romania: 43 per cent is concentrated in Cluj, Bihor and Satu Mare counties. Cluj-Napoca airport registered 750 thousand passengers in 2008; the terminal which opened that same year can house 2 million passengers.

In terms of development, the Western Region has a high position in the country. The economy benefits well from its traditionally Western orientation, its historical and gradually reviving economic-spatial structural connections and the existence of developed and high quality cross-border transport networks. Various elements of the transport system (different types of railways and main road is, the international airport in Timişoara with 1 million passengers in 2008) enabled this area to become a transit region for international trade between the EU and countries outside the EU, and to provide increasing opportunities for action for a diversified economy. This region, which is second to Bucharest, provides about one-fifth of Romania's exports. On the basis of its foreign direct investment stock of €2.0 billion, it has the second largest value in the country.

The Centre region, referred to as the heart of Transylvania, produces 12 per cent of the national GDP, and the proportion of industry and construction in40 per cent) is relatively high. The sufficiently advanced system of main roads and railway infrastructure, two airports (Târgu Mureş and Sibiu) and a third under construction (Braşov) and diversified industry were sufficient to attract foreign direct investment of €2.6 billion (7.7 per cent of Romania's). The region already benefits from its location at the intersection of key strategic main roads and railways (three European main routes passing through it) but the lack of significant developments has meant that the region's advantages have not been fully exploited. Capital investments are concentrated in the region's traditionally developed areas once populated by the Saxons (Germans. As a further sign of spatial concentration, 18 out of the region's 30 most prominent companies are located in Braşov and Sibiu counties.

Székler Land[2] is also part of this region. The Székkler (székely) counties are near the Romanian average in terms of GDP per capita. Among the 42 Romanian counties Mureş and Covasna are joint seventeenth and Harghita nineteenth. In his PhD thesis, István Nagy from Miercurea Ciuc examined the three counties' location in the Romanian economic space based on 65 indicators (by rank order calculation) and found that Mureş was twelfth, Covasna eighteenth and Harghita nineteenth, according to the rank order indicators. Regarding temporal dynamics, Mureş is ninth, Covasna is twenty-second , and Harghita is twenty-fourth in ranking of the 42 counties of Romania (Nagy 2009). Forty per cent of Hungarian FDI was allocated to Harghita and Covasna counties.

The autonomous province of Vojvodina is considered to be a developed territory of Serbia. Income values per capita exceed the national average, as the province generates 30 per cent of the national GDP, 33 per cent of the national export and contains 27 per cent of the country's population. The position of Vojvodina and its developmental potential (based not only on the income situation, but economic structure, the quality of human resources and the institutional system) is by no means worse than that of most backward regions of the Carpathian Basin, including some more under-developed regions of Hungary. Disregarding the content, the institutional administrative structure of the autonomous province bears the closest formal resemblance to the decentralised institutional system of most Western European regionalised states.

There are large developmental disparities inside the region. West Bačka is the most developed district of the province. The level of GDP per capita is 2.5 times as high as the provincial average in the area of Apatin, whereas it is only one-third of the amount in the small region of Sremski Karlocki (near Novi Sad). GDP values in the surroundings of larger cities are 1.5 times or twice as high as the provincial average. The value of the complex development index in North Bačka and North Banat, with large Hungarian populations, is twice as high as the provincial average. Industry accounts for 33 per cent of the total employment, and agriculture for 10 per cent. Vojvodina's food industry is the largest supplier to the Serbian market, and 50–80 per cent of a wide range of products are manufactured in the province.

Declining areas

A considerable part of the industry established in the socialist era disappeared due to the economic crisis that preceded systematic change and the privatisation and restructuring process that followed. The demand for low-quality products involving high production costs has considerably diminished in Eastern Europe and also in domestic markets. The decrease in production capacities led to the reduction of most of the workforce. The unemployment rate increased drastically, the income level of the population was reduced and territorial-local conflicts multiplied. The situation was aggravated in regions where one single company was the main employer. The disappearance of the dominant company resulted in the disappearance of a range of services for the population.

The largest group of depressed areas consists of the heavy industrial, mainly mining and metallurgical regions. Mining used to employ 450,000 workers in the 1970s in the Carpathian Basin, and by 2006, the number of jobs in this branch fell by one-quarter, to 114,000 (Illés 2008). These areas struggle with severe structural problems: transport, communication and public services infrastructures are under-developed, agricultural areas polluted and of low quality. Therefore, these regions are unable to attract capital. In several cases we can find ore processing plants and metallurgical centres in the proximity of mining sites.

There are many depressed areas in Eastern Slovakia and in Transylvania (Figure 8.4). A large Hungarian population lives in the backward regions of Southern and Eastern Slovakia. The most under-developed townships contain 33 per cent of Slovakia's Hungarian population. A whole range of areas in South Transylvania (Hunedoara, Reşiţa, Oraviţa, Oţelu Roşu, Cugir and Făgăraş) belong to the group of declining industrial areas. For instance, the number of miners decreased from 45,000 to 18,000 in the Petrosani Basin with a population of 160,000. The most vulnerable areas in North-Western Transylvania are those towns where the local economy is based on non-ferrous ore processing. The regions of Zlatna and Copşa Mică are classified as environmental disaster zones. Only two settlements are categorised as depressed areas in Székler Land: Bălan in Harghita county and Baraolt in Covasna county. In both towns, the difficulties of transformation are linked to the decline of mining industry. The population of the depressed areas of Transylvania, as a result of the inward migration occurring simultaneously with forced industrialisation, is predominantly Romanian.

Successful regions

In the market economy, companies, settlements and regions compete with each other to obtain development resources, institutions, infrastructure and human resources in order to create an increasingly favourable entrepreneurial environment which facilitates social and economic revival of their area. We can find successful areas in every region of the Carpathian Basin.

According to a survey by the Entrepreneur Association of Slovakia (2004), along Slovakian-Hungarian border, the district of Dunajská Streda offers the most favourable entrepreneurial environment. The district predominantly inhabited by ethnic Hungarians (over 83 per cent), occupies the prominent thirteenth position in the list of the country's 79 districts. The district outranks the rest of the country's successful territories (Košice and Banská Bystrica among others).

The former agrarian district has undergone an exemplary process of renewal in the last two decades, becoming an industrial, commercial, logistic and touristic centre and an active region on the growth axis between Vienna, Bratislava and Győr (Finka 2009; Jaššo 2007). The district's centre (populated by 25,000

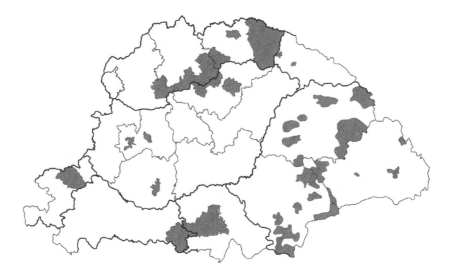

Figure 8.4 Declining areas in the Carpathian Basin
Source: Designed by the author.

inhabitants, and 50,000 with the surrounding agglomeration) exploited its developmental opportunities to an outstanding degree at the time of the change of the regime. The development of Dunajská Streda has been constant for over half a century, transforming the town into one of the most attractive social and economic centres of South Slovakia. Two other settlements with city status, Šamorín (12,500 inhabitants) and Veľký Meder (9,000 inhabitants) which were successful in their transition to the market economy, contribute to the outstanding competitive position of the district.

Székler Land has a reputation as a region with a great respect for tradition which constitutes an insurmountable obstacle to modernisation. Nevertheless, during the last hundred years there have been several remarkable initiatives which were respected not only in Transylvania, but also in Hungary and Europe.

The need for structural renewal and definite intervention was articulated at the Székely Congress of 1902 and during the subsequent attempts of economic development to remedy the general state of backwardness and belated peripheral development prevailing through the centuries. No such comprehensive development strategies were articulated in other areas of the country at the beginning of the last century. The Székely Congress, which integrated the development endeavours of territorial stakeholders into a unified system in an exemplary manner, is duly considered to be an important element of the tradition of Hungarian spatial development. The crises of history eliminated the possibility of the propositions being followed by actual forms of governmental and local action, yet regional development experts may find the in minutes of the congress an interesting and thought provoking methodology even today (Székely Kongresszus, 2001).

Among recent innovations, the Miercurea Ciuc and Târgu-Mureş faculties of the Sapientia Hungarian University in Transylvania are worth noting. Intellectuals of Székler Land recognised that the use of knowledge acquired in the region was more profitable in the development of local economies. The Székler university was not established, and we are right to investigate the reasons for this, yet higher education endeavours originate from the modern idea that development of the knowledge-based society will be inevitable in the future. Intellectual achievements are perceived in the economy, too. Modern industrial clusters (printing and confection industry clusters) are emerging in several parts of the region. Regional development strategies with scientific pretensions are being formulated. Social forums of community planning are being established and the urban planning concept of Odorheiu Secuiesc meets European standards.

Hopefully these factors of the Székler paradigm shift, that may rely heavily on past experiences in history, will continue to gain strength, transforming Székler Land into a key driver of modernisation of the Romanian economic space. All this will not be fed by nostalgic sentiments, but forced by the demand to create European-level living standards. The optimal harmonisation of this triple linkage, which serves as an important driving force in several European regions, requires special managing structures. This summarises the basic essence of the concept of autonomy.

Weak R&D capacities

The change of the regime had a controversial effect on the state of scientific research in the neighbouring countries. On one hand, political and legal frameworks were set up guaranteeing scientific liberty, but on the other hand, R&D capacities decreased from one-half to one-third of their former level, and the number of R&D staff also decreased considerably. At present, only 0.2 to 0.6 per cent of the GNP in neighbouring countries is allocated to R&D purposes (the 1.6 per cent rate of Slovenia is the highest in Central and Eastern Europe). These low rates are further compounded by the presence of significant regional disparities in each of the countries. In counties and regions in Hungarian-populated areas, the value of this index is considerably lower than the national average (e.g. the estimated R&D expenditure values fall within the statistical error ranges in Covasna and Harghita in Székler Land).

The legislation creating scientific liberty in the area of ethnic Hungarian research has proved to be a dynamic force. Formerly latent scientific forces were mobilised, and have taken institutional form. Results of the Hungarian world of science were shortly presented in publications, scientific workshops and independent journals and professional forums. These remarkable results were attributed to the ambitions of leading scientists and the young generation of researchers. Still, the level of R&D expenditure remained quite low. Even though it is possible to achieve results with lower expenditure in the development of a qualified scientific experts group and in individual scientific progress, this will hardly generate progressive and developmental energies for Hungarian communities.

The institutionalisation of Hungarian science witnessed extensive development at the stage of formation. Research teams and workshops were formed at several places in the Carpathian Basin which were organised within the national legal systems for optimal financial resourcing. The common feature the research institutions of different size and nature is that they are primarily financed by Hungarian funds and research programmes. The research units operate in isolation and have short-term plans. The continuous implementation of their programmes and the income of their research staff depend almost entirely on often unpredictable, arbitrary and non-transparent decisions of Hungarian foundation boards of trustees. The lack of resources for basic operation and the dependence on external financing hinders the conscious and long-term planning and organic development process. The need for external financial resources due to inadequate financing does not promote co-operation among research units and the implementation of large-scale, multi-annual research programmes and the application of up-to-date instruments of modern science organisation. The involuntary dependence on minimal financing of basic activities and the low organisational size below the level of scale economies cannot promote international co-operation; moreover, it inhibits the articulation of ambitious research programmes.

Effective co-operation is further hindered by fact that research teams operating in public institutions beyond the borders of Hungary can be supported by Hungarian sources only to a very limited extent. Even the most efficient research units are unable to exploit their competitive advantage for the benefit of Hungarian communities.

New tendencies in regional development

EU-compatible territorial policy

Three factors hindered the elaboration and continuous implementation of long-term strategies to reduce regional development problems in the countries of the Carpathian Basin's in the first phase of the transition lasting from the collapse of communism to the mid-1990s: the limited support of an independent regional policy at the government level, the underdevelopment of institutions of regional development and the unresolved situation of territorial administration. At that time, among the respective countries, only Hungary and Slovenia elaborated governmental regional development programmes. The establishment of regional development institutions began during the second half of the 1990s, partially due to the grave consequences of the continuously deepening territorial crisis in the four countries that applied for EU membership, and also due to pressure from the EU. The first country where paradigm change took place was Hungary. The 1998 Report of the European Commission declared that Hungary appeared to be the best prepared in terms of regional policy.

After Hungary, Romania was the second country to prepare a plan concerning the elaboration of objectives, tools and institutions of regional development. The Green Paper elaborated within the PHARE framework highlighted the problems of spatial development, analysed the situation of the country's spatial structure and made suggestions about the construction of the Romanian model of spatial development (Green Paper, 1997). The document summarised the most urgent tasks of Romanian spatial development policy in nine articles ranging from the establishment of basic institutions of spatial development, the introduction of regional programming, to the organisation of training for regional development professionals. These proposals are quite self-evident and reasonable in developed market economies and civil democracies with articulated institutional systems, yet in case of the Romanian democracy based on new principles while conserving the old structures, obstacles to realisation are considerable.

Due to pressure from the EU, spatial development policy plays an important role in the reform initiatives of Romanian governments. The Act on spatial development (1998) defined the role of regional development as follows: 'to diminish existing regional disparities through promoting balanced development, reducing the backwardness of less favoured areas due to historical, geographical, social and political conditions, and preventing the development of new inequalities (Green Paper 1997: p. 3).

The Soviet type of councils in transition countries were replaced by local governments based on the European model. Local governments became the main stakeholders in the new distribution of power. Due to democratic euphoria and the dislike of former territorial administrative organisations, territorial meso-levels in Romania gained only limited functions. The elected county councils remained, but a system of prefectures with extensive powers were organised. Regions were abolished in Slovakia and public authorities were established in the districts, and public administration offices also operated in the newly formed districts of Serbia. The four-level Soviet administration remained in Ukraine, while elected councils and presidential delegates operate in areas in the Carpathians and their districts.

The revaluation of spatial development had a binding influence on the disintegrated public administration, too. The territorial administration reforms in the mid-1990s led to the setting up of larger territorial units. Eight counties were created in Slovakia and 20 in Croatia.

The objectives and the institutional system of an EU-compatible spatial development, the preparation of planning and structural policy decisions require larger territorial units in the new EU member-states. The economic potential and the size of the 42 Romanian, the 19 Hungarian and eight Slovakian territorial-administrative units are too modest to provide an opportunity for territorial organisations to articulate and implement comprehensive and complex spatial development objectives. Consequently, counties of different socio-economic structure were organised into development regions. In principle, the size of development regions allows the effective utilisation of resources and the elaboration and realisation of regional development strategies. Regions are also the basic units of statistical data collection and processing.

The delimitation of development regions and the selection of their capitals are the most debated questions of the institutional system of spatial development in each country. Several concepts were articulated in Romania about the delimitation of regions and finally the eight-region version following the historical borders of Transylvania, also respecting the existing county based delimitation became the basis of regulation. The internal structure of the Transylvanian regions may give rise to new disputes. The Centre region in Romania provides an unfavourable structural framework for the three Székler counties, and the decision to put the headquarters of the regional development organisation to Alba Iulia further aggravated this situation. Due to historical traditions and urban network features, the conditions are more favourable for the organisation of regions in Romania in certain aspects, for the following reasons:

- Seventeen provinces constituted the territorial meso-level between 1953 and 1965; the administrative structure of the country changed several times in the twentieth century, and, contrary to Hungary, territorial administration is not rooted in century-long traditions. Despite the multiple-decade forced homogenisation, the country's historical regions (Oltenia, Muntenia, Moldova, Transylvania, Banat, etc.) still reveal traces of regional identity upon which a conscious regional policy can be based.
- Romania's network of large cities provides relatively favourable conditions for decentralised spatial development. Cluj-Napoca, Oradea, Timişoara, Arad, Braşov, Sibiu, Târgu-Mureş, Craiova, Constanţa, Galaţi, Iaşi, Ploeşti, Piteşti can be considered as real growth centres both in terms of population and multifunctional profile. Large cities have strong intellectual and cultural functions. At several locations there are R&D capacities with 2,000 to 5,000 employees and universities with 10,000 to 30,000 thousand registered students.

Difficulties should be considered as factors preventing the diffusion of the efficient institutional model of the regional policy of the European Union and its organisational forms encouraging autonomous decision-making in unitary states with a homogenous nation-state ideology. Attempts in Székler Land to elaborate the bottom-up, integrative regional development model were not particularly liked by the local and central Romanian political elite and administration. Regional development scientific forums in Székler Land are regularly followed by sharp counter-opinions. The circles of opposition tend to forget that conclusions of the research laying down the foundation of new regional policy and the scientific debates on the evaluation of results do not point towards the institutionalisation of disintegration; on the contrary, an attempt is being made to elaborate the organisational forms and models boosting economic performance and regional competitiveness.

Extreme Slovak nationalism has left its mark on the institutional system of Slovakian regional development. After gaining independence in 1993, the majority of development policy decisions, the delimitation of territorial units on NUTS 2 and NUTS 3 levels, the regulation of local government powers and spatial development measures (without considering the institutionalisation of decentralisation which was a requirement of the EU) was based on ethnic reasons (namely the breaking up of Hungarian ethnic territory on the north-south axis, the negative discrimination of areas with a Hungarian population in development policy). The approach of spatial development questions on an ethnical basis (dating back to 1918) weakens cohesion, and is a cause of large socio-economic disparities among the country's macro-regions.

Cross-border territorial co-operation

As Europe continues to unite, national and EU regional policy and regional science turn their attention increasingly to examining issues concerning national borders, border areas and cross-border co-operation. The topic of border areas and an examination of the divisive and connective roles of national borders have also become important questions in the countries of transition in East Central Europe. The changes occurring in the late 1980s and early 1990s in Eastern Europe created circumstances which are more favourable for regional co-operation. The relaxing of rigid border controls and the broadening of cross-border connections were also expected in the Carpathian Basin. However, in spite of some encouraging developments, there remain, perhaps understandably, new and inherited problems and superficial contradictions which make co-operation harder (Baranyi 2003).

For a long time, national borders within the expanding European Union hampered the steady growth of economic space, in part slowing the dynamism of co-operation (Hooper and Kramsch 2004; Scott 2000, 2006). This negative influence was exacerbated in Central and Eastern Europe. In spite of the broadening of the European horizon, national borders remained, and, moreover, as new states came into existence, the boundaries of former domestic macro-regions became significant borders. In Central and Eastern Europe, the territorial structure was fragmented and natural connections disappeared, placing obstacles in the way of uniting the European space structure. Differences were often intensified, since the centre-periphery dynamics of individual countries generated movements in the spatial structure on both sides of borders, so influencing old or new divergences, whether economic or social in origin.

The change of political system created, in the Carpathian Basin also, a situation which was, in general, favourable for regional co-operation, even when considering the weaknesses coming to light at the same time, such as the fears, suspicions and conflicts of earlier ages. The Interreg-CBC programme of the European Union played a leading part in creating new attitudes.

The role and importance of cross-border co-operation, redefining the functions of national borders, became more important not only among specialists in regional sciences, but also for EU Structural and Cohesion policy. Dynamic development began in many West European border regions, stimulated by EU programmes and targeting the development of border areas. Most notably, these included the historical-territorial-ethnic and other problems of the past which had blocked European co-operation along the borders between France, Germany, Belgium and the Netherlands, and between Austria and Italy.

Most areas lying alongside national borders in East Central Europe are still under-developed . In Hungary, the Northern and Eastern areas which border Slovakia,

Ukraine and Romania, are among the least developed areas of the European Union (Kozma 2011). The Romanian and Serbian areas across the South-eastern and Southern borders of Hungary show somewhat better results, although productivity in Croatian regions bordering Hungary is also below the national average in GDP terms, and the Burgenland is the least developed *Land* in Austria. The low productivity is primarily the result of an outdated economic structure: high employment in agriculture, coupled with an outdated industrial structure and a weak tertiary sector.

Unfavourable border locations, inadequate urbanisation, a chronic lack of capital, the acute employment crisis, all beg for development support for marginally situated areas and settlements. It is in the basic national interest of countries in transition such as Hungary and its neighbours to eliminate the rigid division of national borders.

An institutional background for cross-border structures has been created in practically every stretch of border in Hungary, and since the ratification of the Madrid Agreement (1993) a strong wave of co-operation has swept along the country's borders. The circumstantial nature of much of this new co-operation is evident in the many problems which are faced and which hinder effective co-operation. Such problems, among many others, are the excessive number of types of organisational structure and circles of actors, tasks which are over- generously and too widely formulated and the modest financial potential attached to them. The peak of institutionalisation reached in East Central Europe to date has been the formation of Euroregion organisations (so named, although not bordering the EU). Based on size and territoriality, on the situation in and connection with the spatial structure, there are two main types of Euroregion.

One is the so-called 'macro-region' model and the other, the 'micro-region' model. The former could also be called the 'provincial' or 'county' model, since they consist of Euroregion organisations including meso-level territorial units, provinces, regions (NUTS 2) and/or counties (NUTS 3) of two or more neighbouring countries (e.g. the Euroregion Carpathians). The latter could equally be named the *urban gravitational* field model, since it builds strongly on direct bilateral connections between micro-regions (NUTS 3) or settlements (NUTS 5). Considering smaller areas from the outset, it defines the territorial interdependencies of the region more narrowly, while preserving a number of strategic elements of the macro-region model (Baranyi 2003).

Euroregions embodying an institutionalised form of co-operation between border regions have a longer history in Western Europe. On the other hand, in East Central Europe this form of cross-border co-operation grew stronger following the change of the political and economic system and the completion of Euro-Atlantic processes. In particular, managing the integrating continent is made significantly easier by the formation of territorial units which normally function as a single economic area, considering that the Euroregions are characteristic geographical structures of cross-border relations. Euroregions are the highest level of institutionalised cross-border co-operation, and, while mostly unifying border regions, they are the most developed organisations with the widest range of powers and with the most functions. The main objective of Euroregions is to be recognised as a form of international organisation which deals with the economic, environmental, social, cultural and other institutional problems of a region. By concentrating these activities at Euroregion level, they hope to reach a critical mass (in the economic sense) which will strengthen the cohesion of the border areas and attract the interest of private and institutional investors.

A pragmatic, final definition of Euroregions would then be: they are a traditional, and the most effective, form of cross-border co-operation, which geographically encompass territories of two or more countries who sign an agreement with the aim of harmonising their activity in order to develop their border areas more effectively.

Hungarian counties are currently taking part in 16 cross-border inter-regional co-operative organisations (Table 8.3). The formal structures and substantive characteristics of these co-operative organisations are very different, as are the motives for co-operation, but, as a general characteristic, we can emphasise that these organisations have the potential to broaden the market for the Hungarian national economy, to push the limits of the economies of size and help the market expansion of companies.

Apart from the problems of cross-border co-operation already mentioned, the huge number of organisations set up without serious reason, the fundamental problem is the territoriality of the new-born Euroregions. The new institutionalised border regions relatively rarely cover real, functional border areas, and while there are positive examples (e.g. Euroregion Košice-Miskolc), it is far more usual that, since the early formation of the huge Euroregion (Euroregions Carpathians and Duna-Tisza-Körös-Maros), the areas involved in any given co-operation have become smaller, more accurately reflecting genuine spatial connections, and also include the Eastern borders of Hungary (Interregio, Euroregion Bihar-Bihor). The motive behind these basically positive processes probably lies in the fact that the micro-regions and settlements on both sides of a border have identified the possibilities in their common interest, especially considering matters of natural geography, space structure and the ethnic make-up of the one against the other in territories divided by the Treaty of Trianon. In this way they circumvent the (still significant) obstacles rising from the principle of the nation-state, and placing the benefits of local co-operation at the forefront (Baranyi 2003; Hardi 2008).

Overall, systematic change has created favourable conditions for regional co-operation in the Carpathian Basin, even if weaknesses and previous conflicts, fears and suspicions were brought to the surface at the same time. The EU's Interregional CBC programmes played a primary role in the formation of the new approach. A number of areas on two sides of Central and Eastern European state borders are under-developed. The Slovakian, Ukrainian and Romanian border areas adjacent to North-east Hungary are among the least developed territories of the new European Community. Romanian and Serbian regions along the South-eastern and Southern Hungarian borders show a slightly better performance. The performance of the two adjoining Croatian macro-regions is below the average national GDP, just as Burgenland is the most under-developed *Land* of Austria.

The currently disadvantageous cross-border situation, the predominance of rural areas, the chronic lack of capital, the acute employment crisis urge the development of marginal areas and their settlements. The dissolution of the rigid dividing role

Table 8.3 Important basic data of cross-border co-operation organisations, 2010

International organisation	Founded in	Territory (km²)	Population ('000s)	Hungarians (%)	No. of territorial units
Euroregion Carpathians	1993	154042	15,708	16.2	20
Euroregion Neogradiensis	1999	3,897	360	60.2	4
Euroregion Ipoly	1999	5,782	450	49.4	4
Euroregion Vag-Danube-Ipoly	1999	14,283	2,082	65.5	6
Euroregion Košice-Miskolc	2000	14,000	1512	49.3	2
Euroregion Sajó-Rima	2000	10,621	930	80.0	4
Euroregion Triple Danube region	2001	8,648	976	77.4	4
Euroregion of Zemplen	2003	3,186	251	59.5	4[1]
Euroregion Ister-Granum	2003	Irrelevant[2]	91	60.4	17
Euroregion Danube-Tisza-Körös-Maros	2001	77, 500	6,110	28.9	9
Euroregion Danube-Drava-Sava	2002	11,760	1,335	33.8	5
West Pannonia Euroregion	2001	15, 148	1,265	78.0	4
Euroregion Drava-Mura	2001	Irrelevant[2]	157	62.4	9
Euroregion Hajdu-Bihar-Bihor	2002	13,765	1,178	46.9	2
Bihar-Bihor	2002	1,759	140	28.3	36[3]

Notes: [1]The members of the inter-regional co-operation are smaller administrative districts and micro-regions; [2]The members do not border each other, and so the size of territory is not relevant; [3] The members are neighbouring settlements.

Source: Designated by the author.

of state borders and their gradual dissolution is a basic national interest for transition countries.

The institutional background of cross-border structures has been implemented on each Hungarian frontier area. Since the ratification of the Madrid Agreement in 1993, a real co-operation and foundation wave has swept through the country's borders. The eventuality of the large number of newly formed organisations and co-operations is accompanied by several problems which hinder their efficient functioning. The extremely wide range of organisational structures and stake-holders, the overly generous and generalised definition of tasks and the related modest sources of financing pose such problems. The institutionalisation of linkages reached its peak in Central and Eastern Europe in the formation of the Euroregional organisations, which, despite their name, do not share borders with the EU.

Hungarian counties are currently involved in 16 organisations of cross-border inter-regional co-operation. The organisations of co-operation change in their formal framework and content. Their motives are varied, yet a common feature is that these organisations have the potential to broaden the market spaces of all co-operating regions, and may raise economies of scale and promote the market expansion of companies. At present, however, only weak signs indicate the presence of this opportunity. Member-states allocate only modest resources to the development of cross-border economic co-operation. Neither the support system for economic planning and economic development, nor the corporate strategies are able to transform cross-border relationships into forces of integration yet.

The new institutionalised border regions rarely overlap real functional frontier areas. Even though positive examples can be found (e.g. the Košice-Miskolc Euroregion); co-operations along the Eastern frontiers have been formed in ever smaller areas respecting real spatial relationships (e.g. Interregion, Bihar-Bihor Euroregion), since the creation of the Euroregions which initially encompassed huge areas (Carpathian Euroregion, Danube-Kriş-Mureş-Tisza Euroregion). The underlying reason for these basically positive processes is that micro-regions and settlements on both sides of the frontier became aware of the opportunities created by their common interests, especially those in the natural geographical, spatial structural and ethnic interdependence of territories divided by frontiers established by the Treaty of Trianon, while evading the still significant nation-state obstacles and focusing on the advantages of local co-operation (Baranyi 2003, 2007; Hardi 2008).

Development plans for the period between 2007–2013

With the elaboration of national development plans for EU member-states for the periods between 2004–2006 and 2007–2013, a new era began in determining development directions of the Carpathian Basin's regions. National development plans were made using the EU planning methodology.

The number and nomination of operational programmes of the national development plans vary from country to country. National programmes are divided into five large groups of activities in harmony with EU requirements. The Economic Competitiveness Operational Programme covers the development of small and medium-sized enterprises, the support of R&D development and investments in technology. The Environmental Protection and Infrastructure Operational Programme focuses on the development of a healthy domestic environment through the creation of environmental infrastructure, the improvement of environmental safety and aims to develop transport infrastructure. The objectives of the Human Resources Development Operational Programme are to raise the standard of training and education, improve the competitiveness of the workforce and to promote social inclusion. The Agricultural and Rural Development Operational Programme focuses on the modernisation and increased efficiency of agricultural production on one hand, partially through the development of production technologies and food processing; and on the other hand, on the development of rural areas, the creation of alternative income opportunities for the population. Regional Operational Programmes cover developments under the responsibility of development regions.

A negative phenomenon is that the process of accession to the European Union has had a centralising effect on all new member-states. National development plans reflected a top-down approach. The central government had an almost exclusive role in the elaboration of programmes. The development regions, not being administrative units, could only partially enforce their interests and development ideas and their role was mostly limited to the collection of projects. National development plans denominate mostly sectoral development tasks. Regional operational programmes were not based on the development ideas of regions; instead, tasks omitted from sectoral operational programmes were regarded as of regional significance. A sign of the undervaluation of the regions is that the rate of development resources allocated to regional operational programmes does not reach 25 per cent of the development resources in any country (Table 8.4).

EU-financed developments will mainly be infrastructure-related (roads, sewage system construction, etc.) and concerned with environmental protection (48 per cent of the expenditure in Romania, 45 per cent in Slovakia), which can temporarily improve the conditions for local entrepreneurs involved in these construction works and develop the local environment, improve the accessibility and living standards, but do not provide adequate resources for sustainable growth. Romanian development policy allocates much fewer resources to the development of a competitive economy and to regional programmes than required. Therefore, other methods should be used for the reinforcement of economic bases. The methods and techniques of the market-based development of the economy (which means the production of internationally marketable products and services) can and must be mastered. This is necessary, because fundamental changes are expected in the support policy of the EU from 2014 onwards. We must be prepared for this. Hungarian communities ought to be involved in this preparation work. It is still a false conception, even in Hungary, that the creation of a competitive society can be based on EU support. However, healthy communities do not require the socio-political control of society.

The result of the strong dependence on the central government is that local and regional synergies are neglected. The experiences of concluded or still effective

Table 8.4 EU support for operational programmes, 2007–2013

	Hungary		Romania		Slovakia	
	Million euros	(%)	Million euros	(%)%	Million euros	(%)
Competitive economy	2,810	11.3	2,724	14.2	2,975	26.4
Environment and infrastructure	10,905	43.8	9,286	48.3	5,007	44.5
Human resources development	5,430	21.8	3,476	18.1	1,750	15.5
Regional development	5,771	23.1	3,726	19.4	1,532	13.6
Total	24,916	100.0	19,212	100.0	11,264	100.0

Source: Eligible areas under the Convergence Objective and the Regional Competitiveness and Employment Objective. http://ec.europa.eu/regional_policy/atlas2007 [2012. 04.19.]

national development plans indicate that the mechanism of centralised decision-making does not support the reduction of spatial disparities but their increase. Regional financial resources are not capable of investments in cross-border co-operation since they are primarily allocated to tasks related to settlement regeneration, education, culture and tourism development. While Interreg programmes extend the frameworks of co-operation between areas overlapping national borders, they are less capable of establishing long-term economic relations. The results of an international research project conducted in the Hungarian-Romanian frontier area warns that the efficiency of centrally controlled programmes for the development of peripheries is low. Offices of central administration located in frontier areas are insensitive to local specificities and the bureaucratic nature of the organisation disables co-operation among the actors of spatial development policies (Baranyi 2006).

Tasks for strengthening territorial cohesion

The group of countries (excluding Ukraine) with 54 million inhabitants, constituting or overlapping the Carpathian Basin is characterised by large disparities in their territorial structure, demographic potential and settlement network. The population distribution in Romania and Slovakia is relatively balanced, and they have a deconcentrated settlement structure. There are several densely populated areas in the settlement network of Romania. Regional centres with a significant population and economic potential developed outside the capital. The capitals in the majority of the eight countries of the Carpathian Basin, while being dominant economic, political decision-making centres and at the same time the most developed territorial units of their countries, are located in this large natural area or in its proximity. This geopolitical position may have an advantageous effect on the integration of the region, since the modernisation of the urban agglomerations of capitals forms the basis for integration into European economic space. Due to the proximity to state frontiers, economies of scale cannot be achieved without taking into account the interests of the neighbouring countries. In the examples of Bucharest and Kiev, which are far from the Carpathian Basin, it is not their agglomeration but their national strategic interests that require strengthening spatial relations. In order to access EU markets, these two countries have to use the transport networks of the Carpathian Basin.

The future of certain elements of the fragmented Hungarian nation is shaped primarily by national development strategies. Only slow and less forceful corrections are brought about by the support policy of Hungarian governments. The logical system of Hungarian development concepts did not incorporate potential effects of cross-border co-operation between several regions. Activities promoting the economic and cultural development of ethnic Hungarian territories do not form a unified system; they disregard the regional distribution of labour but seem to remain isolated initiatives independent of the development of the Hungarian economy. In the absence of organically linked elements, the consequences are incidental and the efficiency of intervention is low. There are no synergic effects, and the chances of sustainable development are limited. As an example, the absence of co-ordination can be mentioned among economic development initiatives of the Hungarian-populated areas and Hungarian higher education and research.

The notion of a national strategy today is primarily present in political documents, keeping in view the requirements to preserve the autonomy of ethnic Hungarian territories and to keep the Hungarian population in their homeland. The obvious and understandable basis of this idea is that the Hungarian population is decreasing. Demographic indices deteriorate, while according to Hungarian labour-market prognoses, economic development cannot be implemented without the settlement of a significant number of workers. A strategic answer has to be given to this significant question, too, keeping in mind that the flow of Hungarian working capital into foreign countries can create and additional workforce for the Hungarian economy in other regions. The content of the term used in political discourse is not elaborated. It has no exact definition and its content is not clarified making its elements and their interrelations unclear.

Besides more or less positive experiences of integration in modern European history, the following arguments support the creation of the Carpathian Basin macro-region:

- Cohesion problems of this area with a population of nearly 25 million show similarities (poor accessibility, outdated economic structure, capital city-based regions of modernisation); common objectives may facilitate the definition of modern European development directions and the financing of the implementation of programmes.
- The efficiency of uniform environmental protection across the Carpathian Basin and of common flood prevention programmes can be improved.
- Economies of scale requirements of modern driving forces of spatial development (high-level business services, R&D) are easier to meet; elements of the economic competitive strength can be more favourably developed.
- The organisation of regional capitals (large and medium-sized cities) into co-operation networks may contribute to the implementation of polycentric development set by the EU and to validate the strategic requirement of a polycentric regional development.
- New cross-border co-operation objectives can be defined and the optimal utilisation of local labour markets and service networks can be strengthened through co-operative linkages between neighbouring territories.
- The territory – due to its ethnic structure unique in Europe – may become the experimental field for the democratic exercise of power and regional autonomies. The institute of trans-national macro-regions may serve to eliminate the national obstacles of transition to a decentralised and regionalised political system.

The EU accession of Hungary and the two neighbouring countries with the largest Hungarian populations has created favourable conditions for long-term strategy making. EU structural policy relies on far-ranging trans-regional (cross-border and interconnected) territorial strategies. The EU is currently preparing plans for eight macro-regions. From the viewpoint of regional policy, the following topics are relevant regarding planning partnership in the Carpathian Basin:

1   The reduction of development disparities between cross-border areas, cross-border infrastructure development and labour market co-operation. Contrary to the present practice, special attention must be paid to the development of co-operation between large cities in the proximity of frontiers (Miskolc, Nyíregyháza, Debrecen, Szeged, Békéscsaba, Pécs, Győr, Košice, Satu Mare, Oradea, Arad, Timişoara, Novi Sad, Subotica, Osijek). A weakness of this territory is the low performance of business services. Its development, however, as the core of a knowledge-based economy, can only be imagined in metropolitan spaces. The quantity and quality of available information has always influenced the intensity of collaboration between labour markets significantly. While neighbouring regions on the former Austro-Hungarian frontier have mutually presented their job offers through existing institutional collaboration for several decades, the necessary information about conditions of employment is still lacking on the Eastern and Southern borders. There is a huge potential in constantly enhancing and upgrading the knowledge base of employees and employers, the exploitation of which may contribute to diminishing the chronic lack of workforce, and simultaneously reduce unemployment.

2   Neighbourhood partnership is a new priority of the EU's support policy for the period 2007–2013. The elaboration and harmonisation of development programmes for frontier regions and the execution of common tasks is unthinkable without taking an institutional form. The present practice of programme co-ordination of decentralised central government offices is inefficient. These tasks are executed by common bodies in Western European border regions. The functional model, organisational structure and operational order of common bodies for regional development (trans-national regional development councils) is to be elaborated.

3   Large cities in the proximity of frontiers (Miskolc, Košice, Debrecen, Nyíregyháza, Oradea, Satu Mare, Uzhhorod, Arad, Timişoara, Szeged, Subotica, Novi Sad, Pécs,) are or can be developed into dominant national knowledge centres. A severe problem in the neighbouring five countries is that their research potential does not attain the competitive size of organisations in the European knowledge market. The establishment of common research centres contributes to strengthening industrial linkages between research in natural sciences and engineering, promotes product development, the spread of knowledge-intensive small and medium-sized companies, and serves to raise the export potential of regions. The elaboration of the concept on the establishment of technological centres is to be encouraged. The development strategy ought to rely on the specialisation in research and development of a limited number of internationally marketable products and services.

4 A similar opportunity for collaboration is offered by the development of the existing or planned regional airports in the proximity of frontiers. Air transport can significantly improve the accessibility of these territories. Currently, several large Romanian cities maintain third-category regional airports, whereas in Hungary, only Debrecen airport has the potential of moving into a higher category. In order to attain this higher ranking, its agglomeration must be extended to the Romanian Bihor and Satu Mare counties with a population of approximately 1 million. The catchment area of the international airport of Timişoara could comprise the South-east Hungarian counties, and that of Košice's airport could extend to Eastern parts of the North Hungarian region. An efficient distribution of labour has to be achieved between Pécs and Osijek airports.

5 Regional development professionals of new member-states are still quite few in number and they are lacking adequate qualifications. There will be considerable growth in the size of regional development programmes in the new planning period, and in the meantime, their execution will become more complicated. A considerably larger number of regional policy experts will be required not only to organise the implementation of the programmes, but to monitor the anticipated consequences of the new European regional policy paradigm in the Central and Eastern European area struggling with specific problems. There is a need for training and postgraduate training centres which continuously organise the transfer of professional knowledge. The establishment of three major centres seems reasonable: the University of Debrecen (in collaboration with the University of Oradea, Babeş-Bolyai University and the Uzhhorod State University), the other in Pécs (co-operating with the universities of Osijek and Novi Sad) and the third in Győr (co-operating with universities and research institutes of Bratislava and the Selye János University of Komarno). As the leading institute of university training in regional policy and economics, the HAS Centre for Regional Studies could play an active role in the operation of these centres. CRS already operates cross-border documentation centres in Békéscsaba and Győr. The training programme of 50 regional experts could be organised with one and two semester courses.

6 The modernisation of the 15-year-old cross-border institutionalised Hungarian science is advisable. The essence of paradigm change is to articulate well defined objectives and instruments to implement further development, to determine relatively significant scientific capacities, to select leading institutions and to establish co-ordination forums.

The following objectives must be considered in the operation of Hungarian scientific workshops in the neighbouring countries:

1) Enhancing general Hungarian scientific capacities and results in order to strengthen the international position of Hungarian science.
2) Developing the national identity of Hungarian communities and establishing a solid basis for their modernisation programmes.

3) Taking into account the objectives of the dominant national science in order to expand resources of financing on the one hand, and promoting co-operation in European and bilateral research on the hand.
4) Establishing a scientific basis for Hungarian higher education program-mes, co-operation in doctoral programmes.
5) Adopting and developing new scientific branches.

7   The activity of cross-border Hungarian organisations may significantly contribute to strengthening the economy in the Carpathian Basin, to the revival of cross-border economic relations (nevertheless, significant regional dis-parities can be detected in the rate of development along the same frontier, due to the diverse sectoral structures and market relations in the regions). Hungarian-Hungarian economic co-operation networks support primarily the activity of small and medium-sized companies through organising business meetings, providing information services, and organising exhibitions and conferences. The conscious and deliberate development of co-operation results not only in increased trade flow but in common investments and the establish-ment of clusters in the long run.

The new European macro-region could also provide a framework for planning co-operation. It is possible to project the economic and spatial development impacts of the planned co-operative linkages, to estimate cohesion consequences and to call the designed programmes into action. National regional scientific workshops in each country could play a significant role in the implementation of this task. These research, planning and development programmes are also eligible for EU funding.

During the preparation for the next programming period of the EU starting in 2014, Hungarian development policy must take strongly marked positions in determining the scope and content of measures in favour of strengthening economic cohesion in the Carpathian Basin, and this must also be revealed in different forms of Hungarian support policy. The application of this new philo-sophy is a much more complex task, since it produces less spectacular but more efficient results.

The objective of organised handling of cross-border affairs is to continuously maintain and develop national identity. The development of economic relations must be organised by using highly sophisticated methods, countless formal and informal methods of partnership. In the future, the capital expansion in the Hungarian economy must be more intensive. Possible directions for capital export may also include the cross-border Hungarian-populated areas. Economic rationality suggests that these areas must also prepare for the entry of the Hungarian capital. At the same time, Hungarian economic policy must be aware of the fact that in the support policy of capital export, investments undertaken in cross-border Hun-garian-populated areas require special regulations. In their case, more factors need to be considered in order to produce rational decisions.

The development speed of the real economy, the quality of the structure of the economy and its income producing capacity, and this is a lesson to be learnt from the causes of the economic crisis, will be increasingly determined by the spatial co-operation and the quality of partnership between the state, the local governments, and the business stakeholders in the future. Partnership needs to be organised and managed. These functions are successfully practised by regions in several European countries. The institutionalisation of the formal regionalisation of the Carpathian Basin could lead to the economic boost of the area, while indirectly promoting the development of territorial autonomies. This is why Hungary ought to be a positive example in the formation of its regions.

References

Baranyi, B. (2003) 'Euroregional organisations and formations on the Eastern borders of Hungary', *European Spatial Research and Policy,* 1: 85–94.

Baranyi, B. (2006) 'Euroregions along the Eastern borders of Hungary: a question of scale?' in Scott, J.W. (ed.) *EU Enlargement, Region Building and Shifting Borders of Inclusion and Exclusion,* Aldershot: Ashgate, 149–162.

Baranyi, B. (2007) *A határ mentiség dimenziói Magyarországon* [Dimensions of borderland situation in Hungary], Budapest and Pécs: Dialóg Campus Kiadó.

Barta, G. (ed.) (2006) *Hungary – the New Border of the European Union,* Discussion Papers, 54, Pécs: Centre for Regional Studies, HAS.

Berend, T.I. and Ránki, G. (1982) *The European Periphery and Industrialization, 1780–1914,* Cambridge: Cambridge University Press.

Finka, M. (2009) 'Sustainable territorial development and concepts of polycentricity in Slovak territorial development', *Urban Research & Practice,* 3: 332–343.

Fitzmaurice, J. (1993) 'Regional co-operation in Central Europe', *Wes European Politics,* 3: 380–400.

Good, D.E. (1984) *The Economic Rise of the Habsburg Empire. 1750–1914,* Berkeley and Los Angeles, London: University of California Press.

Green Paper: Regional Development Policy in Romania (1997) Bucharest: Romanian Government and European Commission.

Hardi, T. (ed.) (2008) *Transborder Movements and Relations in the Slovakian-Hungarian Border Regions,* Discussion Papers, 68, Pécs: Centre for Regional Studies, HAS.

Hooper, B. and Kramsch, O. (eds) (2004) *Cross-border Governance in the European Union,* London: Routledge.

Horváth, J. (1998) 'Contribution to the history of regional co-operation in the Eastern and Central European region', *Society and Economy in Central and Eastern Europe,* 1: 58–74.

Illés, I. (ed.) (2008) *Visions and Strategies in the Carpathian Area (VASICA),* Discussion Papers Special, Pécs: Centre for Regional Studies, HAS.

Jaššo, M. (2008) 'Cross-border co-operation challenges: positioning the Vienna-Bratislava region' in Leibenath, L., Korcelli-Olejniczak, E. and Knippschild, R. (eds) *Cross-border Governance and Sustainable Spatial Development. Mind the Gaps!* Berlin: Springer, 87–100.

Kozma, G. (ed.) (2011) *New Results of Cross-border Co-operation,* Debrecen: Didakt Kft.

Scott, J.W. (2000) 'Euroregions, governance and transborder co-operation within the EU', *European Research in Regional Science,* 1: 104–115.

Scott, J.W. (ed.) (2006) *EU Enlargement, Region Building and Shifting Borders of Inclusion and Exclusion,* Aldershot: Ashgate.

Székely Kongresszus [Székler Congress], Csíkszereda: Hargita Kiadóhivatal, 2001.

Notes

1   The Carpathian or Pannonian Basin is a large basin in Central Europe. The basin covers all of Hungary and Slovakia, as well as parts of Serbia, Croatia, Slovenia, Austria and Ukraine. It forms a topographically discrete unit set in the European landscape, surrounded by imposing geographic boundaries.

2   Székler (Székely) Land refers to the territories inhabited mainly by the Székely, a Hungarian-speaking ethnic group from Eastern Transylvania. They live in the valleys and hills of the Eastern Carpathian Mountains corresponding to the present-day Harghita, Covasna counties, and parts of the Mureş county in Romania. Originally, the name Székler Land denoted an autonomous region within Transylvania. It existed as a legal entity from medieval times until the Austro–Hungarian Compromise of 1867, when it was incorporated intothe county system. Along with Transylvania, it became part of Romania in 1920. It was returned to Hungary in 1940 and was again cededto Romania in 1945. The area was an autonomous region within Romania between 1952–1968, and today there are Székely initiatives to reach a higher level of self-government for Székler Land within Romania.

9 Conclusions

Since the early stages of the transition, Central and Eastern European regional policies have gained strength, although they are still constrained by limited resources and institutional problems. The EU has not only provided financial and technical assistance to introduce the necessary legislation and improve policy design in all spheres of the economy but has also contributed to changes in the territorial organisation of the countries. New actors for territorial policy are now emerging, and new regional institutions have been given responsibilities for policy implementation. The gradual introduction of the Structural Funds system has increased the participation of lower tiers of government, notably through the partnership mechanisms, and has extended their consultative functions.

The positive and negative effects of processes shaping socio-economic spaces can be observed in the twentieth century development of Central and Eastern Europe, just as in other parts of the continent. Spatial aspects were also represented in the policies of past eras characterised by heterogeneous forms of state organisation. Research results were useful for decision-makers in terms of their ramifications for specific regions. The research results of various social scientific disciplines were incorporated in spatially-related decision-making processes during the last years of the twentieth century as well. Nevertheless, the ruling elite of the communist era required only superficial knowledge about the evolution of spatial processes. Spatial research was conducted within national borders, international professional co-operation – with the exception of Poland and Hungary – remained weak and erratic.

Profound regional transformation was experienced due to the introduction of the market economy after 1989 and the collapse of the Soviet Union. The manageability of these changes naturally called for the thematic and organisational development of spatial research. The preparations for EU accession provided a further incentive for the research and regional studies research groups flourishing in all Central and Eastern European countries at the beginning of the twenty-first century.

However, the new regional policy structure has led to a deconcentration of government administration rather than a truly strengthened decentralisation, and has often complicated rather than simplified the institutional system. Furthermore, local governments are strongly dependent on central governments. As a consequence of this weaknesses, the intermediate level (regions) should be given extended powers and including authority to raise taxes. A philosophy of flexible horizontal co-operation in associations, pacts and partnerships should be promoted to establish functional regions for different public services. Financial and other incentives should be created by raising the share of taxes that remain at local level.

Compatibility with EU Structural Funds regulations and procedures is now understandably one of the main tasks of Central and Eastern European regional policies given the perspective of Structural Funds at the time of accession. Fast progress will probably accelerate accession. It should however be borne in mind that these regulations have been evolving and could change. What is crucial here is more the present learning process and the capacity to develop flexible policy responses. Moreover, compliance with regulations does not suffice to ensure policy efficiency. Other factors such as the quality of partnerships, the ability to make the best use of available funds, selection of targets, project monitoring and professionalism are critical.

The new member-countries are small or medium-sized states of Europe. Their regional inequalities are rooted in their belated industrial development and in the delay their urbanisation processes suffered compared to Western Europe. Their 40 years of planned economy could not significantly reduce either their deficiencies in economic potential, or the reasons underlying their territorial inequalities. At the expense of considerable social costs, the economic and social inequalities among the regions were somewhat reduced during the two decades of socialist regimes. In the early 1980s, it became clear that this process did not guarantee sustainable development. Policies based on the same ideological rudiments, however, went together with different practices in the countries. The pragmatism of Hungarian regional development, also a result of intensive co-operation with Western European professional circles, applied a number of arrangements for development not permitted elsewhere in Eastern Europe. The fact that these attempts had only partial results is explained by the prevailing political system, which worked heavily against economic reforms. To some extent, post-communist regional development in Hungary could rely on nearly two decades of antecedents. As a consequence, well-co-ordinated professional planning commenced in Hungary at the very beginning of the 1990s, even before Hungary signed the agreement to become a candidate for EU accession, with a view to design an up-to-date system for regional policy.

Almost all elements of the system of objectives, tools and institutions of regional development struck root in Hungary for the first time in Eastern Europe. Bulgaria, where the territorial location of economic production followed the Soviet model in the socialist period, only undertook to introduce certain elements of the modern European regional policy later. In these changes, the conditions required by the European Commission were more motivating than internal economic and social needs.

Despite the numerous similarities in the changes that have taken place in the territorial structures of the countries, the differences in the responses individual countries gave to the challenges of regional development and the varied results of their development efforts demonstrate that the 'Eastern European Bloc' is at least as heterogeneous as the European Union. This is a fact which the structural policy reforms of the Union have to take into account.

Today it is not public administrative reasons or accession to the EU that compel the countries to make progress in regionalisation. There is more at stake: the growth of the Central and Eastern European economy, the modernisation of the countries, and their future positions in the European territorial division of labour. The Central and Eastern European administration has been incapable of a paradigm shift during the twentieth century; neither the central nor the territorial organs were interested in sharing power with other actors, and the various decentralisation schemes, in an attempt to simulate reforms, only made minor adjustments in the level of redistri-bution. The emergence of a modern and competitive territorial economic structure is only possible within a new framework. Based on strong, central cities and assigned with political power, proper institutions and financial autonomy, the region can be the basis of this territorial framework.

The analysis of the effective acts and regulations on the building of regions has revealed that the intentions of the legislative power and the government regarding the future of the regions are not clear. Owing to ambiguous legal regulation and the lack of clear-cut concepts, the regions are the weakest element of regional development policy. As soon as a definite political stance is taken regarding the regions, the significant reform of the legal regulation of the regional level will be inevitable. First, the number of regions and their geographical borders have to be defined within the institutional system of regional development. After this, the regions should be assigned with scope of authority and resources, in a process of the parallel decentralisation of government. Underlying this is the fact that the building of regions only helps the emergence of an effective regional policy if it is done through decentralisation and not at the expense of the county's resources and settlement levels. Empirical studies have shown that it is the sectoral ministries that exert the strongest resistance towards the decentralised model of region building; therefore, the government has to act in a very determined and disciplined manner.

In its broad context, therefore, the regional structure of the economy of Central and Eastern European countries cannot currently satisfy the competition requirements of the post-industrial era and of European integration. The notions, concepts and political slogans of decentralisation in the twentieth century proved a failure. The obstacles to progress in almost every attempt at decentralisation were increased both by the combined resistance of central government and sectoral leadership and by the historically shaped introverted behaviour of the country's regional public administration system.

Empirical surveys carried out among the actors involved in the operation of the regional development institution system show that, apart from the problems ensuing from insufficient legal regulation, a number of other difficulties have to be faced in the endeavour to build regions. Although most actors support the efforts of regionalisation in principle, they show no interest or determination in the problematic issues of the present geographical borders and the potential centres of the regions; their territorial links are limited to a narrower area. Nevertheless, it has to be accepted that on the basis of the opinions of the actors, it is impossible to define more consensual region borders than the present ones. In the present phase of region building, therefore, the process should be encouraged within the border of the present region; it will be reasonable, however, to review the issue of borders before the regions are to be made permanent. By that time, enough experience will have been accumulated and research will have been undertaken to make these long-term decisions more substantiated. The actors of regional development tend to find it difficult to place their interests in a regional context and to determine the optimal development objectives for the different territorial categories.

The future of spatial structure of Central and Eastern Europe is basically dependent on the quality of the decentralisation strategy, which these countries will follow in the utilisation of new resources after accession to the European Union. A proper decentralisation seems to offer the most efficient solution for this European macro-region. Strong regions will be required in Central and Eastern Europe because the practice of the European Union unquestionably proved that the subnational level with about 1.5–2.0 million population, administered on the basis of local government principles, based on the economic capacities and structural features is:

- The most optimal spatial framework for the enforcement of the economic development oriented regional development policy.
- The adequate field of the functioning of post-industrial spatial organising forces and their relationships.
- The important action space of interest enforcement.
- The most ideal spatial unit for the establishment of the modern infrastructure and professional organisational-executive apparatus of regional policy.
- A dominant element of the regional and cohesion decision-making system of the European Union.

The decentralised state organisational system can emerge through organic development and complex legal regulation. The principles creating the necessary preconditions are to be included in the constitution. These are the following:

1   The state considers in the course of its development activities and economic policy the inter-relationships and correlation between the territorial features and the spatial elements, insures the necessary preconditions of fulfilling elementary social functions.
2   The state enforcing the principle of social equity and justice contributes with its own means to the moderation of objective territorial inequalities in the living standards.
3   The active regional policy of the state promotes the territorial decentralisation of economic activities and functions.
4   The state shares its regional development tasks and tools with the local and territorial governments and other concerned actors and delegates to the co-

ordination responsibilities and development resources to the territorial decision-makers.

Today, regionalisation in Central and Eastern Europe is inevitable not because of administrative system or membership of the EU. What is at stake is rather the growth of the economy, the modernisation of the countries, and the future positions regions can take in the European territorial division of labour. The states of these parts of Europe state were incapable of bringing a paradigm shift throughout the twentieth century; neither the central nor the territorial authorities were interested in sharing power. Thus, instead of real reforms, the various concepts for decentralisation achieved no more than insignificant modifications in the extent of redistribution. The attitude is the same in the latest plans. It is albeit impossible to join the current trends of the European economy with labour division's present structure of, just as all attempts failed in the last century. The emergence of a modern territorial economic structure can only be conceived within a completely new framework. This territorial framework can only be the region, organised around strong metropolitan centres, with political power, having their own institutions and financial autonomy.

The changes during the previous years imply that the space of regional policy, besides the self-determining rules of economic development, will be determined by two significant factors: first the organisational, functional and financing reforms of the European Union and its eastern enlargements and second, due to a high extent of the previous factor, by the new distribution of power within the national state, decentralisation.

The reforms within the European Union shall receive special attention, since, as we have seen, regions were granted significantly higher subsidies from the structural and cohesion funds of the integration, than from national resources in the course of strengthening European cohesion. The final outcomes of the €700 billion of community subsidies granted for regional development between 2000 and 2013 are not very promising, since the cohesion analyses report a very slow decrease in regional inequalities. One of the reasons for the weak implementation of efficiency requirements is to be detected in the scattered character of subsidies.

The determinative direction of the reforms being prepared is not accidentally the improvement of concentrated utilisation of the resources. In the course of the designation of eligible regions, the indigence must be defined by strict criteria and the proportion of the eligible population must be restricted to one-third of the total population within the Community. The investment practice is to be reconsidered, since the multiple effects of the investments did not reach the desired level and, due to different reasons, the absorption ability of the regions did not develop in accordance with the original expectations. The consistent enforcement of the principle of additionality, the local, regional and national contribution, seems to be the only feasible way. The second key issue is the enforcement of the co-operation between the actors of regional development, the partnership, yet, taking the principle of subsidiarity into account. Within the system of subsistence and incentives of the European Union, the *ex-ante* evaluation of 'cost-benefit' effects are given significant importance which could, depending on the knowledge possessed on the functioning of regional economy and not exclusively on the solid capital, launch a new process of differentiation between European regions.

In the future a principal interest of the national state will be, in order to maintain its influence over the management of economic policy, to counteract the impacts of external (globalisation and integration) pressure by increasing the decision-making potential within the state borders and the improvement of the regions' regulated interest enforcement ability. The traditional regional economic develop-ment practice of Keynesian economic policy cannot be applied any more successfully in the new paradigm. The state regional policy may be replaced by the regions' own policies. Yet, the change of paradigm will not be an automatic process. The interests of the diversely developed regions in institutionalising regionalism show significant differences. The most indigent regions still expect to move away from external (national and international) assistance and therefore their motivations are somewhat bound with the traditional subsidy systems, than the wider autonomy to be achieved in the 'Europe of the Regions'. The engaged followers of regional decentralisation are mostly from among the developed regions, which will be without doubt the beneficiaries of the single market, and economic and monetary union.

Yet, regionalism must face several serious challenges before its general evolution. National governments still have a significant regulatory role in shaping the relationships between the regions and the European Commission. Europe's least advanced regions can enforce their interests rather ineffectively in the inte-gration decisions, since the least affluent states have fewer representatives within the Union's bodies. Also, the competition policy of the Union strengthens the centralisation effects. The common regional policy is not able to balance the inequalities deriving from the competitive abilities.

Parallel with the irreversible deepening of the European integration, the national governments maintained their key positions in at least three policy areas. The first determining national state task is the regulation of the administration of corporate capitalism. Industrial development in the future is impossible without efficient national monetary systems, since the domestic markets and regulation environment will serve as the most stable starting point for corporate strategies. The second important central governmental task remains the co-ordination of national inno-vation and technology development programmes. Finally, the third national priority includes dealing with the labour market and industry policy. Yet, the success of the two latter national functions highly depends on the efficiency of the subnational public administration in partially solving tasks. Therefore, regionalisation is one of the preconditions of the national state's successful functioning since no macro-political task can be implemented without mature human resources, education, training and business development and no balanced competition can be imagined without the co-operation of the social partners either. The implementation of these tasks is the most important in the regional tier.

In the period of the preparation for the new Structural Policy, besides the objectives of aid, resources and mechanisms of structural instruments, the exploitation of the new driving forces of spatial development must also be taken into consideration. The former question is related to the representation of national interests in the EU; the latter belongs to the domain of national sectoral policies and institutional structures. The modification of factors shaping spatial development necessitates the transformation of the system of objectives, instruments and institutions of regional policy. This also implies the enforcement of national interests. The long-term trends of European spatial development require the development of the most heterogeneous institutionalised forms of decentralisation in the countries with different traditions in the continent. The new Eastern and European member-states are able to meet the cohesion requirements of the European Union only with decentralised institutions. This is not only a question of public administration, but also a precondition of efficient research and development with the aim of enhancing competitiveness.

Despite the similarities of the changes in the spatial structure of CEE countries, the various responses to the questions of regional development and the diverse development results all indicate that the Eastern bloc is just as heterogeneous as the European Union. EU Structural Policy reforms must this fact into consideration as well as the strategic factors of regional development policies.

Decentralised and regionalised development policy might provide a means for successfully overcoming the crisis in Europe. This supposes a totally new spatial development paradigm. During the recent one-and-a-half decades, every measure was designed to promote the creation of the system of objectives, instruments and institutions of central regional policy. Besides the radical renewal of state functions, the guarantees of autonomous regional policy-making must be established through legislative regulation and the financing of the operation must be resolved in the coming decade (Table 9.1).

The principle of subsidiarity and its practical utilisation exerts a positive influence on the evolution of European territorial cohesion. Evidently, those countries achieved success which regarded subsidiarity as the basic condition of the transformation of the organisational system of the functioning of the state and applied it

Table 9.1 Some directions of the paradigm shift

	Present paradigm	*New paradigm of spatial policy*
The object of spatial development	Moderation of disadvantages	Increasing economic performance
The perspective of decentralisation	Regional operational programmes meet the requirement of decentralisation	Regional operational programmes receive at least half of the structural expenses
The area of co-ordination	Central intersectorial	Horizontal regional
The objective of the development of public administration	Raising the efficiency of state administration	Developing the spatial frameworks of socio-economic welfare

Source: Author's construction.

in its full complexity. In other words, through the transformation of the total decision-making hierarchy, the reorganisation of the location of powers occurred: centralised functions were redefined just as tasks of lower levels were reorganised. Multiple examples justify that a system of social control can only be competitive if it takes clearly into consideration the organisational requirement according to which lower levels cannot be overburdened with tasks which they are unable to resolve and the transfer of competencies must be coupled with the transfer of sources of financing. Eastern and Central European countries may only be successful and will only be capable of absorbing EU funds primarily for the objective of cohesion between various regions if they take these requirements into consideration.

The region is considered to be a spatial unit serving the sustainable growth of the economy and the modernisation of the spatial structure, with independent financial resources, fulfilling autonomous development policy, and equipped with local government rights. On the basis of this term, whose factors naturally developed differently in the different periods of European development, regions have not so far existed in Eastern and Central Europe, despite the fact that some geographers (on the basis of the indisputable results obtained by geographic science in regional research) assert that we do possess some well-defined, natural regions. Such 'form without content', as in previous decades, cannot, in itself, steer the spatial structure of the country in a favourable direction, decentralise the new space-forming forces, and create the prerequisites for multi-polar development. The region, if defined as a framework for regional research, is not capable of organising the space-forming powers of the twenty-first century without the competences, institutions, and tools.

Naturally, creating political, public administration regions is a time-consuming task, but, in relation to the future, it was at this historically important time of the country's modernisation prior to EU accession that agreement should have been reached. At the same time, it has to be said that bitter political disputes do no favours to large-scale regional political reform, but, apart from that, it is difficult to find arguments against the decentralising trends of modernisation and rationalisation. Disputes notwithstanding, the target should be to submit to parliament the basic projected legislation necessary for changing to a regional public service and administration organisation system, 'the sooner the better.'

The pressure for regionalisation in Eastern and Central Europe today has been created not in relation to public administration or even for reasons associated with EU membership. The increasing size of the economies, the modernisation of the countries, the decline in regional differences, and the future of the positions to be gained in the Europe-wide regional division of labour constitute the stake. Regionalism can be the new motivating force for modernisation at the beginning of the twenty-first century.

The current institutional system of regional development cannot even meet the original targets. Some regional agencies have the task of gathering projects together, and, consequently, they promote the execution of the will of central government rather than the realisation of regional concepts. In the performance of regional agencies, some basic differences can be seen. There are, indeed, some innovative examples willing to use the methods of modern regional economic development agencies, but there are also a number of traditional agencies operating in an executive role.

On the basis of empirical research, the greatest protest against the decentralised model has been provoked within the circle of the ministries. Balanced against this can be the fact that most of the stakeholders involved in regional formation theoretically support reform, but are not convinced of the appropriateness of current regional borders and of regional centres, their regional relationships being in a narrower circle. It seems, however, in the opinion of the actors, that it is impossible to create more acceptable regional borders than the current ones, and it is most important not to distract attention from significant questions, such as the decentralisation of the state and the strengthening of regional autonomy, with a debate about regional borders and the tug-of-war over regional centres. At the moment these last two questions are the ones that excite most the various county elite.

Never discussed or debated are the core questions such as: What functions should a region have? What responsibilities should central government devolve to the regions? (since the ministries also now realise that, perhaps, they are facing a change)? Why does the central administration deal with the evaluation of an application for a couple of million Hungarian forints? While hundreds and thousands of applications are evaluated and decided on, the same level of intensity is nowhere to be seen in any debate on strategic questions. Why is not the most important task for the central state administration to work out the sectoral operative programs so important for EU accession? Why are there no intricately elaborated long-term development ideas?

Not only operative, but also important planning-strategy tasks can be delegated to the regions. This is rather more the case, since what is suggested by central offices will not be a realistic solution in the new programming period 2014–2020, namely, that the methods tested in one corner of the country can be used in another. Each region should be allowed to find its own way. Those EU member-states are successful where the country is developing along different regional orbits.

To reduce underdevelopment and to develop the regions are the most important strategic aims of the European Community, and almost 40 per cent of its budget is used for these purposes. Member-states, or, rather their regions (depending on their level of development), are given considerable support from the common budget for catching up. At the same time, we also have to see that, besides the large support in the ranking list of the regions in the individual member-states, changes could only happen if, in the utilisation of EU support, a long-term (several decades-long) structural policy were used. Regional development policy concentrated not only on the development of traditional infrastructural elements, but also on the modern regional development driving forces (innovation, business services, modern industrial organisation methods, and human resources development). Those regions that expected success exclusively from the EU's support policy and tried to fulfil the actual development policy aims at that specific moment, were unable to improve their relative position.

The basic concepts valid for all member-states and related to fulfilling structural policy – subsidiarity, decentralisation, in addition, concentration, programming, partnership, transparency – also demanded the modernisation of the national-regional political institutional system, and these points of view must also be taken into account when the reform of public administration is being planned. The consistent application of these concepts in the EU member-states has increased the efficiency of regional development and strengthened cohesion, and in the latest period a more frequently voiced new support policy aim, the development of competitiveness, is targeting the sustainable development of the regions. What is, perhaps, most important, is that the main aim of EUs membership is not to obtain structural support, but to exploit the privileges of the 450 million market. Deriving from this is that the method for further development of regional policy should be found not merely (and exclusively) in the expansion of redistribution, but in the opportunities for mobilising resources.

In most EU member-states today, it is obvious that the division of power and the institutions of multilevel government increase both the economic performance capacity and welfare in the individual regions. The lobbyist politician will be replaced by the developer-type politician who regulates, with directives and laws, the long-term guarantees of local autonomous development, who promotes European co-operation, and builds partnership connections among the region's actors. The success of this approach is proved by the successful development of numerous West European regions and by their outstanding role as the creator of regional identity.

If we examine the spatial location of R&D activity, which should be one of the factors supporting the dynamic of European regional development, we can see that the systemic change and the transition have had the effect of preserving the *status quo ante* in the new member-states in Central and Eastern Europe. Major regional inequalities are still evident in the regional structure of developed innovative institutions, and the core areas and capital cities still have their privileged position. The regional and structural policies based on EU norms have not stimulated the development of R&D in the new member-states, as the operational programmes for 2007–2013 demonstrate. There is no CEE country with a regional or competitiveness-related operational programme targeting a comprehensive transformation of human resource development in respect of research.

Changes in the factors influencing regional development require the regional policy system of objectives, together with the related instruments and institutions, to be transformed. The long-term trends of European spatial development require the widest range of institutionalised forms of decentralisation to be established in the countries of Europe in the face of their different traditions. The new, Central and Eastern European member-states can only meet EU cohesion requirements with the help of decentralised institutions. This is not only a public administration issue, but also a prerequisite for the success of R&D in helping to improve competitiveness. If regionalism progresses, it can bring about the modernisation of regional structures and the need for multi-polar regional development may change quite profoundly the hierarchies of power in those countries still in transition. The subnational level of the power structure, the region, is a territorial entity which supports the sustainable development of the economy and the modernisation of the spatial structure, with its own financial resources and having at its disposal an autonomous development policy based upon local governmental rights. The regions are becoming the stage for innovative development, and the degree of embeddedness at regional level of the fundamental institutions of innovation output is becoming stronger.

The decentralisation of science and R&D has a number of positive effects on the improvement of the regions. The formation of research-intensive sectors increases the number of quality jobs and the business development effects of the setting up of spin-off companies are clearly evident. Innovative business develops the region's export capacity and helps the region to integrate into the European and international research area. Companies which demand or rely on research contribute to the re-industrialisation of the region and to the spread of modern services. All of these improve the income-generating ability of the regions and contribute to the enhancement of regional cohesion. In lack of state reforms aiming at decentralisation, the Lisbon criteria will not be realisable in the unitary states of Europe,

Without hopefully strengthening economic performance of countries, the results of EU cohesion policy will remain limited. Decentralised and regionalised development policy may be the only EU-conformity solution for Eastern and Central Europe. This requires a totally new spatial development paradigm. During the recent one-and-a half decades, every measure was directed at the creation of the system of objectives, instruments and institutions of central regional policy. During the coming decade the guarantees of regional individual policy-making would have to be established via legislation and the problem of the financing their operations will have to be resolved.

Index

For Product Safety Concerns and Information please contact our EU
representative GPSR@taylorandfrancis.com Taylor & Francis Verlag GmbH,
Kaufingerstraße 24, 80331 München, Germany

Printed and bound by CPI Group (UK) Ltd, Croydon, CR0 4YY
08/05/2025
01864368-0002